MW00845550

React Design Patterns and Best Practices

Second Edition

Design, build and deploy production-ready web applications using standard industry practices

Carlos Santana Roldán

BIRMINGHAM - MUMBAI

`mapt.io`

Mapt is an online digital library that gives you full access to over 5,000 books and videos, as well as industry leading tools to help you plan your personal development and advance your career. For more information, please visit our website.

Why subscribe?

- Spend less time learning and more time coding with practical eBooks and Videos from over 4,000 industry professionals

- Improve your learning with Skill Plans built especially for you

- Get a free eBook or video every month

- Mapt is fully searchable

- Copy and paste, print, and bookmark content

Packt.com

Did you know that Packt offers eBook versions of every book published, with PDF and ePub files available? You can upgrade to the eBook version at `www.packt.com` and as a print book customer, you are entitled to a discount on the eBook copy. Get in touch with us at `customercare@packtpub.com` for more details.

At `www.packt.com`, you can also read a collection of free technical articles, sign up for a range of free newsletters, and receive exclusive discounts and offers on Packt books and eBooks.

React Design Patterns and Best Practices
Second Edition

Copyright © 2019 Packt Publishing

All rights reserved. No part of this book may be reproduced, stored in a retrieval system, or transmitted in any form or by any means, without the prior written permission of the publisher, except in the case of brief quotations embedded in critical articles or reviews.

Every effort has been made in the preparation of this book to ensure the accuracy of the information presented. However, the information contained in this book is sold without warranty, either express or implied. Neither the author, nor Packt Publishing or its dealers and distributors, will be held liable for any damages caused or alleged to have been caused directly or indirectly by this book.

Packt Publishing has endeavored to provide trademark information about all of the companies and products mentioned in this book by the appropriate use of capitals. However, Packt Publishing cannot guarantee the accuracy of this information.

Commissioning Editor: Kunal Chaudhari
Acquisition Editor: Larissa Pinto
Content Development Editor: Mohammed Yusuf Imaratwale
Technical Editor: Leena Patil
Copy Editor: Safis Editing
Project Coordinator: Pragati Shukla
Proofreader: Safis Editing
Indexer: Tejal Daruwale Soni
Graphics: Alishon Mendonsa
Production Coordinator: Tom Scaria

First published: January 2017
Second edition: March 2019

Production reference: 1290319

Published by Packt Publishing Ltd.
Livery Place
35 Livery Street
Birmingham
B3 2PB, UK.

ISBN 978-1-78953-017-9

www.packtpub.com

Contributors

About the author

Carlos Santana Roldán is a senior web developer with more than 12 years of experience. Currently, he is working as a Senior React Developer at MindBody Inc. He is the founder of Dev Education, one of the most popular developer communities in Latin America, training people in web technologies such as React, Node.js, GraphQL, and JavaScript in general.

About the reviewer

Mayur Tanna is a senior software consultant with over 10 years of experience. He has worked on various high-value projects with international clients such as the World Bank and the United Nations, and played a key role in creating the architecture of those projects using the latest technologies, including React, Angular, Node.js, MongoDB, Spring Boot, Firebase, Amazon Web Services, and Google Cloud Platform. Mayur is the coauthor of *Serverless Web Applications with React and Firebase* by *Packt Publishing*. He holds a master's degree in computer applications and has trained lot of engineering students through tech workshops. In his free time, he plays table tennis and cricket.

I want to thank my wife, Dr. Purna; my parents, Mr. Ratilal and Mrs. Nirmala; my little child, Dhyey; and the rest of my family for their valuable support. Without their support, the review of this book would not have been possible. I would also like to thank the Packt team for giving me the opportunity to review this book.

Packt is searching for authors like you

If you're interested in becoming an author for Packt, please visit authors.packtpub.com and apply today. We have worked with thousands of developers and tech professionals, just like you, to help them share their insight with the global tech community. You can make a general application, apply for a specific hot topic that we are recruiting an author for, or submit your own idea.

Table of Contents

Preface

This book will take you on a journey through the most valuable design patterns in React, demonstrating how to apply design patterns and best practices in real-life situations. This book will help make your applications more flexible, perform better, and will make them easier to maintain, while giving your workflow a huge boost by improving speed, but crucially without affecting quality.

We'll begin by understanding the internals of React, before gradually moving on to writing clean and maintainable code. We'll build components that are reusable across the application, structure applications, and create forms that actually work.

We will then style React components and optimize them to make applications faster and more responsive. Finally, we'll write tests effectively, and you'll learn how to contribute to React and its ecosystem.

By the end of the book, you'll be saved from a lot of trial and error and developmental headaches, and you will be on the road to becoming a React expert.

Who this book is for

The book can be used by any developer who has a basic knowledge of building web applications. This is mainly aimed at JavaScript developers, but any other type of devs will benefit from this book.

What this book covers

Chapter 1, *Taking Your First Steps with React*, covers some basic concepts that are important for following the rest of the book, and that are crucial to working with React daily. We will learn how to write declarative code, and will gain a clear understanding of the difference between the components we create, and the elements React uses to display their instances on the screen. We'll then learn the reasons behind the choice of co-locating logic and templates together, and why that unpopular decision has been a big win for React. We will go through the reasons why it is common to feel fatigue in the JavaScript ecosystem, but we'll also see how to avoid those problems by following an iterative approach. Finally, we will see what the new create-react-app CLI is, and with that, we'll be ready to start writing some real code.

Chapter 2, *Clean Up Your Code*, teaches the reader a great deal about how JSX works and how to use it in the right way in our components. We start from the basics of the syntax to create a solid knowledge base that will enable us to master JSX and its features. In the second part, we will look at how ESLint and its plugins can help us find problems faster and enforce a consistent style guide across our code base. Finally, we will go through the basics of functional programming to understand the important concepts to use when writing a React application. Now that our code is clean, we are ready to start digging deeper into React and learn how to write truly reusable components.

Chapter 3, *Create Truly Reusable Components*, starts from a deep study of the basics, outlining the differences between stateful and stateless components, and providing an example of how to make a tightly-coupled component reusable. We'll look at the internal state of a component and at when it is better to avoid using it. We will also learn the basics of prop types, and will apply those concepts to the reusable components we created. Finally, we'll look at how living style guides can help us to communicate better with other members of our team, so as to avoid creating duplicated components and to enforce consistency within the application.

Chapter 4, *Compose All the Things*, explains how to compose our reusable components and make them communicate effectively. Then, we will go through some of the most interesting composition patterns in React. We will also see how React tried to solve the problem of sharing functionalities between components with mixins. We'll then learn how to deal with the context without needing to couple our components to it, thanks to HoCs. Finally, we'll see how we can compose components dynamically by following the `FunctionAsChild` pattern.

Chapter 5, *Proper Data Fetching*, goes through some of the most common patterns to make a child and parent communicate using callbacks. We'll then learn how we could use a common parent to share data across components that are not directly connected. We then start with a simple component, which will be able to load data from GitHub, and we make it reusable with HoC, and then go on to learn how we could use react-refetch to apply data fetching patterns to our components and avoid reinventing the wheel. Finally, we learn how to use the new Context API.

Chapter 6, *Write Code for the Browser*, looks at different things we can do when we target the browser with React, from form creation to events; from animations to SVGs. React gives us a declarative way to manage all the aspects we need to deal with when we create a web application. React gives us access to the actual DOM nodes in a way that we can perform imperative operations with them, which is useful if we need to integrate React with an existing imperative library.

Chapter 7, *Make Your Components Look Beautiful*, studies the reasons why regular CSS may not be the best approach for styling components, along with the various alternative solutions. Moving through the chapter, we'll learn to use inline styles in React, along with the downsides of this, which can be fixed by using Radium Library. At the end, a new library, styled-components, will be introduced, along with an outline of the modern approach that it offers.

Chapter 8, *Server-Side Rendering for Fun and Profit*, invites you to follow certain steps to set up a server-side rendered application. By the end of this chapter, we will be able to build a universal application, and be aware of its pros and cons.

Chapter 9, *Improve the Performance of Your Applications*, takes a quick look at the basic components of the performance of React, and how we can use some APIs to help the library find the optimal path to update the DOM without degrading the user experience. We will also learn how to monitor performance and find bottlenecks using some tools that we can import into our code base. At the end, we'll see how immutability and PureComponent are the perfect tools to build fast React applications.

Chapter 10, *About Testing and Debugging*, explains why it is important to test our applications, along with an outline of the most popular tools that we could use to create tests with React. We also learn to set up a Jest environment to test components using Enzyme, along with a discussion of what Enzyme is and why it is a must for testing React applications. By covering all these topics, at the end of the chapter, we will be able to create a test environment from scratch and write tests for our application's components.

Chapter 11, *React Router*, looks at certain steps that will help us to implement React Router in our application. Moving ahead, as we complete each section, we will be able to add dynamic routes and understand how exactly React Router works. We will learn how to install and configure React Router, along with adding a <Switch> component, exact prop, and parameters to routes.

Chapter 12, *Anti-Patterns to be Avoided*, is all about the common anti-patterns we should avoid when using React. We will study why mutating the state is harmful for performance. Choosing the right keys and helping the reconciler will also be covered in this chapter, along with the reason why spreading props on DOM elements is bad and how can we avoid doing that.

Chapter 13, *Deploying to Production*, covers how to deploy our React application using Node.js and nginx on an Ubuntu server from Digital Ocean, along with configuring nginx, PM2, and a domain. Implementing CircleCI for continuous integration will also be covered.

Chapter 14, *Next Steps*, demonstrates how we can contribute to the React library by opening issues and pull requests, and explains why it is important to give back to the community and share our code. At the end, we will cover the most important aspects to keep in mind when pushing open source code, along with how we can publish an npm package and how to use semantic versioning.

To get the most out of this book

To master React, you need to have a fundamental knowledge of JavaScript and Node.js. This book is mostly targeting web developers, and, at the time of writing, the following assumptions were made of the reader:

- The reader knows how to install the latest version of Node.js.
- The reader is an intermediate developer who can understand JavaScript ES6 syntax.
- Some experience of CLI tools and Node.js syntax is required.

Download the example code files

You can download the example code files for this book from your account at www.packt.com. If you purchased this book elsewhere, you can visit www.packt.com/support and register to have the files emailed directly to you.

You can download the code files by following these steps:

1. Log in or register at www.packt.com.
2. Select the **SUPPORT** tab.
3. Click on **Code Downloads & Errata**.
4. Enter the name of the book in the **Search** box and follow the onscreen instructions.

Once the file is downloaded, please make sure that you unzip or extract the folder using the latest version of:

- WinRAR/7-Zip for Windows
- Zipeg/iZip/UnRarX for Mac
- 7-Zip/PeaZip for Linux

The code bundle for the book is also hosted on GitHub at `https://github.com/ PacktPublishing/React-Design-Patterns-and-Best-Practices-Second-Edition`. In case there's an update to the code, it will be updated on the existing GitHub repository.

We also have other code bundles from our rich catalog of books and videos available at `https://github.com/PacktPublishing/`. Check them out!

Download the color images

We also provide a PDF file that has color images of the screenshots/diagrams used in this book. You can download it here: `https://www.packtpub.com/sites/default/files/ downloads/9781789530179_ColorImages.pdf`.

Conventions used

There are a number of text conventions used throughout this book.

`CodeInText`: Indicates code words in text, database table names, folder names, filenames, file extensions, pathnames, dummy URLs, user input, and Twitter handles. Here is an example: "Again, with `createClass`, we use a function, while, with the ES6 classes, we set an attribute of the instance."

A block of code is set as follows:

```
const Button = React.createClass({
    getInitialState() {
      return {
        text: 'Click me!'
      };
    },
    render() {
      return <button>{this.state.text}</button>;
    }
});
```

When we wish to draw your attention to a particular part of a code block, the relevant lines or items are set in bold:

```
React.createElement("img", {
    src: "https://www.dev.education/images/logo.png",
    alt: "DEV Education"
});
```

Any command-line input or output is written as follows:

```
npm install -g create-react-app
```

Bold: Indicates a new term, an important word, or words that you see on screen. For example, words in menus or dialog boxes appear in the text like this. Here is an example: "Let's start with a basic example—displaying a form with an input field and a **Submit** button."

 Warnings or important notes appear like this.

 Tips and tricks appear like this.

Get in touch

Feedback from our readers is always welcome.

General feedback: If you have questions about any aspect of this book, mention the book title in the subject of your message and email us at customercare@packtpub.com.

Errata: Although we have taken every care to ensure the accuracy of our content, mistakes do happen. If you have found a mistake in this book, we would be grateful if you would report this to us. Please visit www.packt.com/submit-errata, selecting your book, clicking on the Errata Submission Form link, and entering the details.

Piracy: If you come across any illegal copies of our works in any form on the internet, we would be grateful if you would provide us with the location address or website name. Please contact us at copyright@packt.com with a link to the material.

If you are interested in becoming an author: If there is a topic that you have expertise in, and you are interested in either writing or contributing to a book, please visit authors.packtpub.com.

Reviews

Please leave a review. Once you have read and used this book, why not leave a review on the site that you purchased it from? Potential readers can then see and use your unbiased opinion to make purchase decisions, we at Packt can understand what you think about our products, and our authors can see your feedback on their book. Thank you!

For more information about Packt, please visit `packt.com`.

Section 1: Hello React!

In this section, we will learn about the basics of React and modern JavaScript concepts. We will then move on to understanding concepts including JSX, spread attributes, JavaScript templating, and common patterns and code styles. Finally, we will take a look at the basics of functional programming.

The following chapters will be covered in this section:

- Chapter 1, *Taking Your First Steps with React*
- Chapter 2, *Clean Up Your Code*

Taking Your First Steps with React

1

Hello, readers!

This book assumes that you already know what React is and what problems it can solve for you. You may have written a small/medium application with React, and you want to improve your skills and answer all of your open questions. You should know that React is maintained by developers at Facebook and hundreds of contributors within the JavaScript community. React is one of the most popular libraries for creating user interfaces, and it is well-known to be fast, thanks to its smart way of touching the **Document Object Model (DOM)**. It comes with JSX, a new syntax to write markup in JavaScript, which requires you to change your mind regarding the separation of concerns. It has many cool features, such as server-side rendering, which gives you the power to write universal applications.

To follow this book, you will need to know how to use the terminal to install and run `npm` packages in your Node.js environment. All the examples are written in modern JavaScript, which you should be able to read and understand.

In this first chapter, we will go through some basic concepts that are essential to master in order to use React effectively, but are straightforward enough for beginners to figure out:

- The difference between imperative and declarative programming
- React components and their instances, and how React uses elements to control the UI flow
- How React changes the way we build web applications, enforcing a different new concept of separation of concerns, and the reasons behind its unpopular design choice
- Why people feel the JavaScript fatigue, and what you can do to avoid the most common errors developers make when approaching the React ecosystem

Declarative programming

Reading the React documentation or blog posts about React, you have undoubtedly come across the term **declarative**. One of the reasons why React is so powerful is because it enforces a declarative programming paradigm.

Consequently, to master React, it is essential to understand what declarative programming means and what the main differences between imperative and declarative programming are. The easiest way to approach the problem is to think about imperative programming as a way of describing how things work, and declarative programming as a way of describing what you want to achieve.

A real-life parallel in the imperative world would be entering a bar for a beer, and giving the following instructions to the bartender:

1. Take a glass from the shelf.
2. Put the glass in front of the draft.
3. Pull down the handle until the glass is full.
4. Pass me the glass.

In the declarative world, you would just say: *Beer, please.*

The declarative approach of asking for a beer assumes that the bartender knows how to serve one, and that is an important aspect of the way declarative programming works.

Let's move into a JavaScript example, writing a simple function that, given an array of uppercase strings, returns an array with the same strings in lowercase:

```
toLowerCase(['FOO', 'BAR']) // ['foo', 'bar']
```

An imperative function to solve the problem would be implemented as follows:

```
const toLowerCase = input => {
  const output = [];
  for (let i = 0; i < input.length; i++) {
    output.push(input[i].toLowerCase());
  }
  return output;
};
```

First of all, an empty array to contain the result gets created. Then, the function loops through all the elements of the input array and pushes the lowercase values into the empty array. Finally, the output array gets returned.

A declarative solution would be as follows:

```
const toLowerCase = input => input.map(value => value.toLowerCase());
```

The items of the input array are passed to a map function that returns a new array containing the lowercase values. There are some significant differences to note: the former example is less elegant and it requires more effort to be understood. The latter is terser and easier to read, which makes a huge difference in big code bases, where maintainability is crucial.

Another aspect worth mentioning is that, in the declarative example, there is no need to use variables nor to keep their values updated during the execution. Declarative programming tends to avoid creating and mutating a state.

As a final example, let's see what it means for React to be declarative.

The problem we will try to solve is a common task in web development: showing a map with a marker.

The JavaScript implementation (using the Google Maps SDK) is as follows:

```
const map = new google.maps.Map(document.getElementById('map'), {
    zoom: 4,
    center: myLatLng
});
const marker = new google.maps.Marker({
    position: myLatLng,
    title: 'Hello World!'
});
marker.setMap(map);
```

It is imperative because all the instructions needed to create the map, and create the marker and attach it to the map, are described inside the code one after the other.

A React component to show a map on a page would look like this instead:

```
<Gmaps zoom={4} center={myLatLng}>
    <Marker position={myLatLng} title="Hello world!" />
</Gmaps>
```

In declarative programming, developers only describe what they want to achieve, and there's no need to list all the steps to make it work.

The fact that React offers a declarative approach makes it easy to use, and consequently, the resulting code is simple, which often leads to fewer bugs and more maintainability.

React elements

This book assumes that you are familiar with components and their instances, but there is another object you should know if you want to use React effectively – the element.

Whenever you call `createClass`, extend `Component`, or declare a stateless function, you are creating a component. React manages all the instances of your components at runtime, and there can be more than one instance of the same component in memory at a given point in time.

As mentioned previously, React follows a declarative paradigm, and there's no need to tell it how to interact with the DOM; you declare what you want to see on the screen and React does the job for you.

As you might have already experienced, most other UI libraries work oppositely: they leave the responsibility of keeping the interface updated to the developer, who has to manage the creation and destruction of the DOM elements manually.

To control the UI flow, React uses a particular type of object, called an element, that describes what has to be shown on the screen. These immutable objects are much simpler compared to the components and their instances, and contain only the information that is strictly needed to represent the interface.

The following is an example of an element:

```
{
  type: Title,
  props: {
    color: 'red',
    children: 'Hello, Title!'
  }
}
```

Elements have a type, which is the most important attribute, and some properties. There is also a particular property, called `children`, that is optional and represents the direct descendant of the element.

The type is important because it tells React how to deal with the element itself. If the type is a string, the element represents a DOM node, while if the type is a function, the element is a component.

DOM elements and components can be nested with each other as follows, to represent the render tree:

```
{
  type: Title,
  props: {
    color: 'red',
    children: {
      type: 'h1',
      props: {
        children: 'Hello, H1!'
      }
    }
  }
}
```

When the type of the element is a function, React calls it, passing the props to get back the underlying elements. It keeps on performing the same operation recursively on the result until it gets a tree of DOM nodes that React can render on the screen. This process is called **reconciliation**, and it is used by both React DOM and React Native to create the user interfaces of their respective platforms.

Unlearning everything

Using React for the first time usually requires an open mind because it is a new way of designing web and mobile applications. React tries to innovate the way we build user interfaces following a path that breaks most of the well-known best practices.

In the last two decades, we learned that the separation of concerns is important, and we used to think about it regarding separating the logic from the templates. Our goal has always been to write the JavaScript and the HTML in different files.

Various templating solutions have been created to help developers achieve this.

The problem is that, most of the time, that kind of separation is just an illusion and the truth is that the JavaScript and the HTML are tightly coupled, no matter where they live.

Let's see an example of a template:

```
{{#items}}
  {{#first}}
    <li><strong>{{name}}</strong></li>
  {{/first}}
  {{#link}}
```

```
<li><a href="{{url}}">{{name}}</a></li>
  {{/link}}
{{/items}}
```

The preceding snippet is taken from the Mustache website, one of the most popular templating systems.

The first row tells Mustache to loop through a collection of items. Inside the loop, there is some conditional logic to check whether the #first and the #link properties exist, and, depending on their values, a different piece of HTML is rendered. Variables are wrapped into curly braces.

If your application has only to display some variables, a templating library could represent a good solution, but when it comes to starting to work with complex data structures, things change. Templating systems and their **Domain-Specific Language** (**DSL**) offer a subset of features, and they try to provide the functionalities of a real programming language without reaching the same level of completeness.

As shown in the example, templates highly depend on the models they receive from the logic layer to display the information.

On the other hand, JavaScript interacts with the DOM elements rendered by the templates to update the UI, even if they are loaded from separate files. The same problem applies to styles – they are defined in a different file, but they are referenced in the templates, and the CSS selectors follow the structure of the markup, so it is almost impossible to change one without breaking the other, which is the definition of coupling. That is why the classic separation of concerns ended up being more a separation of technologies, which is, of course, not a bad thing, but it doesn't solve any real problems.

React tries to move a step forward by putting the templates where they belong – next to the logic. The reason it does that is because React suggests you organize your applications by composing small bricks called components. The framework should not tell you how to separate the concerns, because every application has its own, and only the developers should decide how to limit the boundaries of their applications.

The component-based approach drastically changes the way we write web applications, which is why the classic concept of separation of concerns is gradually being taken over by a much more modern structure. The paradigm enforced by React is not new, and it was not invented by its creators, but React has contributed to making the concept mainstream and, most importantly, popularized it in such a way that is easier to understand for developers with different levels of expertise.

The `render` method of a React component looks like this:

```
render() {
  return (
    <button style={{ color: 'red' }} onClick={this.handleClick}>
      Click me!
    </button>
  );
}
```

We all agree that it seems a bit weird in the beginning, but it is just because we are not used to that kind of syntax. As soon as we learn it and we realize how powerful it is, we understand its potential. Using JavaScript for both logic and templating not only helps us separate our concerns in a better way, but it also gives us more power and more expressivity, which is what we need to build complex user interfaces.

That is why, even if the idea of mixing JavaScript and HTML sounds weird in the beginning, it is vital to give React five minutes. The best way to get started with a new technology is to try it in a small side project and see how it goes. In general, the right approach is always to be ready to unlearn everything and change your mindset if the long-term benefits are worth it.

There is another concept that is pretty controversial and hard to accept, and that the engineers behind React are trying to push to the community: moving the styling logic inside the component, too. The end goal is to encapsulate every single technology used to create our components and separate the concerns according to their domain and functionalities.

Here is an example of a style object taken from the React documentation:

```
const divStyle = {
  color: 'white',
  backgroundImage: `url(${imgUrl})`,
  WebkitTransition: 'all', // note the capital 'W' here
  msTransition: 'all' // 'ms' is the only lowercase vendor prefix
};
ReactDOM.render(<div style={divStyle}>Hello World!</div>, mountNode);
```

This set of solutions, where developers use JavaScript to write their styles, is known as #CSSinJS, and we will talk about it extensively in `Chapter 7`, *Make Your Components Look Beautiful*.

Common misconceptions

There is a prevailing opinion that React is a vast set of technologies and tools, and if you want to use it, you are forced to deal with package managers, transpilers, module bundlers, and an infinite list of different libraries. This idea is so widespread and shared among people that it has been clearly defined, and has been given the name **JavaScript fatigue**.

It is not hard to understand the reasons behind this. All the repositories and libraries in the React ecosystem are made using shiny new technologies, the latest version of JavaScript, and the most advanced techniques and paradigms.

Moreover, there is a massive number of React boilerplates on GitHub, each with tens of dependencies to offer solutions for any problems. It is straightforward to think that all these tools are required to start using React, but this is far from the truth. Despite this common way of thinking, React is a pretty tiny library, and it can be used inside any page (or even inside a JSFiddle) in the same way everyone used to use jQuery or Backbone, just by including the script on the page before the closing `body` element.

There are two scripts, because React is split into two packages:

- `react`: Implements the core features of the library
- `react-dom`: Contains all the browser-related features

The reason behind this is because the core package is used to support different targets, such as React DOM in browsers, and React Native on mobile devices. Running a React application inside a single HTML page does not require any package manager or complex operation. You can just download the distribution bundle and host it yourself (or use `https://unpkg.com/`), and you are ready to get started with React and its features in a few minutes.

Here are the URLs to be included in the HTML to start using React:

- `https://unpkg.com/react@16.7.0/umd/react.production.min.js`
- `https://unpkg.com/react-dom@16.7.0/umd/react-dom.production.min.js`

If we add the core React library only, we cannot use JSX because it is not a standard language supported by the browser; but, the whole point is to start with the bare minimum set of features and add more functionalities as soon as they are needed. For a simple UI, we could just use `createElement` and, only when we start building something more complex, we can include a transpiler to enable JSX and convert it into JavaScript. As soon as the app grows a bit more, we may need a router to handle different pages and views, and we can include that as well.

At some point, we may want to load data from some API endpoints, and, if the application keeps growing, we will reach the point where we need some external dependencies to abstract complex operations. Only at that very moment should we introduce a package manager. Then, the time will come to split our application into separate modules and organize our files in the right way. At that point, we should start thinking about using a module bundler.

Following this simple approach, there's no fatigue. Starting with a boilerplate that has one hundred dependencies and tens of npm packages of which we know nothing is the best way to get lost. It is important to note that every programming-related job (and frontend engineering in particular) requires continuous learning. It is the nature of the web to evolve at a breakneck pace and change according to the needs of both users and developers. This is the way our environment has worked since the beginning, and is what makes it very exciting.

As we gain experience working on the web, we learn that we cannot master everything and we should find the right way to keep ourselves updated to avoid the fatigue. We become able to follow all the new trends without jumping into the new libraries for the sake of it unless we have time for a side project.

It is astonishing how, in the JavaScript world, as soon as a specification is announced or drafted, someone in the community implements it as a transpiler plugin or a polyfill, letting everyone else play with it while the browser vendors agree and start supporting it.

This is something that makes JavaScript and the browser a completely different environment compared to any other language or platform. The downside of it is that things change very quickly, but it is just a matter of finding the right balance between betting on new technologies versus staying safe.

In any case, Facebook developers care a lot about the **Developer Experience** (**DX**), and they listen carefully to the community. So, even if it is not true that to use React we are required to learn hundreds of different tools, they realized that people were feeling the fatigue and they released a CLI tool that makes it incredibly easy to scaffold and run a real React application.

The only requirement is to use a node.js/npm environment and install the CLI tool globally as follows:

```
npm install -g create-react-app
```

When the executable is installed, we can use it to create our application passing a folder name:

```
create-react-app hello-world
```

Finally, we move into the folder of our application with `cd hello-world`, and we just run the command:

```
npm start
```

Magically, our application is running with a single dependency, but with all the features needed to build a complete React application using the most advanced techniques. The following screenshot shows the default page of an application created with `create-react-app`:

 This is the new version of `create-react-app` (v2), which includes the new Babel 7.

Summary

In this first chapter, we have learned some basic concepts that are very important for following the rest of the book, and that are crucial to working with React daily.

We now know how to write declarative code, and we have a clear understanding of the difference between the components we create and the elements React uses to display their instances on the screen.

We learned the reasons behind the choice of locating logic and templates together, and why that unpopular decision has been a big win for React.

We went through the reasons why it is common to feel fatigue in the JavaScript ecosystem, but we have also seen how to avoid those problems by following an iterative approach.

Finally, we have seen what the new `create-react-app` CLI is, and we are now ready to start writing some real code.

Clean Up Your Code 2

This chapter assumes that you already have experience with JSX and you want to improve your skills to use it effectively. To use JSX without any problems or unexpected behaviors, it is essential to understand how it works under the hood, and the reasons why it is a useful tool for building UIs.

Our goal is to write clean and maintainable JSX code, and to achieve that we have to know where it comes from, how it gets translated to JavaScript, and which features it provides.

In the first section, we will do a little step back, but please bear with me because it is crucial to master the basics to apply the best practices.

In this chapter, we will cover the following topics:

- What is JSX, and why should we use it?
- What is Babel and how can we use it to write modern JavaScript code?
- The main features of JSX and the differences between HTML and JSX
- Best practices to write JSX in an elegant and maintainable way
- How linting, and ESLint in particular, can make our JavaScript code consistent across applications and teams
- The basics of functional programming and why following a functional paradigm will make us write better React components

JSX

In the previous chapter, we saw how React changes the concept of separation of concerns, moving the boundaries inside components. We also learned how React uses the elements returned by the components to display the UI on the screen.

Let's now look at how we can declare our elements inside our components.

React provides two ways to define our elements. The first one is by using JavaScript functions, and the second one is by using JSX, an optional XML-like syntax. Here is the examples section of the official React.js website (`https://reactjs.org/#examples`):

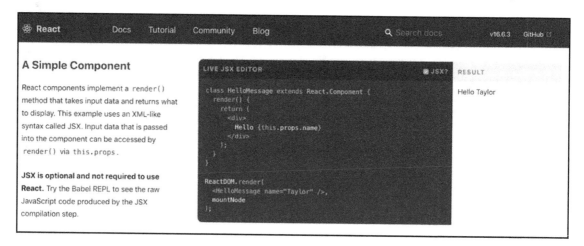

To begin with, JSX is one of the main reasons why people fail to approach React, because looking at the examples on the home page and seeing JavaScript mixed with HTML for the first time seems strange to most of us.

As soon as we get used to it, we realize that it is very convenient, precisely because it is similar to HTML and looks very familiar to anyone who has already created UIs on the web. The opening and closing tags make it easier to represent nested trees of elements, something that would have been unreadable and hard to maintain using plain JavaScript.

Babel 7

To use JSX (and some features of ES6) in our code, we have to install the new Babel 7.

First of all, it is important to clearly understand the problems it can solve for us and why we need to add a step to our process. The reason is that we want to use features of the language that have not yet been added in the browser, our target environment. Those advanced features make our code cleaner for developers, but the browser cannot understand and execute it.

The solution is to write our scripts in JSX and ES6, and, when we are ready to ship, we compile the sources into ES5, the standard specification implemented in major browsers today.

Babel is a popular JavaScript compiler widely adopted within the React community.

Babel can compile ES6 code into ES5 JavaScript, as well as compile JSX into JavaScript functions. The process is called transpilation, because it compiles the source into a new source rather than into an executable.

In older versions of Babel 6.X, you installed the `babel-cli` package and you got `babel-node` and `babel-core` now everything is separated: `@babel/core`, `@babel/cli`, `@babel/node`, and so on.

To install it, we need to install `@babel/core` and `@babel/node` as follows:

```
npm install -g @babel/core @babel/node
```

If you do not want to install it globally (developers usually tend to avoid this), you can install Babel locally to a project and run it through an `npm` script, but for this chapter, a global instance is fine.

When the installation is complete, we can run the following command to compile any JavaScript file:

```
babel source.js -o output.js
```

One of the reasons Babel is so powerful is because it is highly configurable. Babel is just a tool to transpile a source file into an output file, but to apply some transformations, we need to configure it.

Luckily, there are some very useful presets of configurations that we can easily install and use:

```
npm install -g @babel/preset-env @babel/preset-react
```

Once the installation is complete, we create a configuration file called `.babelrc` in the root folder, and put the following lines into it to tell Babel to use those presets:

```
{
  "presets": [
    "@babel/preset-env",
    "@babel/preset-react"
  ]
}
```

From this point on, we can write ES6 and JSX in our source files and execute the output files in the browser.

Hello, World!

Now that our environment has been set up to support JSX, we can dive into the most basic example: generating a `div` element.

This is how you would create a `div` element with React's `createElement` function:

```
React.createElement('div')
```

And this is the JSX for creating a `div` element:

```
<div />
```

It looks similar to regular HTML.

The big difference is that we are writing the markup inside a `.js` file, but it is important to note that JSX is only syntactic sugar, and it gets transpiled into JavaScript before being executed in the browser.

In fact, our `<div />` element is translated into `React.createElement('div')` when we run Babel, which is something we should always keep in mind when we write our templates.

DOM elements and React components

With JSX, we can create both HTML elements and React components; the only difference is whether or not they start with a capital letter.

For example, to render an HTML button, we use `<button />`, while to render the `Button` component we use `<Button />`.

The first button is transpiled into the following:

```
React.createElement('button');
```

The second one is transpiled into the following:

```
React.createElement(Button);
```

The difference here is that in the first call we are passing the type of the DOM element as a string, while in the second call we are passing the component itself, which means that it should exist in the scope to work.

As you may have noticed, JSX supports self-closing tags, which are pretty good for keeping the code terse and do not require us to repeat unnecessary tags.

Props

JSX is very convenient when your DOM elements or React components have props. Using XML is pretty easy to set attributes on elements:

```
<img src="https://www.dev.education/images/logo.png" alt="DEV
Education" />
```

The equivalent in JavaScript would be as follows:

```
React.createElement("img", {
  src: "https://www.dev.education/images/logo.png",
  alt: "DEV Education"
});
```

This is far less readable, and even with only a couple of attributes it is harder to read without a bit of reasoning.

Children

JSX allows you to define children to describe the tree of elements and compose complex UIs.

A basic example is a link with text inside it, as follows:

```
<a href="https://dev.education">Click me!</a>
```

This would be transpiled into the following:

```
React.createElement(
  "a",
  { href: "https://www.dev.education" },
  "Click me!"
);
```

Our link can be enclosed inside a `div` element for some layout requirements, and the JSX snippet to achieve that is as follows:

```
<div>
  <a href="https://www.dev.education">Click me!</a>
</div>
```

The JavaScript equivalent is as follows:

```
React.createElement(
  "div",
  null,
  React.createElement(
    "a",
    { href: "https://www.dev.education" },
    "Click me!"
  )
);
```

It should now be clear how the XML-like syntax of JSX makes everything more readable and maintainable, but it is always important to know the JavaScript parallel of our JSX to have control over the creation of elements.

The good part is that we are not limited to having elements as children of elements, but we can use JavaScript expressions, such as functions or variables.

To do this, we have to enclose the expression within curly braces:

```
<div>
  Hello, {variable}.
  I'm a {() => console.log('Function')}.
</div>
```

The same applies to non-string attributes, as follows:

```
<a href={this.createLink()}>Click me!</a>
```

Differences with HTML

So far, we have looked at the similarities between JSX and HTML. Let's now look at the little differences between them and the reasons they exist.

Attributes

We must always keep in mind that JSX is not a standard language, and that it gets transpiled into JavaScript. Because of this, some attributes cannot be used.

For example, instead of `class` we have to use `className`, and instead of `for` we have to use `htmlFor`, as follows:

```
<label className="awesome-label" htmlFor="name" />
```

The reason for this is that `class` and `for` are reserved words in JavaScript.

Style

A pretty significant difference is the way the `style` attribute works. We will look at how to use it in more detail in `Chapter 7`, *Make Your Components Look Beautiful*, but now we will focus on the way it works.

The `style` attribute does not accept a CSS string as the HTML parallel does, but it expects a JavaScript object where the style names are **camelCased**:

```
<div style={{ backgroundColor: 'red' }} />
```

Root

One important difference with HTML worth mentioning is that, since JSX elements get translated into JavaScript functions, and you cannot return two functions in JavaScript, whenever you have multiple elements at the same level you are forced to wrap them into a parent.

Let's look at a simple example:

```
<div />
<div />
```

This gives us the following error:

```
Adjacent JSX elements must be wrapped in an enclosing tag.
```

On the other hand, the following works:

```
<div>
  <div />
  <div />
</div>
```

Before, React forced you to return an element wrapped with a `<div>` element or any other tag; since React 16.2.0, it is possible to return an array or string directly:

```
// Example 1: Returning an array of elements.
render() {
  // Now you don't need to wrap list items in an extra element
  return [
    <li key="1">First item</li>,
    <li key="2">Second item</li>,
    <li key="3">Third item</li>
  ];
}

// Example 2: Returning a string
render() {
  return 'Hello World!';
}
```

Also, React now has a new feature called `Fragment` that also works as a special wrapper for elements. It can be specified with empty tags (`<></>`) or directly using `React.Fragment`:

```
// Example 1: Using empty tags <></>
render() {
  return (
    <>
      <ComponentA />
      <ComponentB />
      <ComponentC />
    </>
  );
}

// Example 2: Using React.Fragment
render() {
  return (
    <React.Fragment>
      <h1>An h1 heading</h1>
      Some text here.
      <h2>An h2 heading</h2>
      More text here.
```

```
      Even more text here.
    </React.Fragment>
  );
}


// Example 3: Importing Fragment
import React, { Fragment } from 'react';

render() {
  return (
    <Fragment>
      <h1>An h1 heading</h1>
      Some text here.
      <h2>An h2 heading</h2>
      More text here.
      Even more text here.
    </Fragment>
  );
}
```

Spaces

There's one thing that could be a little bit tricky in the beginning and, again, it concerns the fact that we should always keep in mind that JSX is not HTML, even if it has an XML-like syntax.

JSX handles the spaces between text and elements differently from HTML, in a way that's counter-intuitive.

Consider the following snippet:

```
<div>
  <span>My</span>
  name is
  <span>Carlos</span>
</div>
```

In the browser, which interprets HTML, this code would give you "My name is Carlos", which is exactly what we expect.

In JSX, the same code would be rendered as `MynameisCarlos`, which is because the three nested lines get transpiled as individual children of the `div` element, without taking the spaces into account. A common solution to get the same output is putting a space explicitly between the elements as follows:

```
<div>
  <span>My</span>
  {' '}
  name is
  {' '}
  <span>Carlos</span>
</div>
```

As you may have noticed, we are using an empty string wrapped inside a JavaScript expression to force the compiler to apply the space between the elements.

Boolean attributes

A couple more things are worth mentioning before starting for real regarding the way you define Boolean attributes in JSX. If you set an attribute without a value, JSX assumes that its value is `true`, following the same behavior of the HTML `disabled` attribute, for example.

This means that if we want to set an attribute to `false`, we have to declare it explicitly as false:

```
<button disabled />
React.createElement("button", { disabled: true });
```

The following is another example:

```
<button disabled={false} />
React.createElement("button", { disabled: false });
```

This can be confusing in the beginning, because we may think that omitting an attribute would mean `false`, but it is not like that. With React, we should always be explicit to avoid confusion.

Spread attributes

An important feature is the **spread attribute** operator (. . .), which comes from the rest/spread properties for ECMAScript proposal, and is very convenient whenever we want to pass all the attributes of a JavaScript object to an element.

A common practice that leads to fewer bugs is not to pass entire JavaScript objects down to children by reference, but to use their primitive values, which can be easily validated, making components more robust and error-proof.

Let's see how it works:

```
const attrs = {
  id: 'myId',
  className: 'myClass'
};
return <div {...attrs} />;
```

The preceding code gets transpiled into the following:

```
var attrs = {
  id: 'myId',
  className: 'myClass'
};

return React.createElement('div', attrs);
```

JavaScript templating

Finally, we started with the assumption that one of the advantages of moving the templates inside our components instead of using an external template library is that we can use the full power of JavaScript, so let's start looking at what that means.

The spread attributes is an example of this, and another common example is that JavaScript expressions can be used as attribute values by enclosing them within curly braces, as follows:

```
<button disabled={errors.length} />
```

Common patterns

Now that we know how JSX works and can master it, we are ready to see how to use it in the right way following some useful conventions and techniques.

Multi-line

Let's start with a very simple one. As stated previously, one of the main reasons we should prefer JSX over React's `createElement` function is because of its XML-like syntax, and because balanced opening and closing tags are perfect to represent a tree of nodes.

Therefore, we should try to use it in the right way and get the most out of it.

One example is as follows; whenever we have nested elements, we should always go multiline:

```
<div>
  <Header />
  <div>
    <Main content={...} />
  </div>
</div>
```

This is preferable to the following:

```
<div><Header /><div><Main content={...} /></div></div>
```

The exception is if the children are not elements, such as text or variables. In that case, it makes sense to remain on the same line and avoid adding noise to the markup, as follows:

```
<div>
  <Alert>{message}</Alert>
  <Button>Close</Button>
</div>
```

Always remember to wrap your elements inside parentheses when you write them in multiple lines. JSX always gets replaced by functions, and functions written on a new line can give you an unexpected result because of automatic semicolon insertion. Suppose, for example, that you are returning JSX from your render method, which is how you create UIs in React.

The following example works fine because the `div` element is on the same line as the return:

```
return <div />;
```

The following, however, is not right:

```
return
  <div />;
```

The reason for this is because you would then have the following:

```
return;
React.createElement("div", null);
```

This is why you have to wrap the statement in parentheses, as follows:

```
return (
  <div />
);
```

Multi-properties

A common problem in writing JSX comes when an element has multiples attributes. One solution is to write all the attributes on the same line, but this would lead to very long lines that we do not want in our code (see the following section for how to enforce coding style guides).

A common solution is to write each attribute on a new line, with one level of indentation, and then align the closing bracket with the opening tag:

```
<button
  foo="bar"
  veryLongPropertyName="baz"
  onSomething={this.handleSomething}
/>
```

Conditionals

Things get more interesting when we start working with **conditionals**, for example, if we want to render some components only when certain conditions are matched. The fact that we can use JavaScript in our conditions is a big plus, but there are many different ways to express conditions in JSX, and it is important to understand the benefits and problems of each one of these to write code that is both readable and maintainable.

Suppose we want to show a logout button only if the user is currently logged into our application.

A simple snippet to start with is as follows:

```
let button;
if (isLoggedIn) {
  button = <LogoutButton />;
}
return <div>{button}</div>;
```

This works, but it is not very readable, especially if there are multiple components and multiple conditions.

In JSX, we can use an inline condition:

```
<div>
  {isLoggedIn && <LoginButton />}
</div>
```

This works because if the condition is `false`, nothing gets rendered, but if the condition is `true`, the `createElement` function of the `LoginButton` gets called, and the element is returned to compose the resulting tree.

If the condition has an alternative (the classic `if...else` statement), and we want, for example, to show a logout button if the user is logged in and a login button otherwise, we can use JavaScript's `if...else` statement as follows:

```
let button;

if (isLoggedIn) {
  button = <LogoutButton />;
} else {
  button = <LoginButton />;
}
return <div>{button}</div>;
```

Alternatively, and better still, we can use a ternary condition that makes the code more compact:

```
<div>
  {isLoggedIn ? <LogoutButton /> : <LoginButton />}
</div>
```

You can find the ternary condition used in popular repositories, such as the Redux real-world example (`https://github.com/reactjs/redux/blob/master/examples/real-world/src/components/List.js#L28`), where the ternary is used to show a loading label if the component is fetching the data, or *load more* inside a button depending on the value of the `isFetching` variable:

```
<button [...]>
  {isFetching ? 'Loading...' : 'Load More'}
</button>
```

Let's now look at the best solution for when things get more complicated and, for example, we have to check more than one variable to determine whether to render a component or not:

```
<div>
  {dataIsReady && (isAdmin || userHasPermissions) &&
    <SecretData />
  }
</div>
```

In this case, it is clear that using the inline condition is a good solution, but the readability is strongly impacted. Instead, we can create a helper function inside our component and use it in JSX to verify the condition:

```
canShowSecretData() {
  const { dataIsReady, isAdmin, userHasPermissions } = this.props;
  return dataIsReady && (isAdmin || userHasPermissions);
}
return (
  <div>
    {this.canShowSecretData() && <SecretData />}
  </div>
);
```

As you can see, this change makes the code more readable and the condition more explicit. If you look at this code in six months, you will still find it clear just by reading the name of the function.

If you do not like using functions, you can use an object's getters, which makes the code more elegant.

For example, instead of declaring a function, we define a getter as follows:

```
get canShowSecretData() {
  const { dataIsReady, isAdmin, userHasPermissions } = this.props;
  return dataIsReady && (isAdmin || userHasPermissions);
}
```

```
return (
  <div>
    {this.canShowSecretData() && <SecretData />}
  </div>
);
```

The same applies to computed properties. Suppose you have two single properties for currency and value. Instead of creating the price string inside your `render` method, you can create a class function:

```
getPrice() {
  return `${this.props.currency}${this.props.value}`;
}
return <div>{this.getPrice()}</div>;
```

This is better because it is isolated and you can easily test it in case it contains logic.

Alternatively, you can go a step further and, as we have just seen, use getters:

```
get price() {
  return `${this.props.currency}${this.props.value}`;
}
return <div>{this.price()}</div>;
```

Going back to conditional statements, other solutions require using external dependencies. A good practice is to avoid external dependencies as much as we can to keep our bundle smaller, but it may be worth it in this particular case, because improving the readability of our templates is a big win.

The first solution is `render-if`, which we can install with the following:

```
npm install --save render-if
```

We can then easily use it in our projects, as follows:

```
const { dataIsReady, isAdmin, userHasPermissions } = this.props;

const canShowSecretData = renderIf(
  dataIsReady && (isAdmin || userHasPermissions)
);
return (
  <div>
    {canShowSecretData(<SecretData />)}
  </div>
);
```

We wrap our conditions inside the `renderIf` function.

The utility function that gets returned can be used as a function that receives the JSX markup to be shown when the condition is `true`.

One goal we should always keep in mind is to never add too much logic inside our components. Some of them will require a bit of it, but we should try to keep them as simple as possible so that we can easily spot and fix errors.

We should at least try to keep the `renderIf` method as clean as possible, and, to do that, we can use another utility library called `react-only-if`, which lets us write our components as if the condition is always `true` by setting the conditional function using a **higher-order component (HoC)**.

We will talk about HoC extensively in `Chapter 4`, *Compose All the Things*, but, for now, you need to know that they are functions that receive a component and return an enhanced one by adding some properties or modifying its behavior.

To use the library, we need to install it as follows:

```
npm install --save react-only-if
```

Once it is installed, we can use it in our apps in the following way:

```
import onlyIf from 'react-only-if';

const SecretDataOnlyIf = onlyIf(
  ({ dataIsReady, isAdmin, userHasPermissions }) => dataIsReady &&
  (isAdmin || userHasPermissions)
) (SecretData);

return (
  <div>
    <SecretDataOnlyIf
      dataIsReady={...}
      isAdmin={...}
      userHasPermissions={...}
    />
  </div>
);
```

As you can see here, there is no logic at all inside the component itself.

We pass the condition as the first parameter of the `onlyIf` function, and when the condition is matched, the component is rendered.

The function used to validate the condition receives the props, state, and context of the component.

In this way, we avoid polluting our component with conditionals so that it is easier to understand and reason about.

Loops

A very common operation in UI development is to display lists of items. When it comes to showing lists, using JavaScript as a template language is a very good idea.

If we write a function that returns an array inside our JSX template, each element of the array gets compiled into an element.

As we have seen before, we can use any JavaScript expressions inside curly braces, and the most common way to generate an array of elements, given an array of objects, is to use `map`.

Let's dive into a real-world example. Suppose you have a list of users, each one with a name property attached to it.

To create an unordered list to show the users, you can do the following:

```
<ul>
  {users.map(user => <li>{user.name}</li>)}
</ul>
```

This snippet is incredibly simple and incredibly powerful at the same time, where the power of the HTML and JavaScript converge.

Control statements

Conditionals and loops are very common operations in UI templates, and you may feel wrong using the JavaScript ternary or the map function to perform them. JSX has been built in such a way that it only abstracts the creation of the elements, leaving the logic parts to real JavaScript, which is great except that, sometimes, the code becomes less clear.

In general, we aim to remove all the logic from our components, and especially from our render methods, but sometimes we have to show and hide elements according to the state of the application, and very often we have to loop through collections and arrays.

If you feel that using JSX for that kind of operation will make your code more readable, there is a Babel plugin available to do just that: `jsx-control-statements`.

This follows the same philosophy as JSX, and it does not add any real functionality to the language; it is just syntactic sugar that gets compiled into JavaScript.

Let's see how it works.

First of all, we have to install it:

```
npm install --save jsx-control-statements
```

Once it is installed, we have to add it to the list of our babel plugins in our `.babelrc` file:

```
"plugins": ["jsx-control-statements"]
```

From now on we can use the syntax provided by the plugin and Babel will transpile it together with the common JSX syntax.

A conditional statement written using the plugin looks like the following snippet:

```
<If condition={this.canShowSecretData}>
  <SecretData />
</If>
```

This gets transpiled into a ternary expression as follows:

```
{canShowSecretData ? <SecretData /> : null}
```

The `If` component is great, but if, for some reason, you have nested conditions in your render method, it can easily become messy and hard to follow. Here is where the `Choose` component comes in handy:

```
<Choose>
  <When condition={...}>
    <span>if</span>
  </When>
  <When condition={...}>
    <span>else if</span>
  </When>
  <Otherwise>
    <span>else</span>
  </Otherwise>
</Choose>
```

Please note that the preceding code gets transpiled into multiple ternaries.

Finally, there is a component (always remember that we are not talking about real components but just syntactic sugar) to manage the loops that are also very convenient:

```
<ul>
  <For each="user" of={this.props.users}>
    <li>{user.name}</li>
  </For>
</ul>
```

The preceding code gets transpiled into a map function – no magic there.

If you are used to using **linters**, you might wonder why the linter is not complaining about that code. The `user` variable does not exist before the transpilation, nor is it wrapped into a function. To avoid those linting errors, there is another plugin to install: `eslint-plugin-jsx-control-statements`.

If you did not understand the previous sentence, don't worry; we will talk about linting in the following section.

Sub-rendering

It is worth stressing that we always want to keep our components very small and our render methods very clean and simple.

However, that is not an easy goal, especially when you are creating an application iteratively, and in the first iteration you are not sure exactly how to split the components into smaller ones. So, what should we be doing when the `render` method becomes too big to maintain? One solution is to split it into smaller functions in a way that lets us keep all the logic in the same component.

Let's look at an example:

```
renderUserMenu() {
  // JSX for user menu
}
renderAdminMenu() {
  // JSX for admin menu
}
render() {
  return (
    <div>
      <h1>Welcome back!</h1>
      {this.userExists && this.renderUserMenu()}
      {this.userIsAdmin && this.renderAdminMenu()}
    </div>
```

```
    );
  }
```

This is not always considered best practice because it seems more obvious to split the component into smaller ones. However, sometimes it helps to keep the render method cleaner. For example, in the Redux real-world examples, a sub-render method is used to render the load more button.

Now that we are JSX power users, it is time to move on and see how to follow a style guide within our code to make it consistent.

Code style

In this section, you will learn how to implement EditorConfig and ESLint to improve your code quality by validating your code style.

EditorConfig

EditorConfig helps developers to maintain consistent coding styles between different IDEs.

Configuring EditorConfig

EditorConfig is supported by a lot of editors. You can check whether your editor is supported or not on the official website, https://www.editorconfig.org.

You need to create a file called .editorconfig in your root directory – the configuration I use is this one:

```
root = true

[*]
indent_style = space
indent_size = 2
end_of_line = lf
charset = utf-8
trim_trailing_whitespace = true
insert_final_newline = true

[*.html]
indent_size = 4

[*.css]
```

```
indent_size = 4

[*.md]
trim_trailing_whitespace = false
```

You can affect all the files with [], and specific files with [.extension].

ESLint

We always try to write the best code possible, but sometimes errors happen, and spending a few hours catching a bug due to a typo is very frustrating. Luckily, some tools can help us check the correctness of our code as soon as we type it. These tools are not able to tell us if our code is going to do what it's supposed to do, but they can help us to avoid syntactical errors.

If you come from a static language, such as C#, you are used to getting that kind of warning inside your IDE. Douglas Crockford made linting popular in JavaScript with JSLint (initially released in 2002) a few years ago; then we had JSHint, and finally, the de-facto standard in the React world nowadays is ESLint.

ESLint is an open source project released in 2013 that became popular thanks to the fact that it is highly configurable and extensible.

In the JavaScript ecosystem, where libraries and techniques change very quickly, it is crucial to have a tool that can be easily extended with plugins, and rules that can be enabled and disabled when needed. Most importantly, nowadays we use transpilers, such as Babel, and experimental features that are not part of the standard version of JavaScript, so we need to be able to tell our linter which rules we are following in our source files. Not only does a linter help us to make fewer errors, or at least, find those errors sooner, but it enforces some common coding style guides, which is important, especially in big teams with many developers, each one with their favorite coding style.

It is very hard to read the code in a code base where different files, or even various functions, are written using inconsistent styles.

Installation

First of all, we have to install ESLint as follows:

```
npm install --global eslint
```

Once the executable is installed, we can run it with the following command:

```
eslint source.js
```

The output will tell us if there are errors within the file.

When we install and run it for the first time, we do not see any errors because it is completely configurable and it does not come with any default rules.

Configuration

Let's start configuring it.

ESLint can be configured using a `.eslintrc` file that lives in the root folder of the project.

To add some rules, we use the `rules` key.

For example, let's create a `.eslintrc` file and disable the semicolon:

```
{
    "rules": {
        "semi": [2, "never"]
    }
}
```

This configuration file needs a bit of explanation: `"semi"` is the name of the rule and `[2, "never"]` is the value. It is not very intuitive the first time you see it.

ESLint rules have three levels that determine the severity of the problem:

- **off (or 0)**: The rule is disabled
- **warn (or 1)**: The rule is a warning
- **error (or 2)**: The rule throws an error

We are using the 2 value because we want ESLint to throw an error every time our code does not follow the rule. The second parameter tells ESLint that we want the semicolon to never be used (the opposite is always). ESLint and its plugins are very well documented, and for any single rule you can find the description of the rule and some examples of when it passes and when it fails.

Now, create an `index.js` file with the following content:

```
var foo = 'bar';
```

Note that we are using `var` here because ESLint does not know yet that we want to write code in ES6 (ES2015).

If we run `eslint index.js` we get the following:

```
Extra semicolon (semi)
```

This is great; we set up the linter, and it is helping us follow our first rule.

We can enable and disable every single rule manually, or we can enable the recommended configuration in one go by putting the following code into our `.eslintrc` file:

```
{
    "extends": "eslint:recommended"
}
```

The `extends` key means that we are extending the recommended rules from the ESLint configuration, but we can always override single rules manually inside our `.eslintrc` file using the `rules` key, as we have done before.

Once the recommended rules are enabled, and we run ESLint again, we should not receive an error for the semicolon (which is not part of the recommended configuration), but we should see the linter complaining about the fact that the `foo` variable has been declared and never used.

The `no-unused-vars` rule is pretty useful for keeping our code clean.

As we have said since the beginning, we want to write ES6 (ES2015) code, but changing the code to the following returns an error:

```
const foo = 'bar';
```

This is the error in question:

```
Parsing error: The keyword 'const' is reserved
```

So, to enable ES6 (ES2015), we have to add the `parserOptions` configuration option:

```
{
    "extends": "eslint:recommended",
    "parserOptions": {
        "ecmaVersion": 6
    }
}
```

Once we have done this, we will get the unused error again, which is fine.

Finally, to enable JSX, we use the following:

```
{
  "extends": "eslint:recommended",
  "parserOptions": {
    "ecmaVersion": 6,
    "ecmaFeatures": {
      "jsx": true
    }
  }
}
```

At this point, if you have written any React applications before and have never used a linter, a good exercise to learn the rules and get used to it is to run ESLint against the source and fix all the issues.

There are different ways in which we make ESLint help us write better code. One is what we have done until now – run it from the command line and get the list of errors.

This works, but it is not very convenient to run it manually all the time. It would be great to add the linting process inside our editor to get immediate feedback as soon as we type. To do that, there are ESLint plugins for Atom, **Visual Studio Code** (**VSC**), and the other most popular editors.

In the real world, running ESLint manually or getting the feedback live in the editor, even if it is very useful, is not enough, because we can miss some warnings or errors, or we can simply ignore them.

Git hooks

To avoid having unlinted code in our repository, what we can do is add ESLint at one point of our process using Git hooks. For example, we can use Husky to run our linter in a Git hook called pre-commit, and it is also useful to run our unit tests on the hook pre-push.

To install husky, you need to run:

```
npm install --save-dev husky
```

Then in our `package.json` file, we can add this node to configure the tasks we want to run in the Git hooks:

```
{
  "scripts": {
    "lint": "eslint --ext .jsx,.js src",
    "lint:fix": "eslint --ext .jsx,.js --fix src",
    "test": "jest src"
  },
  "husky": {
    "hooks": {
      "pre-commit": "npm lint",
      "pre-push": "npm test"
    }
  }
}
```

There is a special option (flag) for the ESlint command called `--fix` – with this option, ESLint will try to fix all our linter errors automatically (not all of them), be careful with this option because sometimes can affect a little bit of our code style. Another useful flag is `--ext` to specify the extensions of the files we want to validate, in this case just the `.jsx` and `.js` files.

React plugin

As mentioned previously, one of the main reasons ESLint is popular is because it is extensible with plugins; the most important one for us is `eslint-plugin-react`.

ESLint can parse JSX without any plugins (just by enabling the flag), but we want to do more. For example, we may want to enforce one of the best practices we have seen in the previous section and keep our templates consistent across developers and teams.

To use the plugin, we first have to install it:

```
npm install --global eslint-plugin-react
```

Once it is installed, we instruct ESLint to use it by adding the following line to the configuration file:

```
"plugins": [
  "react"
]
```

As you can see, it is pretty straightforward, and it does not require any complex configuration or set up. Just like ESLint, without any rules it doesn't do anything, but we can enable the recommended configuration to activate a basic set of rules.

To do that, we update the "extends" key in our .eslintrc file as follows:

```
"extends": [
  "eslint:recommended",
  "plugin:react/recommended"
]
```

Now, if we write something wrong, for example, we try to use the same prop twice in a React component, we are going to get an error:

```
<Foo bar bar />
```

The preceding code returns the following:

No duplicate props allowed (react/jsx-no-duplicate-props)

There are a lot of rules available to be used in our project. Let's go through some of them and see how they can help us to follow the best practices.

As discussed in the previous chapter, it is very helpful to indent our JSX following the tree structure of the elements to improve the readability.

The problem comes when the indentation is not consistent through the code base and components.

So, here is an example of how ESLint can be useful to help everyone in the team follow a style guide without having to memorize it.

Notice how, in this case, having the wrong indentation is not an actual error and the code works; it is just a matter of consistency.

First of all, we have to activate the rule:

```
"rules": {
  "react/jsx-indent": [2, 2]
}
```

The first 2 means that we want ESLint to raise an error in case the rule is not followed within the code, and the second 2 means that we want every JSX element to be indented with two spaces. ESLint does not make any decisions for you, so it is up to you to decide which rules to enable. You can even choose to force a non-indentation using 0 as a second parameter.

Write something like the following:

```
<div>
  <div />
</div>
```

ESLint complains, as follows:

```
Expected indentation of 2 space characters but found 0
    (react/jsx-indent)
```

A similar rule regards the way we indent our attributes when we write them on a new line.

As we have seen in the previous section, when the attributes are too many or too long, it is a good practice to write them on a new line.

To enforce formatting where the attributes are indented by two spaces in relation to the element name, we can just enable the following rule:

```
"react/jsx-indent-props": [2, 2]
```

From now on, if we do not indent the attributes with two spaces, ESLint will fail.

The question is, when do we consider a line too long? How many attributes are too many? Every developer will have a different opinion about this. ESLint helps us to maintain consistency with the `jsx-max-props-per-line` rule so that every component is written in the same way.

The React plugin for ESLint not only gives us some rules to write better JSX, but also some rules to write better React components.

For example, we can enable a rule to enforce the sorting of the prop types into alphabetical order, a rule to give us an error when we are using a prop that has not been declared, a rule to force us to prefer stateless functional components over classes (we will see the difference in detail in `Chapter 3`, *Create Truly Reusable Components*), and so on.

Airbnb React/JSX style guide

The Airbnb React/JSX style guide is the most popular style guide for coding in React.

To implement the Airbnb React/JSX style guide, we need to install some packages:

```
npm install --save-dev babel-eslint eslint eslint-config-airbnb eslint-
plugin-import eslint-plugin-jsx-a11y eslint-plugin-react
```

You can check all the ESLint rules on the official website (`https://eslint.org/docs/rules`) and all the special React ESLint rules at `https://github.com/yannickcr/eslint-plugin-react/tree/master/docs/rules`.

The rules that I prefer not to use, or that I prefer to change the default values of, are as follows:

- `comma-dangle`: Off
- `arrow-parens`: Off
- `max-len`: 120
- `no-param-reassign`: Off
- `function-paren-newline`: Off
- `react/require-default-props`: Off

First, you need to create a new file called `.eslintrc` at the root level:

```
{
  "parser": "babel-eslint",
  "extends": "airbnb",
  "rules": {
    "arrow-parens": "off",
    "comma-dangle": "off",
    "function-paren-newline": "off",
    "max-len": [1, 120],
    "no-param-reassign": "off",
    "react/require-default-props": "off"
  }
}
```

To run your linter, you have to add a lint script into your `package.json` file:

```
{
  "scripts": {
    "lint": "eslint --ext .jsx,.js src"
  }
}
```

Now you can lint your files using the Airbnb React/JSX style guide.

The basics of functional programming

Apart from following the best practices when we write JSX and use a linter to enforce consistency and find errors earlier, there is one more thing we can do to clean up our code: follow a **functional programming** (**FP**) style.

As discussed in `Chapter 1`, *Taking Your First Steps with React*, React has a declarative programming approach that makes our code more readable.

FP is a declarative paradigm, where side-effects are avoided, and data is considered immutable to make the code easier to maintain and to reason about.

Don't consider the following section an exhaustive guide to functional programming; it is only an introduction to get started with some concepts that are commonly used in React of which you should be aware.

First-class objects

In JavaScript, functions are *first-class objects*, which means that they can be assigned to variables and passed as parameters to other functions.

This allows us to introduce the concept of higher-order functions (HoFs). HoFs are functions that take a function as a parameter, optionally some other parameters, and return a function. The returned function is usually enhanced with some special behaviors.

Let's look at a simple example where there is a function for adding two numbers that gets enhanced with a function that first logs all the parameters and then executes the original one:

```
const add = (x, y) => x + y;

const log = fn => (...args) => {
  console.log(...args);
  return fn(...args);
};

const logAdd = log(add);
```

This concept is pretty important to understand, because, in the React world, a common pattern is to use HoCs, to treat our components as functions, and to enhance them with common behaviors. We will see HoCs and other patterns in `Chapter 4`, *Compose All the Things*.

Purity

An important aspect of FP is to write pure functions. You will encounter this concept very often in the React ecosystem, especially if you look into libraries such as Redux.

What does it mean for a function to be pure?

A function is pure when there are no side-effects, which means that the function does not change anything that is not local to the functions itself.

For example, a function that changes the state of an application, or modifies variables defined in the upper scope, or a function that touches external entities, such as the DOM, is considered impure. Impure functions are harder to debug, and most of the time it is not possible to apply them multiple times and expect to get the same result.

For example, the following function is pure:

```
const add = (x, y) => x + y;
```

It can be run multiple times, always getting the same result, because nothing is stored anywhere and nothing gets modified.

The following function is not pure:

```
let x = 0;
const add = y => (x = x + y);
```

Running add(1) twice, we get two different results. The first time we get 1, but the second time we get 2, even if we call the same function with the same parameter. The reason we get that behavior is that the global state gets modified after every execution.

Immutability

We have seen how to write pure functions that don't mutate the state, but what if we need to change the value of a variable? In FP, a function, instead of changing the value of a variable, creates a new variable with a new value and returns it. This way of working with data is called **immutability**.

An immutable value is a value that cannot be changed.

Let's look at an example:

```
const add3 = arr => arr.push(3);
const myArr = [1, 2];

add3(myArr); // [1, 2, 3]
add3(myArr); // [1, 2, 3, 3]
```

The preceding function doesn't follow immutability because it changes the value of the given array. Again, if we call the same function twice, we get different results.

We can change the preceding function to make it immutable using `concat`, which returns a new array without modifying the given one:

```
const add3 = arr => arr.concat(3);
const myArr = [1, 2];
const result1 = add3(myArr); // [1, 2, 3]
const result2 = add3(myArr); // [1, 2, 3]
```

After we have run the function twice, `myArr` still has its original value.

Currying

A common technique in FP is currying. **Currying** is the process of converting a function that takes multiple arguments into a function that takes one argument at a time, returning another function. Let's look at an example to clarify the concept.

Let's start with the `add` function we have seen before and transform it into a curried function.

Instead of writing the following code:

```
const add = (x, y) => x + y;
```

We define the function as follows:

```
const add = x => y => x + y;
```

And we use it in the following way:

```
const add1 = add(1);
add1(2); // 3
add1(3); // 4
```

This is a pretty convenient way of writing functions because, since the first value is stored after the application of the first parameter, we can reuse the second function multiple times.

Composition

Finally, an important concept in FP that can be applied to React is composition. Functions (and components) can be combined to produce new functions with more advanced features and properties.

Consider the following functions:

```
const add = (x, y) => x + y;
const square = x => x * x;
```

These functions can be composed together to create a new function that adds two numbers and then doubles the result:

```
const addAndSquare = (x, y) => square(add(x, y));
```

Following this paradigm, we end up with small, simple, testable pure functions that can be composed together.

FP and user interfaces

The last step to take is to learn how we can use FP to build UIs, which is what we use React for.

We can think about a UI as a function to which is applied the state of the application, as follows:

```
UI = f(state);
```

We expect this function to be idempotent so that it returns the same UI given the same state of the application.

Using React, we create our UIs using components we can consider functions, as we will see in the following chapters.

Components can be composed to form the final UI, which is a property of FP.

There are a lot of similarities in the way we build UIs with React and the principles of FP, and the more we are aware of it, the better our code will be.

Summary

In this chapter, we learned a great deal about how JSX works and how to use it in the right way in our components. We started from the basics of the syntax to create a solid knowledge base that will enable us to master JSX and its features.

In the second part, we looked at how ESLint and its plugins can help us find problems faster and enforce a consistent style guide across our code base.

Finally, we went through the basics of functional programming to understand the important concepts to use when writing a React application.

Now that our code is clean, we are ready to start digging deeper into React and learn how to write truly reusable components.

Section 2: How React works 2

In this section, we begin by learning how to create reusable components in order to keep the code base clean and maintainable. We will learn how to organize our components and make them communicate with each other by applying consolidate patterns. We will also look at how to keep the code clean and DRY. We will then go through the different techniques and approaches we can use to fetch data in the React way. And finally, we will take a look at forms and events.

In this section, we will cover the following chapters:

3
Creating Truly Reusable Components

To create truly reusable components, we have to understand the different possibilities that React gives us for defining components, and when it is better to choose one or another. A new type of component has been introduced in React that lets us declare a component as a **stateless function**. It is crucial to understand this component and learn when and why it should be used.

You may have already utilized the internal state of components, but you may still be unclear about when it should be used and the problems it can cause us. The best way to learn is by looking at examples, and we will do that by starting from a component that serves a single purpose and transforming it into a reusable one.

In this chapter, we will cover the following topics:

- The different methods we can follow to create React components, and when we should use one rather than the other
- What stateless functional components are, and the differences between functional and stateful ones
- How the state works and when to avoid using it
- Why it is important to define clear prop types for each component, and how to generate documentation dynamically from them with React Docgen
- Introduction to React Hooks
- A real example of transforming a coupled component into a reusable one
- Understanding Fragments

Creating classes

We saw in the first chapter how React uses elements to display the components on the screen.

Let's now look at the different ways in which we can define our components with React, and the reasons why we should use one or other technique.

Again, this book assumes that you've already played with React in a small/medium application, which means that you must have created some components before.

You may have chosen one method according to the examples on the React website, or by following the style of the boilerplate you used to scaffold the project.

Concepts such as props, state, and life cycle methods should be clear at this point, and we are not going to look at them in detail.

The createClass factory

Looking at the React documentation (at the time of writing), the first example we find shows us how to define components using `React.createClass`.

Let's start with a very simple snippet:

```
const Button = React.createClass({
  render() {
    return <button />;
  }
});
```

With the preceding code, we created a button, and we can reference it inside other components in our application.

We can change the snippet to use plain JavaScript as follows:

```
const Button = React.createClass({
  render() {
    return React.createElement('button');
  }
});
```

We can run the code everywhere without needing to use Babel for transpiling, which is a good way to start with React, avoiding the effort of learning different tools in the React ecosystem.

Extending React.Component

The second way to define a React component is by using the ES2015 classes.
The `class` keyword is widely supported in modern browsers, but we can safely transpile it with Babel, which, supposedly, we already have in our stack if we are writing JSX.

Let's see what it means to create the same button from the previous example using a class:

```
class Button extends React.Component {
  render() {
    return <button />;
  }
}
```

This new way to define a component was released with React 0.13, and Facebook developers are pushing the community to use it. For example, Dan Abramov, an active member of the community and a Facebook employee, recently said:

> *"ES6 classes: better the devil that's standardized while talking about createClass vs. extends Component."*

They want developers to use the latter since it's an ES2015 standard feature, while the `createClass` factory is not.

The main differences

Apart from the discrepancies regarding the syntax, there are some major differences that we have to keep in mind when we decide to use one or another.

Let's go through all of them in detail so you can have all the information you need to choose the best way for the needs of your team and your projects.

Props

The first difference is in how we can define the props that a component expects to receive, and the default values for each one of the props.

We will see how props work in detail further into this chapter, so let's now concentrate on how we can define them.

With `createClass`, we declare the props inside the object that we pass as a parameter to the function, and we use the `getDefaultProps` function to return the default values:

```
const Button = React.createClass({
  propTypes: {
    text: React.PropTypes.string
  },
  getDefaultProps() {
    return {
      text: 'Click me!'
    };
  },
  render() {
    return <button>{this.props.text}</button>;
  }
});
```

As you can see, we use the `propTypes` attribute to list all the props that we can pass to the component.

We then use the `getDefaultProps` function to define the values that the props are going to have by default, and which will be overwritten by the props passed from the parent, if they are present.

To achieve the same result using classes, we have to use a slightly different structure:

```
class Button extends React.Component {
  render() {
    return <button>{this.props.text}</button>;
  }
}
Button.propTypes = {
  text: React.PropTypes.string
};
Button.defaultProps = {
  text: 'Click me!'
};
```

Since class properties are still in draft (they are not part of the ECMAScript standard yet), to define the properties of the class we have to set the attributes on the class itself, after it has been created.

As you can see in the example, the `propTypes` object is the same we used with `createClass`.

When it comes to setting the default props instead, we used to use a function to return the default properties object; but with classes, we have to define a defaultProps attribute on the class and assign the default props to it.

The good thing about using classes is that we define properties on the JavaScript object without having to use React-specific functions, such as getDefaultProps.

State

Another big difference between the createClass factory and the extends React.Component method is the way you define the initial state of the components.

Again, with createClass, we use a function, while with the ES6 classes we set an attribute of the instance.

Let's see an example of that in the following code snippet:

```
const Button = React.createClass({
  getInitialState() {
    return {
      text: 'Click me!'
    };
  },
  render() {
    return <button>{this.state.text}</button>;
  }
});
```

The getInitialState method expects an object with the default values for each one of the state properties.

However, with classes, we define our initial state using the state attribute of the instance and setting it inside the constructor method of the class:

```
class Button extends React.Component {
  constructor(props) {
    super(props);
    this.state = {
      text: 'Click me!'
    };
  }
  render() {
    return <button>{this.state.text}</button>;
  }
}
```

These two ways of defining the state are equivalent but, again, with classes we just define properties on the instance without using any React-specific APIs, which is good.

In ES6, to use `this` in sub-classes, we first must call `super`. In the case of React, we also pass the props to the parent.

Autobinding

`createClass` has a cool feature that is pretty convenient, but it can also hide the way JavaScript works, which is misleading, especially for beginners. This feature lets you create event handlers assuming that, when they get called, `this` references the component itself.

We will see how event handlers work in Chapter 6, *Write Code for the Browser*. For now, we are only interested in the way they are bound to the components we are defining.

Let's start with a simple example:

```
const Button = React.createClass({
  handleClick() {
    console.log(this);
  },
  render() {
    return <button onClick={this.handleClick} />;
  }
});
```

With `createClass`, we can set an event handler in this way and rely on the fact that `this` inside the function refers to the component itself. Because of this, we can, for example, call other methods of the same component instance.
Calling `this.setState()`, or any other functions, would work as expected.

Let's now see how `this` works differently with classes, and what we can do to create the same behavior. We could define a component in the following way, extending `React.Component`:

```
class Button extends React.Component {
  handleClick() {
    console.log(this);
  }
  render() {
    return <button onClick={this.handleClick} />;
  }
}
```

The result would be a `null` output in the console when the button is clicked. This is because our function gets passed to the event handler and we lose the reference to the component.

That does not mean that we cannot use event handlers with classes, we just have to bind our functions manually.

Let's see what solutions we can adopt, and in which scenario we should prefer one or another.

As you probably know already, the new ES6 arrow function automatically binds the current `this` keyword to the body of the function.

So, let's look at the following example:

```
() => this.setState();
```

The preceding code gets transpiled into the following code with Babel:

```
var _this = this;
(function () {
  return _this.setState();
});
```

As you can imagine, one possible solution to the **autobinding** problem is using the arrow function directly in the `render` method. Let's look at the following example:

```
class Button extends React.Component {
  handleClick() {
    console.log(this);
  }
  render() {
    return <button onClick={() => this.handleClick()} />;
  }
}
```

This would work as expected without any particular problems. The only downside is that if we care about performance, we have to understand what the code is doing.

Binding a function inside the render method has, in fact, an unexpected side-effect, because the arrow function gets fired every time the component is rendered (which happens multiple times during the lifetime of the application).

Firing a function inside the render multiple times, even if it is not optimal, it is not a problem by itself.

The issue is that, if we are passing the function down to a child component, it receives a new prop on each update, which leads to inefficient rendering, and that represents a problem – especially if the component is pure (we will talk about performance in `Chapter 9, Improve the Performance of Your Applications`).

The best way to solve it is to bind the function with an arrow function but in the method itself, and pass the reference to the `onClick` property:

```
class Button extends React.Component {
  handleClick = () => {
    console.log(this);
  }
  render() {
    return <button onClick={this.handleClick} />;
  }
}
```

Another way to solve it is to bind the function inside the construction in a way that it doesn't ever change, even if the component renders multiple times:

```
class Button extends React.Component {
  constructor(props) {
    super(props);
    this.handleClick = this.handleClick.bind(this);
  }
  handleClick() {
    console.log(this);
  }
  render() {
    return <button onClick={this.handleClick} />;
  }
}
```

That's it. Problem solved!

Stateless components

So far, we have only learned how to create class components in React. These components are useful when you need to handle local states, but in some cases, we will need to render static markup. For static components, we need to use functional components, also known as stateless components. This will improve the performance of our application.

Let's see how it works and what it provides first, and then we will dig into the cases where one solution fits better than another.

The syntax is particularly terse and elegant – let's see an example:

```
() => <button />
```

The preceding code creates an empty button and, thanks to the concise arrow function syntax, it is straightforward and expressive. As you can see, instead of using the `createClass` factory or extending the component, we only define a function that returns the elements to be displayed.

We can, of course, use the JSX syntax inside the body of the function.

Props and context

Components that are not able to receive any props from the parents are not particularly useful, and the stateless functional components can receive `props` as parameters:

```
props => <button>{props.text}</button>;
```

Alternatively, we can use an even more concise syntax with the ES6 destructuring:

```
({ text }) => <button>{text}</button>;
```

We can define the `props` so that a stateless function can receive using the propTypes attribute in a similar way as we do when we extend components:

```
import { string } from 'prop-types';

const Button = ({ text }) => <button>{text}</button>;

Button.propTypes = {
  text: string
}
```

Stateless functional components also receive a second parameter that represents the context:

```
(props, context) => (
  <button>{context.currency}{props.value}</button>
);
```

The this keyword

One thing that makes the stateless functional components different from their stateful counterparts is the fact that `this` does not represent the component during their execution.

For this reason, it is not possible to use functions such as `setState`, or life cycle methods that are associated with the component instance.

State

The name stateless tells us clearly that the stateless functional components do not have any internal state, and the fact that this does not exist enforces it. That makes them extremely powerful and easy to use at the same time.

The stateless functional components only receive props (and context), and they return the elements. This should remind us of the principles of functional programming that we saw in `Chapter 2`, *Clean Up Your Code*.

Life cycle

Stateless functional components do not provide any life cycle hooks, such as `componentDidMount`; they implement a render-like method, and everything else has to be handled by the parent.

Refs and event handlers

Since there is no component instance, to use refs or event handlers with stateless functional components, you can define them in the following way:

```
() => {
  let input;

  const onClick = () => input.focus();

  return (
    <div>
      <input ref={el => (input = el)} />
      <button onClick={onClick}>Focus</button>
    </div>
  )
}
```

Optimization

One thing we should keep in mind when we use stateless functional components is that, even if Facebook developers say that in the future they would be able to provide performance optimizations for components without a state, at the time of writing, they perform a little bit less well.

The `shouldComponentUpdate` function does not exist, and there is not a way to tell React that a functional component should not be rendered if the props (or a particular prop) are not changed.

This is not a big issue, but it is something to consider.

Layout components

Normally, you can use stateless components for layout components, such as headers, content, or footers, since you just need to render static markup.

Let's create a new application with `create-react-app`. If you run your project with npm start you will see something like this:

If you open the file located in `src/App.js` you will see this code:

```
import React, { Component } from 'react';
import logo from './logo.svg';
import './App.css';

class App extends Component {
  render() {
```

```
      return (
        <div className="App">
          <header className="App-header">
            <img src={logo} className="App-logo" alt="logo" />
            <p>
              Edit <code>src/App.js</code> and save to reload.
            </p>
            <a
              className="App-link"
              href="https://reactjs.org"
              target="_blank"
              rel="noopener noreferrer"
            >
              Learn React
            </a>
          </header>
        </div>
      );
  }
}

export default App;
```

Now, let's break our code into layout files – that means we will create the `Header`, `Content`, and `Footer` components to simplify our code.

The first component is the `Header` component; let's look at the code we need:

```
import React from 'react';
import { string } from 'prop-types';

const Header = ({ title }) => (
  <header className="App-header">
    <h1>{title}</h1>
  </header>
);

Header.propTypes = {
  title: string.isRequired
};

export default Header;
```

As you can see, I created a new directory called `components` to separate our components, and inside another one called `layout` to group our layout components. Also, we are destructuring our `props` to pass a title in the component and just render it, after we created this component we need to change `App.js` to import and render the `Header` component:

```
import React, { Component } from 'react';
import Header from './components/layout/Header';
import './App.css';

class App extends Component {
  render() {
    return (
      <div className="App">
        <Header title="Dev Education" />
      </div>
    );
  }
}

export default App;
```

I changed a little bit the styles – I moved the gray background to the body, and I removed `min-height: 100vh;` from the `.App-header` class, and this is the result:

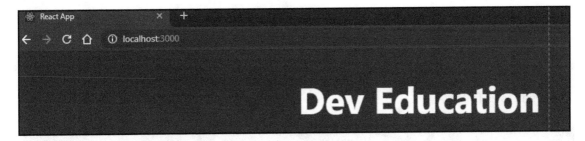

Now, let's create a new component to add the `Content` component of the site:

```
import React from 'react';
import { node } from 'prop-types';

const Content = ({ children }) => (
  <div className="Content">
    {children}
  </div>
);

Content.propTypes = {
  children: node.isRequired
```

```
};

export default Content;
```

For this component, we need to pass the special prop children to include the injected HTML inside the `Content` component, if we look at `App.js` it should now look like this:

```
import React, { Component } from 'react';
import Header from './components/layout/Header';
import Content from './components/layout/Content';
import './App.css';

class App extends Component {
  render() {
    return (
      <div className="App">
        <Header title="Dev Education" />

        <Content>
          {/* This content is sending as the children prop */}
          <p>
            This is our <strong> <Content></strong> component
          </p>
        </Content>
      </div>
    );
  }
}

export default App;
```

The result is as follows:

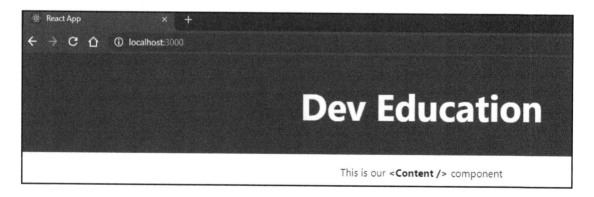

Finally, let's create a `Footer` component:

```
import React from 'react';
import { string } from 'prop-types';

const Footer = ({ copyright }) => (
  <div className="Footer">
    <p>&copy; {copyright}</p>
  </div>
);

Footer.propTypes = {
  copyright: string.isRequired
};

export default Footer;
```

We also need to render our `Footer` component in `App.js`:

```
import React, { Component } from 'react';
import Header from './components/layout/Header';
import Content from './components/layout/Content';
import Footer from './components/layout/Footer';
import './App.css';

class App extends Component {
  render() {
    return (
      <div className="App">
        <Header title="Dev Education" />

        <Content>
          {/* This content is received with the children prop */}
          <p>
            This is our <strong> <Content></strong> component
          </p>
        </Content>

        <Footer
          copyright={`Dev.education ${new Date().getFullYear()}`}
        />
      </div>
    );
  }
}

export default App;
```

As you can see, breaking our components in this way help us to create clean and modular components. The final result with the `Footer` component is this one:

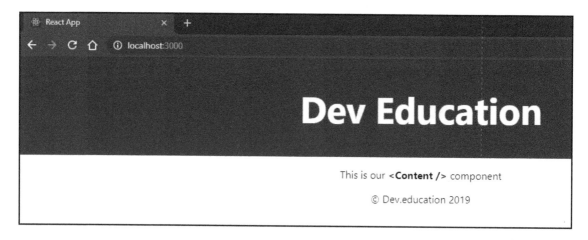

The state

We have seen how to create a component with the factory, extending the React class, or using stateless functional components.

Let's now go deeper into the topic of state and see exactly why it is important to use it and find out how it works.

We will learn when we should use stateless functions rather than stateful components, and why that represents a fundamental decision in designing components.

External libraries

First of all, it is important to understand why we should consider using the state inside our components, and why it can help us in different ways.

Most of the tutorials or boilerplates for React already include external libraries to manage the state of the application, such as **Redux** or **MobX**.

This leads to a common misconception that you cannot write a stateful application using React only, which is far from the truth.

The direct consequence is that many developers try to learn React and Redux together, so they never find out how to use the React state correctly.

This section is our opportunity to make it clear how we can use the state in the right way and understand why, in some cases, we do not need any external libraries.

 Since the version 16.3.0, React introduced a new Context API that is more efficient and supports both static type checking and deep updates.

How it works

Apart from the differences in declaring the initial state using the factory or extending the component, the important concept we've learned is that each stateful React component can have an initial state.

During the lifetime of the component, the state can be modified multiple times using `setState` inside life cycle methods or event handlers. Every time the state changes, React renders the component again with the new state, which is why documentation often says that a React component is similar to a state machine.

When the `setState` method is called with a new state (or part of it), the object gets merged into the current state. For example, if we have an initial state as the following one:

```
this.state = {
  text: 'Click me!'
};
```

And we run `setState` with a new parameter as follows:

```
this.setState({
  cliked: true
});
```

The resulting state is as follows:

```
{
  cliked: true,
  text: 'Click it!'
}
```

Every time the state changes, React runs the render function again, so there's no need for us to do anything other than setting the new state.

However, in some cases, we may want to perform some operations when the state is updated, and React provides a callback for that as follows:

```
this.setState({
  clicked: true
}, () => {
  console.log('the state is now', this.state);
});
```

If we pass any function as a second parameter of the setState method, it gets fired when the state is updated, and the component has been rendered.

Asynchronous

The setState function should always be considered asynchronous, as the official documentation says:

> "There is no guarantee of synchronous operation of calls to setState [...]"

If we try to log the current value of the state into the console after we fire setState in an event handler, we get the old state value:

```
handleClick() {
  this.setState({
    clicked: true,
  });
  console.log('the state is now', this.state);
}
render() {
  return <button onClick={this.handleClick}>Click me!</button>;
}
```

For example, the preceding snippet now renders the state as null.

Into the console. The reason this happens is that React knows how to optimize the state update inside event handlers and it batches the operation for better performance.

However, if we change our code a little as follows:

```
handleClick() {
  setTimeout(() => {
    this.setState({
      clicked: true
    });

    console.log('the state is now', this.state);
```

```
  });
}
```

The result is going to be as follows:

```
the state is now Object {clicked: true}
```

This is what we may have expected in the first place, and it's because React does not have any way to optimize the execution and it tries to update the state as soon as possible.

Please notice that `setTimeout` has been used in the example only to show the behavior of React, but you should never write event handlers in that way.

Using the state

Now that we know how the state works, it is important to understand when it should be used and when we should avoid storing a value in the state.

If we follow the rules, we can easily figure out when a component should be stateless or stateful, and how to deal with the state to make our component reusable across the application.

First of all, we should always keep in mind that only the minimal amount of data needed should be put into the state.

For example, if we have to change a label when a button is clicked, we should not store the text of the label, but we should only save a Boolean flag that tells us if the button has been clicked or not.

In that way, we are using the state properly, and we can always recalculate different values according to it.

Secondly, we should add to the state only the values that we want to update when an event happens, and for which we want to make the component re-render.

The `isClicked` flag is an example of that, and another one could be the value of an input field before it gets submitted.

In general, we should store into the state only the information needed to keep track of the current user interface state, such as the currently selected tab of a tabbed menu.

Another way to figure out whether the state is the right place to store information is to check if the data we are persisting is needed outside the component itself or by its children.

If multiple components need to keep track of the same information, we should consider using a state manager such as Redux at the application level.

We will now look at the cases where we should avoid using the state if we want to follow the best practice guidelines.

Derivables

Every time we can compute the final value from the props, we should not store any data into the state.

So, for example, if we receive the currency and the price from the props, and we always show them together, we may think that it would be better to store it in the state and use the state value inside the render as follows:

```
class Price extends React.Component {
  constructor(props) {
    super(props);
    this.state = {
      price: `${props.currency}${props.value}`
    };
  }
  render() {
    return <div>{this.state.price}</div>;
  }
}
```

This would work if we create it like this in the parent component:

```
<Price currency="$" value="100" />
```

The problem is that, if the currency or the value changes during the lifetime of the Price component, the state never gets recalculated (because the constructor is called once) and the application shows the wrong price.

Therefore, we should use the props to calculate a value whenever we can.

As we saw in Chapter 2, *Clean Up Your Code*, we could use a helper function directly in our render method as follows:

```
getPrice() {
  return `${this.props.currency}${this.props.value}`;
}
```

The render method

We should always keep in mind that setting the state causes the component to re-render and, for that reason, we should only store in the state those values that we are using inside the `render` method.

For example, if we need to persist API subscriptions or timeout variables that we use inside our components, but that do not affect the render in any way, we should consider keeping them in a separate module.

The following code is wrong, because we are storing a value in the state to use it later, but we do not access it in our `render` method, and we fire an unnecessary `render` when we set the new state:

```
componentDidMount() {
  this.setState({
    request: API.get(...);
  });
}
componentWillUnmount() {
  this.state.request.abort();
}
```

In a scenario like the previous one, it would be preferable to keep the API request stored in an external module.

Another common solution for this kind of situation is to store the request as a private member of the component instance:

```
componentDidMount() {
  this.request = API.get(...);
}
componentWillUnmount() {
  this.request.abort();
}
```

In that way, the request is encapsulated into the component without affecting the state, so it does not trigger any additional rendering when the value changes.

The following cheat sheet from Dan Abramov will help you make the right decision:

```
function shouldIKeepSomethingInReactState() {
  if (canICalculateItFromProps()) {
    // Don't duplicate data from props in state
    // Calculate what you can in render() method
    return false;
  }
```

```
if (!amIUsingItInRenderMethod()) {
  // Don't keep something in the state
  // if you don't use it for rendering.
  // For example, API subscriptions are
  // better off as custom private fields
  // or variables in external modules.
  return false;
}

// You can use React state for this!
return true;
}
```

React hooks

React Hooks are a new feature in React 16.8. They let us use state, and other React features, without writing a class component, for example:

```
import React, { useState } from 'react';

function Counter() {
  // times is our new state variable and setTimes the function to update
that state.
  const [times, setTimes] = useState(0); // 0 is the initial value of
times

  return (
    <div className="Times">
      <p>Times clicked: {times}</p>
      <button onClick={() => setTimes(times + 1)}>Click it!</button>
    </div>
  );
}

export default Counter;
```

As you can see, useState creates the new state and the function to update the state, you have to define the initial value when you called – not just numbers, you can add any type of value, even objects:

```
import React, { useState } from 'react';

function Form() {
  const [data, setData] = useState({
    name: '',
    age: 0
```

```
  });

  return (
    <div className="Form">
      <p>
        <input
          name="name"
          type="text"
          onChange={(e) => setData({
            name: e.target.value,
            age: data.age
          })}
        />
      </p>

      <p>
        <input
          name="age"
          type="number"
          onChange={(e) => setData({
            age: e.target.value,
            name: data.name
          })}
        />
      </p>

      <p>
        Name: {data.name} <br />
        Age: {data.age}
      </p>
    </div>
  );
}

export default Form;
```

Prop types

Our goal is to write truly reusable components, and to do that we have to define their interface in the clearest possible way.

If we want our components to be reused across the application, it is crucial to make sure that our components and their parameters are well-defined and straightforward to use.

With React, there is a powerful tool that lets us express, in a very simple way, the name of the props that a component expects to receive, and some validation rules for each one of them.

The rules relate to the type of property, as well as to whether the property is optional or required. There is also the option to write custom validation functions.

 Since React 15.5.0, the `PropTypes` attributes are no longer part of the React core. Instead, you need to install a separate package called `prop-types` to use it.
`npm install --save-dev prop-types`

Let's start with a very simple example:

```
import PropTypes from 'prop-types';
const Button = ({ text }) => <button>{text}</button>;
Button.propTypes = {
  text: PropTypes.string
};
```

In the previous snippet, we created a stateless functional component that receives a text prop of the `string` type.

Great – now every developer that comes across our component knows how to use it in the right way.

However, adding the property only sometimes is not enough, because it does not tell us if the component works without the `prop`.

The button, for example, does not operate properly without text, and the solution is to mark the `prop` as required:

```
Button.propTypes = {
  text: PropTypes.string.isRequired
};
```

If a developer uses the button inside another component without setting the text property, they receive the following warning in the browser console:

Failed prop type: Required prop `text` was not specified in `Button`.

It is important to say that the warning is emitted only in development mode. In the production version of React, the `propTypes` validation is disabled for performance reasons.

React provides ready-to-use validators for various numbers of types: from arrays, to numbers, to components.

It gives us also some utilities, such as `oneOf`, which accept an array of types that are valid for a particular property.

It is important to keep in mind that we should always try to pass primitive props to components, because they are simpler to validate and to compare (we will see the benefits in `Chapter 10`, *About Testing and Debugging*).

Passing single primitive props helps us to find whether a component surface is too wide and whether or not it should be split into smaller surfaces.

If we realize that we are declaring too many props for a single component, and they are not related to each other, it may be better to create multiple vertical components, each one with fewer props and responsibilities.

However, in some cases it is unavoidable to pass objects, and in those cases, we should declare our `propType` object using shapes.

The `shape` function lets us declare objects with nested properties and, for each one of those, we can define their types.

For example, if we are creating a `Profile` component that needs a user object with a required name and an optional surname, we can define it as follows:

```
import { shape, string } from 'prop-types';
const Profile = ({ user }) => (
  <div>{user.name} {user.surname}</div>
);

Profile.propTypes = {
  user: shape({
    name: string.isRequired,
    surname: string
  }).isRequired
};
```

If none of the existing React `propTypes` satisfies our needs, we can create a custom function to validate a property:

```
user: shape({
  age: (props, propName) => {
    if (!(props[propName] > 0 && props[propName] < 100)) {
      return new Error(`${propName} must be between 1 and 99`);
    }
```

```
        return null;
    }
})
```

For example, in the preceding snippet, we verify whether the `age` field fits inside a certain range; and if it doesn't, an error is returned.

React Docgen

Now that the boundaries of our component are well-defined thanks to the prop types, there is another operation that we can do to make them easy to use and share.

We can automatically create documentation for our components starting from the definition of the prop types.

To do this, there is a library called `react-docgen` that we can install with the following command:

```
npm install -g react-docgen
```

React Docgen reads the source code of our component and extracts the relevant information from the prop types and their comments.

For example, if we go back to the first button we created:

```
import { string } from 'prop-types';

const Button = ({ text }) => <button>{text}</button>;
Button.propTypes = {
  text: string
};
```

And then run the following command:

```
react-docgen button.js
```

We get the following object in return, as follows:

```
{
  "description": "",
  "methods": [],
  "props": {
    "text": {
      "type": {
        "name": "string"
      },
```

```
      "required": false,
      "description": ""
    }
  }
}
```

This is a JSON object that represents the interface of our components. As you can see, there is a `props` attribute that has our text property of type string defined inside it.

Let's see whether we can do even better by adding comments:

```
/**
 * A generic button with text.
 */
const Button = ({ text }) => <button>{text}</button>;
Button.propTypes = {
  /**
   * The text of the button.
   */
  text: string
};
```

If we run the command again, the result is as follows:

```
{
  "description": "A generic button with text.",
  "methods": [],
  "props": {
    "text": {
      "type": {
        "name": "string"
      },
      "required": false,
      "description": "The text of the button."
    }
  }
}
```

We can now use the returned object to create the documentation and share it across our team or publish it on GitHub.

The fact that the output is in JSON makes the tool very flexible, because it is very easy to generate web pages applying JSON objects to templates.

A real-world example of components documented using `docgen` is the Material UI library, where all the docs are automatically generated from the source code.

Reusable components

We have seen what the best ways to create components are, and the scenarios where it makes sense to use a local state. We have also seen how we can make our components reusable defining a clear interface with the `prop` types.

Let's now dive into a real-world example and take a look at how we can transform a non-reusable component into a reusable one with a generic, and cleaner, interface.

Suppose we have a component that loads a collection of posts from an API endpoint, and it shows the list on the screen.

It is a simplified example, but it is useful for understanding the necessary steps we need to take to make components reusable.

The component is defined as follows:

```
class PostList extends React.Component
```

With the `constructor` and a life cycle method, an empty array gets assigned to posts to represent the initial state:

```
constructor(props) {
  super(props);
  this.state = {
    posts: []
  };
}
componentDidMount() {
  Posts.fetch().then(posts => {
    this.setState({ posts });
  });
}
```

During `componentDidMount`, the API call gets fired, and as soon as the data is available, the posts are stored in the state.

This is a very common data fetching pattern, and we will see the other possible approaches in `Chapter 5`, *Proper Data Fetching*.

Posts is a helper class that we use to communicate with the API, and it has a `fetch` method that returns a promise that gets resolved with a list of posts.

We can now move into the part where the posts are displayed:

```
render() {
  return (
    <ul>
      {this.state.posts.map(post => (
        <li key={post.id}>
          <h1>{post.title}</h1>
          {post.excerpt && <p>{post.excerpt}</p>}
        </li>
      ))}
    </ul>
  );
}
```

Inside the `render` method, we loop through the posts, and we map each one of them into a `<li>` element.

We assume that the title field is always present, and we show it inside an `<h1>` element while the excerpt is optional, and we show it inside a paragraph only if it exists.

The preceding component works fine, and it has no problems.

Now, suppose that we need to render a similar list, but this time, we want to display a list of users received from the `props` type rather than the state (to make clear that we can serve different scenarios):

```
const UserList = ({ users }) => (
  <ul>
    {users.map(user => (
      <li key={user.id}>
        <h1>{user.username}</h1>
        {user.bio && <p>{user.bio}</p>}
      </li>
    ))}
  </ul>
);
```

Given a collection of users, the preceding code renders an unordered list very similar to the posts one.

The differences are that the heading, in this case, is the username rather than title and the optional field, that has to be shown only if present, is the bio of the user.

Duplicating the code is usually not the best solution, so let's see how React can help us to keep our code with **Don't Repeat Yourself** (**DRY**). The first step to creating a reusable `List` component is to abstract it a little and decouple it from the data it has to display, and we do that by defining a generic collection property. The main requirement is that, for the posts, we want to display the title and the excerpt, while, for the users, we have to show the username and the bio.

To do this, we create two props: one called `titleKey`, where we specify the name of the attribute to be displayed, and one called `textKey` that we use to specify the optional field.

The props of the new reusable `List` component are the following:

```
import { array, string } from 'prop-types';
...
List.propTypes = {
  collection: array,
  textKey: string,
  titleKey: string,
}
```

Since the `List` component is not going to have any state or function, we can write it as a stateless functional component:

```
const List = ({ collection, textKey, titleKey }) => (
  <ul>
    {collection.map(item =>
      <Item
        key={item.id}
        text={item[textKey]}
        title={item[titleKey]}
      />
    )}
  </ul>
);
```

The `List` component receives the props, and iterates over the collection, mapping all the items into another component (that we are going to create next). As you can see, we are passing to the children titles and text `props` that represent the values of the main attribute and the optional one, respectively.

The `Item` component is very simple and clean:

```
import { string } from 'prop-types';

const Item = ({ text, title }) => (
  <li>
```

```
    <h1>{title}</h1>
    {text && <p>{text}</p>}
  </li>
);
Item.propTypes = {
  text: string,
  title: string
};
```

So, we've created two components with a well-defined surface area that can we use together to display posts, users or any other kinds of lists. Smaller components are better for several reasons: for example, they are more maintainable and testable, which makes it easier to find and fix bugs.

Great – we can now rewrite our two components, PostsList, and UsersList, to make them use the generic reusable list and avoid duplicating code.

Let's modify the render method of PostsLists as follows:

```
render() {
  return (
    <List
      collection={this.state.posts}
      textKey="excerpt"
      titleKey="title"
    />
  );
}
```

Then, we will modify the UserList function as follows:

```
const UserList = ({ users }) => (
  <List
    collection={users}
    textKey="bio"
    titleKey="username"
  />
);
```

We went from a single-purpose component to a reusable one using the props to create a generic and well-defined interface.

It is now possible to reuse this component as many times as we need in our application, and every developer can easily understand how to implement it thanks to the prop types.

We could also go a step further using react-docgen to document our reusable list, as we have seen in the previous section.

The benefits of using a reusable component over a component that is coupled with the data it handles are many.

Suppose, for example, that we want to add logic to hide and show the optional field only when a button is clicked.

Alternatively, perhaps there is a new requirement to add a check and, if the title attribute is longer than twenty-five characters, it gets cut and hyphenated.

We can now make the change at one single point, and all the components that are using it will benefit from the modification.

Fragments

Since version React 16.2.0 we are able to return arrays and strings from the render method. Before, React forced us to return an element wrapped with `<div>` or any other tag; it was not possible to return an array or string directly:

```
// Example 1: Returning an array of elements.

render() {
  // Now you don't need to wrap list items in an extra element
  return [
    <li key="1">First item</li>,
    <li key="2">Second item</li>,
    <li key="3">Third item</li>
  ];
}

// Example 2: Returning a string

render() {
  return 'Hello World!';
}
```

Also, React has implemented a new feature called Fragment, which also works as a special wrapper for elements. It can be specified with empty tags (`<></>`) or directly by using `React.Fragment`:

```
// Example 1: Using empty tags <></>
render() {
  return (
    <>
      <ComponentA />
      <ComponentB />
      <ComponentC />
    </>
  );
}

// Example 2: Using React.Fragment
render() {
  return (
    <React.Fragment>
      <h1>An h1 heading</h1>
      Some text here.
      <h2>An h2 heading</h2>
      More text here.
      Even more text here.
    </React.Fragment>
  );
}

// Example 3: Importing the Fragment
import React, { Fragment } from 'react';

render() {
  return (
    <Fragment>
      <h1>An h1 heading</h1>
      Some text here.
      <h2>An h2 heading</h2>
      More text here.
      Even more text here.
    </Fragment>
  );
}
```

Summary

The journey to learn how to make reusable components has come to the end.

We started from a deep study of the basics and looking at the differences between stateful and stateless components, and we saw an example of how to make a tightly coupled component reusable. We've looked at the internal state of a component, and at what point it is better to avoid using it. We learned the basics of prop types and applied those concepts to the reusable components we created.

Finally, we looked at how living style guides can help us to communicate better with other members of our team, to avoid creating duplicated components and to enforce consistency within the application.

We are now ready to learn the various techniques we can put in place to compose our components.

In the next chapter, we will talk about the communication between components and HoC.

Compose All the Things

In the previous chapter (Chapter 3, *Create Truly Reusable Components*), we saw how to create reusable components with a clean interface. Now, it's time to learn how to make those components communicate with each other effectively.

React is powerful because it lets you build complex applications composing small, testable, and maintainable components. Applying this paradigm, you can take control of every single part of the application.

In this chapter, we will go through some of the most popular composition patterns and tools.

We will cover the following topics:

- How components communicate with each other using props and children
- The container and presentational pattern and how it can make our code more maintainable
- The problem mixins tried to solve and why they failed
- What HOCs are and how we can structure our applications in a better way, thanks to them
- The `recompose` library with its ready-made functions
- How we can interact with the context and avoid coupling our components to it
- What the function of the child component pattern is and what its benefits are

Communication between components

Reusing functions is one of our goals as developers, and we have seen how React makes it easy to create reusable components. **Reusable components** can be shared across multiple domains of your application to avoid duplication.

Small components with a clean interface can be composed together to create complex applications that are powerful and maintainable at the same time.

Composing React components is pretty straightforward; you just have to include them in the render method:

```
import { object } from 'prop-types';
const Profile = ({ user }) => (
  <div>
    <Picture profileImageUrl={user.profileImageUrl} />
    <UserName name={user.name} screenName={user.screenName} />
  </div>
);
Profile.propTypes = {
  user: object
};
```

For example, you can create a Profile component by simply composing a Picture component to display the profile image and a UserName component to display the name and the screen name of the user.

In this way, you can produce new parts of the user interface very quickly, writing only a few lines of code. Whenever you compose components, as in the preceding example, you share data between them using props. Props are the way a parent component can pass its data down the tree to every component that needs it (or part of it).

When a component passes some props to another component, it is called the **owner**, irrespective of the parent-child relationship between them.

For example, in the preceding snippet, Profile is not the direct parent of Picture (the div tag is), but Profile owns Picture because it passes down the props to it.

Children

There is a special prop that can be passed from the owners to the components defined inside their `render` method—**children**.

In the React documentation, it is described as **opaque** because it is a property that does not tell you anything about the value it contains. Subcomponents defined inside the `render` method of a parent component usually receive props that are passed as attributes of the component itself in JSX, or as a second parameter of the `createElement` function. Components can also be defined with nested components inside them, and they can access those children using the children `prop`.

Consider that we have a `Button` component that has a text property representing the text of the button:

```
import { string } from 'prop-types';

const Button = ({ text }) => (
  <button className="btn">{text}</button>
);
Button.propTypes = {
  text: string
};
```

It can be used in the following way:

```
<Button text="Click me!" />
```

It can render the following code:

```
<button class="btn">Click me!</button>
```

Now, suppose we want to use the same button with the same class name in multiple parts of our application, and we also want to be able to display more than a simple string. Our UI consists of buttons with text, buttons with text and icons, and buttons with text and labels.

In most cases, a good solution would be to add multiple parameters to the `Button` or to create different versions of the `Button`, each one with its single specialization, for example, `IconButton`.

However, if we realize that our `Button` could be just a wrapper, and we want to be able to render any element inside it, we can use the `children` property.

We can do that easily by changing the `Button` component from the preceding example to be similar to the following snippet:

```
import { array } from 'prop-types';

const Button = ({ children }) => (
  <button className="btn">{children}</button>
);
Button.propTypes = {
  children: array
};
```

Applying this change, we are not limited to a simple single text property, but we can pass any element to `Button`, and it is rendered in place of the `children` property.

In this case, any element that we wrap inside the `Button` component will be rendered as a child of the button element with the `btn` class name.

For example, if we want to render an image inside the button and some text wrapped into a span, we can do this:

```
<Button>
  <img src="..." alt="..." />
  <span>Click me!</span>
</Button>
```

The preceding snippet gets rendered in the browser as follows:

```
<button className="btn">
  <img src="..." alt="..." />
  <span>Click me!</span>
</button>
```

This is a pretty convenient way to allow components to accept any `children` elements and wrap those elements inside a predefined parent.

Now, we can pass images, labels, and even other React components inside the `Button`, and they will be rendered as its children.

As you can see in the preceding example, we defined the `children` property as an array, which means that we can pass any number or elements as the component's children.

We can pass a single child, as shown in the following code:

```
<Button>
  <span>Click me!</span>
</Button>
```

If we pass a single child, we get the following output:

```
Failed prop type: Invalid prop `children` of type `object` supplied to
`Button`, expected `array`.
```

This is because, when a component has a single child, React optimizes the creation of the elements and avoids allocating an array for performance reasons.

We can easily fix this warning by setting the `children` prop to accept the following prop types:

```
import { oneOfType, array, element } from 'prop-types';

Button.propTypes = {
  children: oneOfType([
    array,
    element
  ])
};
```

The container and presentational pattern

In the last chapter, we saw how to take a coupled component and make it reusable step by step. In this section, we will see how to apply a similar pattern to our components to make them cleaner and more maintainable.

React components typically contain a mix of **logic** and **presentation**. By logic, we refer to anything that is unrelated to the UI, such as API calls, data manipulation, and event handlers. The presentation is, instead, the part inside the `render` method where we create the elements to be displayed on the UI.

In React, there is a simple and powerful pattern, known as **container** and **presentational**, which we can apply when creating components that help us to separate those two concerns.

Creating well-defined boundaries between logic and presentation not only makes components more reusable, but it provides many other benefits, which you will learn about in this section. Again, one of the best ways to learn new concepts is by seeing practical examples, so let's delve into some code.

Suppose we have a component that uses geolocation APIs to get the position of the user, and it displays the latitude and longitude on the page in the browser.

First, we create a `Geolocation.js` file in our components folder (`components/Geolocation/index.jsx`) and define the `Geolocation` component using a `class` component:

```
class Geolocation extends Component
```

We then define a `constructor`, where we initialize the internal state and bind the event handlers:

```
constructor(props) {
  super(props);
  this.state = {
    latitude: null,
    longitude: null
  };
  this.handleSuccess = this.handleSuccess.bind(this);
}
```

Now, we can use the `componentDidMount` callback to fire the request to the APIs:

```
componentDidMount() {
  if (navigator.geolocation) {
    navigator.geolocation.getCurrentPosition(this.handleSuccess);
  }
}
```

When the browser returns the data, we store the result into the state using the following function:

```
handleSuccess({ coords: { latitude, longitude } }) {
  this.setState({
    latitude,
    longitude
  });
}
```

Finally, we show the `latitude` and `longitude` using the `render` method:

```
render() {
  return (
    <div>
      <h1>Geolocation:</h1>
      <div>Latitude: {this.state.latitude}</div>
      <div>Longitude: {this.state.longitude}</div>
    </div>
  );
}
```

It is important to note that, during the first render, `latitude` and `longitude`
are `null` because we ask the browser for the coordinates when the component is mounted.
In a real-world component, you might want to display a spinner until the data gets
returned; to do that, you can use one of the conditional techniques we saw in Chapter
2, *Clean Up Your Code*.

Now, this component does not have any problems, and it works as expected. Wouldn't it be
nice to separate it from the part where the position gets requested and loaded to iterate
faster on it?

We will isolate the presentational part of the main component by when following the
container and presentational pattern.

In this pattern, every component is split into two smaller ones, each one with its clear
responsibilities.

The container knows everything about the logic of the component, and it's where the APIs
are called. It also deals with data manipulation and event handling.

The presentational component is where the UI is defined, and it receives data in the form of
props from the container. Since the presentational component is usually logic-free, we can
create it as a functional, stateless component.

There are no rules that say that the presentational component must not have a state. For
example, it could keep a UI state inside it. In this case, we need a component to display the
latitude and longitude, so we are going to use a simple function.

First of all, we should rename our `Geolocation` component to `GeolocationContainer`:

```
class GeolocationContainer extends Component
```

We will also change the filename from `Geolocation.js` to `GeolocationContainer.jsx`.

This rule is not strict, but it is a best practice that's widely used in the React community to
append `Container` to the end of the `Container` component name and give the original
name to the presentational one.

We also have to change the implementation of the `render` method and remove all the UI
parts of it, as follows:

```
render() {
  return (
    <Geolocation {...this.state} />
  );
}
```

As you can see in the preceding snippet, instead of creating the HTML elements inside the `render` method of the container, we just use the presentational one (which we will create next), and we pass the state to it.

The `state` has the latitude and longitude properties, which are `null` by default, and they contain the real position of the user when the browser fires the callback.

We are using the spread attribute operator, which we saw in Chapter 2, *Clean Up Your Code*; it is a convenient way to pass the attributes of the `state`, which lets us avoid writing `prop` by `prop` manually.

Let's create a new file, called `Geolocation.js`, where we define the stateless functional component, as follows:

```
import React from 'react';
import { number } from 'prop-types';
const Geolocation = ({ latitude, longitude }) => (
  <div>
    <h1>Geolocation:</h1>
    <div>Latitude: {latitude}</div>
    <div>Longitude: {longitude}</div>
  </div>
);

export default Geolocation;
```

Stateless functional components are an incredibly elegant way to define UIs. They are pure functions that, given a `state`, return the elements of it.

In this case, our function receives the `latitude` and `longitude` from the owner, and it returns the markup structure to display it.

We surely want to follow the best practices and define a clear interface for our component, so we use `propTypes` to declare the properties that the component needs:

```
Geolocation.propTypes = {
  latitude: number,
  longitude: number
};
```

If you run the components in the browser the first time, the browser will require your permission to allow it to know about your location:

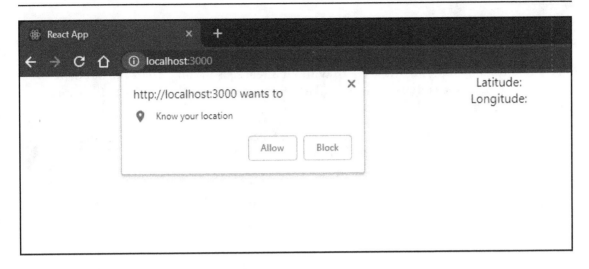

After you allow the browser to know your location, you will see something like this:

Following the container and presentational pattern, we created a dumb reusable component that we can put in our Style Guide so that we can pass fake coordinates to it.

If in some other parts of the application we need to display the same data structure, we do not have to create a new component; we just wrap this one into a new container that, for example, could load the latitude and longitude from a different endpoint.

At the same time, other developers in our team can improve the container that uses geolocation by adding some error-handling logic, without affecting its presentation.

They can even build a temporary presentational component just to display and debug data and then replace it with the real presentational component when it is ready.

Being able to work in parallel on the same component is a big win for teams, especially for those companies where building interfaces is an iterative process.

This pattern is simple but very powerful, and when applied to big applications, it can make a difference when it comes to the speed of development and maintainability of the project.

On the other hand, applying this pattern without a real reason can give us the opposite problem and make the **codebase** less useful as it involves the creation of more files and components.

So, we should think carefully when we decide that a component has to be refactored following the container and presentational pattern.

In general, the right path to follow is starting with a single component and splitting it only when the logic and the presentation become too coupled where they shouldn't be.

In our example, we began from a single component, and we realized that we could separate the API call from the markup.

Deciding what to put in the container and what goes into the presentation is not always straightforward; the following points should help you make that decision:

Container components:

- They are more concerned with behavior
- They render their presentational components
- They make API calls and manipulate data
- They define event handlers
- They are written as classes

Presentational components:

- They are more concerned with visual representation
- They render the HTML markup (or other components)
- They receive data from the parents in the form of props
- They are often written as stateless functional components

Mixins

Components are great to achieve reusability, but what if different components in different domains share the same behavior?

We do not want duplicated code in our applications and React give us a tool that we can use when we want to share functionalities across various components—**mixins**.

Using mixins is deprecated, but it is worth understanding the problems they try to solve and see what the possible alternative solutions are. Also, it could happen that you might have to work on a legacy project that uses an older version of React, and it makes sense to know what mixins are and how to deal with them.

First of all, mixins work only with the `createClass` factory, so if you are using classes, you cannot use mixins, and that is one of the reasons why their use is discouraged.

Suppose you are using `createClass` in your application and you find yourself needing to write the same code into different components. For example, you need to listen to the window resize event to get the size of the window and do some operations accordingly.

One way of using a mixin is to write it once and share it across the different components. Let's delve into the code.

A mixin can be defined as an object literal that has the same functions and attributes of a component:

```
const WindowResize = {...};
```

To communicate with the component, mixins usually use the state.
With `getInitialState`, the state gets initialized with the initial `innerWidth` of a window:

```
getInitialState() {
  return {
    innerWidth: window.innerWidth
  };
}
```

Now, we want to keep track of the changes, so when the component mounts, we start listening to the window resize event:

```
componentDidMount() {
  window.addEventListener('resize', this.handleResize);
}
```

We also want to remove the event listener as soon as the component unmounts, which is critical, thus freeing the memory and not leaving unused listeners attached to the window:

```
componentWillUnmount() {
  window.removeEventListener('resize', this.handleResize);
}
```

Finally, we define the callback to be called every time the window resize event is fired.

The callback function is implemented to update the state with the new `innerWidth` component so that the component that is using the mixin re-renders itself with the fresh value that's available:

```
handleResize() {
  this.setState({
    innerWidth: window.innerWidth
  });
}
```

As you can see from the preceding snippet, creating a mixin is very similar to creating a component.

Now, if we want to use the mixin in our component, we just have to assign it to the array of mixins, which is a property of the object:

```
const MyComponent = React.createClass({
  mixins: [WindowResize],
  render() {
    console.log('window.innerWidth', this.state.innerWidth);
    ...
  }
});
```

From this point on, the value of `innerWidth` of the window will be available in the state of our component, and the component will re-render with the updated value any time `innerWidth` changes.

We can use the mixin in many components at a time and also use multiple mixins for each component. A nice feature of mixins is that they can merge life cycle methods and the initial state.

For example, if we use our `WindowResize` mixin in a component where we also define a `componentDidMount` hook, both will be executed in order.

The same happens in the case of multiple mixins that use the same life cycle hooks.

Now, let's go through the problems of mixins. In the next section, we will see what the best technique is to achieve the same result without all the issues it usually brings.

First of all, mixins sometimes use internal functions to communicate with the component.

For example, our `WindowResize` mixin could expect the component to implement a `handleResize` function and give developers the freedom of doing some operations when the size changes, instead of using the state to trigger the update.

Alternatively, instead of setting the new value into the state, the mixin could require the component to call a function—something like `getInnerWidth`, in our example—to get the actual value.

Unfortunately, there is no way for us to know of the list of methods that have to be implemented.

This is particularly bad for maintainability because, if a component uses multiple mixins, it ends up implementing different methods, which makes it difficult to eliminate the code when some mixins are removed, or they change their behavior.

A very common problem with mixins is clashing. Though it is true that React is smart enough to merge life cycle callbacks, it cannot do anything if two mixins define or require the same function name or use the same attribute in the state.

This is pretty bad in big codebases because it can give us unexpected behaviors and it makes it very hard to debug issues.

As we saw in the `WindowResize` example, mixins tend to communicate with the component using the state. So, for example, a mixin can update a special attribute in the state of a component, and then the component re-renders, taking into account the new attribute.

This makes components use the state even if it is not needed, which is bad because we have seen that we should avoid using it as much as we can to improve reusability and maintainability.

Last but not least, sometimes it can happen that some mixins depend on other mixins. For example, we could create **ResponsiveMixin**, which changes the visibility of some components according to the size of the window, which is provided in the `WindowResize` mixin.

This coupling between mixins makes it very hard to refactor the components and scale the application.

Higher order components

In the previous section, we saw how mixins are useful for sharing functionalities between components and the problems that they bring to our applications.

In the *Functional Programming* section of `Chapter 2`, *Clean Up Your Code*, we mentioned the concept of **higher order functions** (**HoFs**), which are functions that, given a function, enhance it with some extra behaviors, returning a new one.

Let's see if we can apply the same concept to React components and achieve our goal of sharing functionalities between components while avoiding the downsides of mixins.

When we apply the idea of HoFs to components, we call this **higher order components** (**HoCs**) for brevity.

First of all, let's see what an `HoC` looks like:

```
const HoC = Component => EnhancedComponent;
```

HoCs are functions that take a component as input and return an enhanced one as the output.

Let's start with a very simple example to understand what an enhanced component looks like.

Suppose you need to attach the same `className` property to every component for some reason. You could go and change all the render methods adding the `className` property to each of them, or you could write an HoC such as the following one:

```
const withClassName = Component => props => (
  <Component {...props} className="my-class" />
);
```

The preceding code can be a little difficult to understand initially; let's try to understand it.

We declare a `withClassName` function that takes a `Component` and returns another function.

The returned function is a stateless functional component that receives some props and renders the original component. The collected props are spread, and a `className` property with the `"my-class"` value is passed to it.

The reason why HoCs usually spread the props they receive on the component is because they tend to be transparent and only add the new behavior.

This is pretty simple and not very useful, but it should give you a better understanding of what HoCs are and what they look like.

Let's now see how we can use the `withClassName` HoC in our components.

First of all, we create a stateless functional component that receives the class name and applies it to a `div` tag:

```
import { string } from 'prop-types';

const MyComponent = ({ className }) => (
  <div className={className} />
);
MyComponent.propTypes = {
  className: string
};
```

Instead of using it directly, we pass it to an HoC, as follows:

```
const MyComponentWithClassName = withClassName(MyComponent);
```

Wrapping our components into the `withClassName` function, we ensure that it receives the `className` property.

Now, let's move on to something more exciting and let's try to transform the `WindowResize` mixin we saw in the previous section into an HoC function that we can reuse across our application.

The mixin was simply listening to the window resize event and making the updated `innerWidth` property of the window available into the state.

One of the biggest problems with that mixin was, that it was using the state of the component to provide the `innerWidth` value.

Doing that is bad because it pollutes the state with additional attributes, and those attributes may also clash with the attributes that are used in the components itself.

First of all, we have to create a function that receives a `Component`:

```
const withInnerWidth = Component => (
  class extends React.Component { ... }
);
```

You may have spotted a pattern in the way HoCs are named. It is a common practice to prefix HoCs that provide some information to the components they enhance using the *with* pattern.

Our `withInnerWidth` function will return a class component instead of
a functional stateless component because, as we saw in the previous example, we need
additional functions and state.

Let's see what the returned class looks like.

In the constructor, the initial state gets defined, and the `handleResize` callback is bound to
the current class:

```
constructor(props) {
  super(props);
  this.state = {
    innerWidth: window.innerWidth
  };
  this.handleResize = this.handleResize.bind(this);
}
```

The life cycle hooks and the event handler are identical to the mixin's:

```
componentDidMount() {
  window.addEventListener('resize', this.handleResize);
}
componentWillUnmount() {
  window.removeEventListener('resize', this.handleResize);
}
handleResize() {
  this.setState({
    innerWidth: window.innerWidth
  });
}
```

Finally, the original component gets rendered in the following way:

```
render() {
  return <Component {...this.props} {...this.state} />;
}
```

As you may note here, we are spreading the props as we saw before, but we are also
spreading the `state`.

We are storing the `innerWidth` value inside the state to achieve the original behavior, but
we do not pollute the state of the component; we use props instead.

As you learned in Chapter 3, *Create Truly Reusable Components*, using props is always a
good solution to enforce reusability.

Now, using an HoC and getting the `innerWidth` value is pretty straightforward.

We create a stateless functional component that expects `innerWidth` as a property:

```
const MyComponent = ({ innerWidth }) => {
  console.log('window.innerWidth', innerWidth);
  ...
};
MyComponent.propTypes = {
  innerWidth: number
};
```

We enhance it as follows:

```
const MyComponentWithInnerWidth = withInnerWidth(MyComponent);
```

There are various advantages of doing this rather than using a mixin. First of all, we do not pollute any state, and we do not require the component to implement any function.

This means that the component and the HoC are not coupled, and they can both be reused across the application.

Again, using props instead of state lets us make our component dumb so that we can use it in our style guide, ignoring any complex logic and just passing down the props.

In this particular case, we could create a component for each of the different `innerWidth` sizes we support.

Consider the following example:

```
<MyComponent innerWidth={320} />
```

Or consider the following:

```
<MyComponent innerWidth={960} />
```

Recompose

As soon as we become familiar with HoCs, we realize how powerful they are and how we can get the most out of them.

There is a popular library called `recompose` which provides many useful HoCs and also a way to compose them nicely.

The HoCs that the library offers are small utilities that we can use to wrap our components, moving away from some of their logic and making them dumber and more reusable.

Consider that your component is receiving a user object from an API and that this user object has many attributes.

Letting components receive arbitrary objects is not a good practice because it relies on the fact that the component knows the shape of the object and, most importantly, if the object changes, the component breaks.

A better way for a component to receive props from the parent is to define each single property using primitives.

We have a Profile component to display username and age, as follows:

```
const Profile = ({ user: { username, age } }) => (
  <div>
    <div>Username: {username}</div>
    <div>Age: {age}</div>
  </div>
);
Profile.propTypes = {
  user: object
};
```

If you want to change its interface to receive single props instead of the full user object, we can do so with the flattenProp HoC provided by recompose.

Let's see how it works.

We first change the component to declare single properties, as follows:

```
const Profile = ({ username, age }) => (
  <div>
    <div>Username: {username}</div>
    <div>Age: {age}</div>
  </div>
);
Profile.propTypes = {
  username: string,
  age: number
};
```

Then, we enhance it with the HoC:

```
const ProfileWithFlattenUser = flattenProp('user')(Profile);
```

You may have noted here that we are using the HoC in a slightly different way. Some of them, in fact, use the partial application to receive the parameters first, which is a functional approach.

Their signature is something similar to the following:

```
const HoC = args => Component => EnhancedComponent;
```

What we can do is create a function using the first call and wrap our component into it:

```
const withFlattenUser = flattenProp('user');
const ProfileWithFlattenUser = withFlattenUser(Profile);
```

Great! Now, suppose for some reason that we want to change the attribute username to make this component more generic and reusable.

We can use renameProp, which the recompose library gives us, and update our component like this:

```
const Profile = ({ name, age }) => (
  <div>
    <div>Name: {name}</div>
    <div>Age: {age}</div>
  </div>
);
Profile.propTypes = {
  name: string,
  age: number
};
```

Now, we want to apply multiple HoC components: one for flattening the user prop and one to rename a single prop from the user object, but concatenating functions does not seem like a good idea.

Here is where the compose function of recompose comes in handy.

We can pass multiple HoCs to it and get a single enhanced HoC:

```
const enhance = compose(
  flattenProp('user'),
  renameProp('username', 'name')
);
```

Then, we can apply it to our component in the following way:

```
const EnhancedProfile = enhance(Profile);
```

This is more convenient and elegant.

With recompose, we are not limited to using only the HoCs provided by the library—we can compose our HoC in the same way or even use them all together:

```
const enhance = compose(
  flattenProp('user'),
  renameProp('username', 'name'),
  withInnerWidth
);
```

As you can see here, the `compose` function is very powerful, and it makes the code more readable.

We can concatenate multiple HoCs to keep our components as simple as possible.

It is important not to abuse HoCs because with every abstraction comes problems; in this case, the trade-off is related to performance.

You have to think that every time you wrap a component into a higher order one, you are adding a new render function, a new life cycle method call, and memory allocation.

For that reason, it is important to think carefully about when it makes sense to use an HoC and when it is better to rethink your structure.

Context

HoCs come in very handy when we have to deal with context.

Context is a feature that has always been present in React, and it is used in many libraries, even if it hasn't been documented much.

The documentation still advises that it be used very sparingly because it is experimental and likely to change in the future.

However, in some scenarios, it is a very powerful tool that can help us pass information down to the tree without using props at every level.

To get the benefits of context without coupling our components to its APIs, we can use an HoC.

An HoC can get the data from the context, transform it into props, and pass the props down to the component. In this way, the component is unaware of the context, and it can be reused easily in different parts of the application.

Also, if the APIs of the context change in the future, the only part of the application that has to be changed is the HoC because the components are decoupled from it, which is a big win.

There is a function that's provided by recompose that makes using context in a transparent way and receiving props very easy and straightforward; let's see how it works.

Suppose you have a `Price` component that you use to display the currency and the value. The context is widely used to pass down common configuration from the root to the leaves, and currency is one of those values.

Let's start with a context-aware component and let's transform it step by step into a reusable one, thanks to HoCs:

```
const Price = ({ value }, { currency }) => (
  <div>{currency}{value}</div>
);
Price.propTypes = {
  value: number
};
Price.contextTypes = {
  currency: string
};
```

We have a stateless functional component that receives the value as a property and the currency as the second parameter from the context.

We also define the prop types and the context types for both values. As you can see, this component is not truly reusable because it needs a parent with the currency as child context types to work. For example, we cannot use it easily in our style guide and pass a fake currency as a prop.

First of all, let's change the component to get both values from the props:

```
const Price = ({ currency, value }) => (
  <div>{currency}{value}</div>
);
Price.propTypes = {
  currency: string,
  value: number
};
```

Of course, we cannot substitute it with the previous one straightaway because no parents are setting its currency prop. What we can do is wrap it into an HoC that can transform the values that are received from the context into props. We are using the getContext function from recompose, but you can easily write a custom wrapper from scratch.

Again, we use the partial application to specialize the HoC and reuse it multiple times:

```
const withCurrency = getContext({
  currency: string
});
```

Then, we apply it to the component:

```
const PriceWithCurrency = withCurrency(Price);
```

Now, we can replace the old Price component with the resulting one, and it will still work without being coupled with the context.

This is a big win because we did not have to change the parent, we can use the context without worrying about future API changes, and the Price component is now reusable.

We can pass arbitrary currencies and values to the component without needing a custom parent to provide the values.

FunctionAsChild

There is a pattern that is gaining consensus within the React community, and it is known as FunctionAsChild. It is widely used in the popular library react-motion, which we will see in Chapter 6, *Write Code for the Browser*.

The main concept is that, instead of passing a child in the form of a component, we define a function that can receive parameters from the parent.

Let's see what it looks like:

```
const FunctionAsChild = ({ children }) => children();
FunctionAsChild.propTypes = {
  children: func.isRequired
};
```

As you can see, FunctionAsChild is a component that has a children property defined as a function and, instead of being used as a JSX expression, it gets called.

The preceding component can be used in the following way:

```
<FunctionAsChild>
  {() => <div>Hello, World!</div>}
</FunctionAsChild>
```

It is as simple as it looks: the children function is fired in the render method of the parent, and it returns the `Hello, World!` text wrapped in a `div`, which is displayed on the screen.

Let's delve into a more meaningful example where the parent component passes some parameters to the `children` function.

Create a `Name` component that expects a function as `children` and passes it the string `World`:

```
const Name = ({ children }) => children('World');
Name.propTypes = {
  children: func.isRequired
};
```

The preceding component can be used in the following way:

```
<Name>
  {name => <div>Hello, {name}!</div>}
</Name>
```

The snippet renders `Hello, World!` again, but this time the name has been passed by the parent. It should be clear how this pattern works, so let's look at the advantages of this approach.

The first benefit is that we can wrap components, passing them variables at runtime rather than fixed properties, as we do with HoCs.

A good example is a `Fetch` component that loads some data from an API endpoint and returns it to the `children` function:

```
<Fetch url="...">
  {data => <List data={data} />}
</Fetch>
```

Secondly, composing components with this approach does not force the `children` to use some predefined prop names. Since the function receives variables, their names can be decided by the developers who use the component. That makes the `FunctionAsChild` solution more flexible.

Last but not least, the wrapper is highly reusable because it does not make any assumptions about the children it receives—it just expects a function.

Due to this, the same `FunctionAsChild` component can be used in different parts of the application, serving various `children` components.

Summary

In this chapter, we learned how to compose our reusable components and make them communicate effectively. Props are a way to decouple components from each other and create a clean and well-defined interface.

Then, we went through some of the most interesting composition patterns in React. The first one was the so-called container and presentational pattern, which helps us separate the logic from the presentation and create more specialized components with a single responsibility.

We saw how React tried to solve the problem of sharing functionalities between components with mixins. Unfortunately, mixins solve those problems by adding several other ones, and they affect the maintainability of our applications. One way to achieve the same goal without adding complexity is by using HoCs, which are functions that take a component and return an enhanced one.

The `recompose` library provides some useful HoCs that can be used along with our custom ones so that our components have as little logic as possible in their implementation.

We learned how to deal with context without needing to couple our components to it, thanks to HoCs. Finally, we saw how we could compose components dynamically by following the `FunctionAsChild` pattern.

It is now time to talk about data fetching and one-way data flow, which is what we will look at in the next chapter.

5
Proper Data Fetching

The goal of this chapter is to show the different data fetching patterns that we can put in place in a React application. To find the best strategy, we have to understand how the data flows within a tree of components in React.

It is important to know how the parent can communicate with its children and vice versa. It is also crucial to understand how unconnected siblings can share their data. We will look at some real-world examples of data fetching, and transform a base component into a well-structured one using HoCs.

Finally, we will see how existing libraries such as `react-refetch`. can save us a lot of time by providing the core data fetching functionalities we need.

In this chapter, we will cover the following topics:

- The **unidirectional data flow** of React and how it can make our applications easier to reason about
- How a child can communicate with its parent using callbacks
- The way two siblings can share data through their common parent
- How to create a generic HoC, which can fetch data from any API endpoints
- How react-refetch works and why it is a useful tool that we can integrate into our projects to make data fetching easier
- How to use the new Context API

Data flow

In the last two chapters, we saw how to create single reusable components and how to compose them together effectively. Now, it is time to learn how to build a proper data flow for sharing data across multiple components in our application.

React enforces a very interesting pattern to make data go from the root to the leaves. This pattern is usually called unidirectional data flow, and we will look at it in detail in this section.

As the name suggests, in React, data flows in a single direction from the top to the bottom of the tree. This approach has many benefits because it simplifies the components' behavior and the relationship between components, making the code more predictable and maintainable.

Every component receives data from its parent in the form of props, and props cannot be modified. When the data is received, it can be transformed into new information and passed to the other children down the tree. Each of the children can hold a local state and use it as a prop for its nested components.

So far, we have only seen examples where the data is shared from parents to children components using props. However, what happens if a child has to push data up to its parent? Or what if a parent has to be updated when its children's state changes? Also, what if two sibling components need to share data? We will answer all of these questions with a real-world example.

We will start with a simple component that has no children, and we will transform it into a cleaner and structured component.

This approach will let us see the best patterns to apply in each phase to let the data flow across the tree.

Let's delve into the code for creating a `Counter` component, which starts from `0` and has two buttons: one for incrementing the value and one for decrementing it.

We will start by creating a class that extends the `Component` function from React:

```
class Counter extends Component
```

The class has a `constructor` where the counter is initialized to `0`, and the event handlers are bound to the component itself:

```
constructor(props) {
  super(props);
  this.state = {
```

```
      counter: 0
    };
    this.handleDecrement = this.handleDecrement.bind(this);
    this.handleIncrement = this.handleIncrement.bind(this);
  }
```

The event handlers are simple, and they change the state, adding or removing a unit from the current counter:

```
handleDecrement() {
  this.setState({
    counter: this.state.counter - 1
  });
}
handleIncrement() {
  this.setState({
    counter: this.state.counter + 1
  });
}
```

Finally, inside the render method, the current value is displayed, and the buttons with their onClick handlers are defined:

```
render() {
  return (
    <div>
      <h1>{this.state.counter}</h1>
      <button onClick={this.handleDecrement}>-</button>
      <button onClick={this.handleIncrement}>+</button>
    </div>
  );
}
```

Child-parent communication (callbacks)

There are no major issues with this component, apart from the fact that it does multiple things:

- It holds the counter value inside the state.
- It is responsible for showing the data.
- It contains the logic for incrementing and decrementing the counter.

It is always good practice to split components into smaller ones, each with a very specific behavior, to improve the maintainability of the app and make it flexible when requirements change.

Consider that we need the same plus and minus buttons in another part of the application.

It would be great to reuse the buttons we defined inside the `Counter`, but the question is: if we move the buttons away from the component, how do we know when they get clicked on so that the counter can be updated?

In React, when we need to push information or simply trigger an event from children to the parent, we use callbacks. Let's see how they work.

We create a `Buttons` component to display the increment and decrement buttons, which, instead of firing internal functions when they are clicked on, use the functions that are received from the props:

```
const Buttons = ({ onDecrement, onIncrement }) => (
  <div>
    <button onClick={onDecrement}>-</button>
    <button onClick={onIncrement}>+</button>
  </div>
);
Buttons.propTypes = {
  onDecrement: func,
  onIncrement: func
};
```

It is a simple, stateless functional component where the `onClick` event handlers fire the functions received from the props. Now, it is time to see how to integrate this new component into the `Counter`.

We just replace the original markup with the component, passing the internal functions to the new child, as follows:

```
render() {
  return (
    <div>
      <h1>{this.state.counter}</h1>
      <Buttons
        onDecrement={this.handleDecrement}
        onIncrement={this.handleIncrement}
      />
    </div>
  );
}
```

Everything else remains the same, and the logic is still in the parent component. The buttons are now dumb, and they are only able to notify their owner when they are clicked on.

So, every time we need the children to push data into the parent or inform the parent that something happened, we can pass callbacks and implement the rest of the logic inside the parent.

Common parent

Now, the Counter looks a bit better, and the Buttons are reusable. The last thing to be done to clean it up completely is to remove the display logic from it.

To do that, we can create a Display component that receives the value to display and shows it on the screen:

```
const Display = ({ counter }) => <h1>{counter}</h1>;
Display.propTypes = {
  counter: number
};
```

Again, we can use a stateless functional component because there is no need to keep any state. As you may note here, splitting this component is not needed because it just renders an h1 element. However, in your application, you may add CSS classes, display logic to change the color of the counter according to its value, and so on.

In general, our goal is to make components unaware of the data source so that we can reuse them with different sources in various parts of the application.

Using the new component in the Counter is easy. We just have to replace the old markup with the Display component, as follows:

```
render() {
  return (
    <div>
      <Display counter={this.state.counter} />
      <Buttons
        onDecrement={this.handleDecrement}
        onIncrement={this.handleIncrement}
      />
    </div>
  );
}
```

As you can see here, two sibling components are communicating through their common parent.

When the `Buttons` get clicked on, they notify the parent, which sends the updated value to the `Display` component. This is a very common pattern in React, and it is an effective solution to share data across components that do not have a direct relationship.

The data always flows from parents to children, but children can notify the parent and make the tree re-render with the new information.

Every time we need to make two unrelated components communicate, we have to find the common parent between them and keep the state at that level so that, when the state is updated, both components receive fresh data from the props.

Data fetching

In the preceding section, we saw the different patterns we can put in place to share data between components in the tree. It is now time to view how to fetch data in React and where the data fetching logic should be located. The examples in this section use the `fetch` function to make web requests, which is a modern replacement for `XMLHttpRequest`.

At the time of writing, it is natively implemented in Chrome and Firefox, and if you need to support different browsers, you must use the fetch **polyfill** by GitHub: https://github.com/github/fetch.

We are also going to use the public GitHub APIs to load some data, and the endpoint we will use is the one that returns a list of **gists**, given a username, for example, https://api.github.com/users/:username/gists.

Gists are snippets of code that can be shared easily between developers. The first component that we will build is a simple list of the gists that are created by the user, called gaearon (Dan Abramov). Let's delve into some code and create a class.

We use a class because we need to store an internal state and use life cycle methods:

```
import React, { Component } from 'react';
class Gists extends Component {
  ...
}
```

Then, we define a `constructor`, where we initialize the `state`:

```
constructor(props) {
  super(props);
  this.state = {
    gists: []
  };
}
```

Now comes the interesting part: data fetching. There are two life cycle hooks where we can put the data fetching: `componentWillMount` and `componentDidMount`.

The first is fired before the component gets rendered for the first time and the second is fired right after the component is mounted.

Using the first seems to be the right method because we want to load the data as soon as we can, but there is a caveat. The `componentWillMount` function is fired on both server- and client-side rendering.

We will see the server-side rendering in detail in `Chapter 8`, *Server-Side Rendering for Fun and Profit*, but for now, you just need to know that firing an async API call when the component gets rendered on the server can give you unexpected results.

We will then use the `componentDidMount` hook so that we can be sure that the API endpoint is called on the browser only.

This also means that, during the first render, the list of gists is empty and we might want to show a spinner by applying one of the techniques that we saw in `Chapter 2`, *Clean Up Your Code*, which is beyond the scope of the current section.

As we said before, we are going to use the `fetch` function and hit the GitHub APIs to retrieve gaearon's gists:

```
componentDidMount() {
  fetch('https://api.github.com/users/gaearon/gists')
    .then(response => response.json())
    .then(gists => this.setState({ gists }));
}
```

This code needs a little bit of explanation. When the `componentDidMount` hook gets fired, we call the `fetch` function against the GitHub APIs.

The `fetch` function returns a `Promise` and, when it gets resolved, we receive a response object with a JSON function that returns the JSON content of the response itself.

When the JSON is parsed and returned, we can save the raw gists inside the internal state of the component to make them available in the `render` method:

```
render() {
  return (
    <ul>
      {this.state.gists.map(gist => (
        <li key={gist.id}>{gist.description}</li>
      ))}
    </ul>
  );
}
```

The `render` method is simple—we just loop through the gists and map each one of them into an `<li>` element that shows their description.

You might have noted the key attribute of `<li>`. We use it for performance reasons that you will understand by the end of this book. If you try to remove the attribute, you will get a warning from React inside the browser's console.

The component works and everything is fine, but as we learned in the previous sections, we could, for example, separate the rendering logic into a subcomponent to make it more simple and testable.

Moving the component away is not a problem because we have seen how components in different parts of the application can receive the data they need from their parents.

It is very common to need to fetch data from the APIs in different parts of the codebase, and we do not want to duplicate the code. A solution we can apply to remove the data logic from the component and reuse it across the application is to create an HoC.

In this case, the HoC would load the data on behalf of the enhanced component, and it would provide the data to the child in the form of props. Let's see what it looks like.

As we know, an HoC is a function that accepts a component and some parameters and returns a new component that has some special behaviors attached to it.

We are going to use the partial application to receive the parameters first, and then the actual component as the second parameter:

```
const withData = url => Component => (...);
```

We have called the `withData` function, following the `with*` pattern.

The function accepts the URL from which the data has to be loaded and the component that needs the data to work.

The implementation is pretty similar to the component in the preceding example, apart from the fact that the URL is now a parameter and, inside the render method, we use the child component.

The function returns a class that's defined as follows:

```
class extends Component
```

It has a constructor to set the initial empty state.

The property we use to store the data is now called `data` because we are building a generic component and we do not want it to be tied to a particular object shape or collection:

```
constructor(props) {
  super(props);
  this.state = {
    data: []
  };
}
```

Inside the `componentDidMount` hook, the `fetch` function is fired and the data that's returned from the server is converted into JSON and stored in the state:

```
componentDidMount() {
  fetch(url)
    .then(response => response.json())
    .then(data => this.setState({ data }));
}
```

It is important to note that the URL is now set using the first parameter that's received from the HoC. In this way, we can reuse it to make any API call to any endpoint.

Finally, we render the given component, spreading the props because we want our HoC to be transparent.

We also spread the state to pass the JSON data to the child component:

```
render() {
  return <Component {...this.props} {...this.state} />;
}
```

Great! The HoC is ready. We can now wrap any components of our application and provide data to them from any URL.

Let's see how to we can use it.

First of all, we have to create a dumb component that receives the data and displays it, using the markup of the initial example:

```
import React from 'react';
import { array } from 'prop-types';
const List = ({ data: gists }) => (
  <ul>
    {gists.map(gist => (
      <li key={gist.id}>{gist.description}</li>
    ))}
  </ul>
);
List.propTypes = {
  data: array
};
```

We have used a stateless functional component because we do not need to store any state nor define handlers inside it, which is usually a big win.

The prop containing the response from the API is called `data`, which is generic and not useful, but we can easily rename it, thanks to ES6, and give it a more meaningful name.

It is now time to see how to use our `withData` HoC and make it pass the data down to the `List` component we just created. Thanks to the partial application, we can first specialize the HoC to make a specific call and use it many times, as follows:

```
const withGists = withData('https://api.github.com/users/gaearon/gists');
```

This is great because we can now wrap any component with the new `withGists` function and it will receive gaeron's gists without specifying the URL multiple times.

Finally, we wrap the component and get a new one:

```
const ListWithGists = withGists(List);
```

We can now put the enhanced component anywhere within our application, and it just works.

Our `withData` HoC is great, but it is only able to load static URLs, while in the real world URLs often depend on parameters or props.

Unfortunately, the props are unknown at the moment we apply the HoC, so we need a hook that is called when the props are available and before making the API call.

What we can do is change the HoC to accept two types of URLs: a string, as we have done until now, and a function, which receives the component's props and returns a URL that depends on the received parameters.

That is pretty straightforward to do; we have to change the `componentDidMount` hook, as follows:

```
componentDidMount() {
  const endpoint = typeof url === 'function'
    ? url(this.props)
    : url
  fetch(endpoint)
    .then(response => response.json())
    .then(data => this.setState({ data }))
}
```

If the URL is a function, we fire it by passing the props as parameters, while if it is a string, we use it directly.

We can now use the HoC in the following way:

```
const withGists = withData(
  props => `https://api.github.com/users/${props.username}/gists`
);
```

Here, the username for loading the gists can be set in the props of the component:

```
<ListWithGists username="gaearon" />
```

React-refetch

Now, our HoC works as expected and we can reuse it across the codebase without any problems. The question is, what should we do if we need more features?

For example, we may want to post some data to the server or fetch the data again when the props change. Also, we may not want to load the data on `componentDidMount` but apply some lazy loading patterns instead.

We could write all the features we need, but there is an existing library that has a lot of useful functionalities, and it is ready to be used.

The library is called `react-refetch`, and it is maintained by developers from Heroku. Let's see how we can use it effectively to replace our HoC.

From the previous section, we have a `List` component, which is a stateless functional component that can receive a collection of gists; it displays the description for each one of them:

```
import React from 'react';
import { array } from 'prop-types';

const List = ({ data: gists }) => (
  <ul>
    {gists.map(gist => (
      <li key={gist.id}>{gist.description}</li>
    ))}
  </ul>
);

List.propTypes = {
  data: array
};
```

By wrapping this component inside the `withData` HoC, we can provide data to it in a transparent way through props. We can enhance it by passing the URL of the endpoint.

With `react-refetch`, we can do the same thing. First of all, we need to install the library:

```
npm install react-refetch --save
```

Then, we import the `connect` function inside our module:

```
import { connect } from 'react-refetch';
```

Finally, we decorate our component using the `connect` HoC. We use the partial application technique to specialize the function and reuse it:

```
const connectWithGists = connect(({ username }) => ({
  gists: `https://api.github.com/users/${username}/gists`
}));
```

The preceding code needs a bit of an explanation.

We use the `connect` function, passing a function to it as a parameter. The parameter function receives the props (and the context) as parameters so that we can create dynamic URLs based on the current properties of the component.

Our callback function returns an object where the keys are the identifiers of the request, and the values are the URLs. The URL is not limited to being a string; we'll see how we can add multiple parameters to the request later.

At this point, we enhance our component with the function we just created, as follows:

```
const ListWithGists = connectWithGists(List);
```

We now have to make small changes to the initial component to make it work well with the new HoC.

First of all, the parameter is not called `data` anymore; it is called `gists`. React-refetch will inject a property with the same name of the key that we specified in the `connect` function.

The `gists` prop is not the actual data—it is a particular type of object, called `PromiseState`.

A `PromiseState` object is a synchronous representation of a `Promise`, and it has some useful attributes such as pending or fulfilled that we can use to show a spinner or a list of data.

There is also a `rejected` property that we can use in case of errors.

When the request is fulfilled, we can access the data we wanted to load using the `value` property and loop through it to display the gists:

```
const List = ({ gists }) => (
  gists.fulfilled && (
    <ul>
      {gists.value.map(gist => (
        <li key={gist.id}>{gist.description}</li>
      ))}
    </ul>
  )
);
```

As soon as the stateless functional component is rendered, we can check to validate if the request is fulfilled; if it is, we show the list using the `gists.value` property.

Everything else remains the same.

We also have to update the `propTypes` and change the name of the received prop and its type:

```
import { object } from 'prop-types';
...
List.propTypes = {
  gists: object
};
```

Now that we have this library in our project, we can add more functionalities to our `List` component.

For example, we can add a button to start the gists.

Let's start with the UI and then add the real API call, thanks to `react-refetch`.

We do not want to add too many responsibilities to the `List` component as its role is to display the list; so, we change it to use a subcomponent for each row.

We call the new component `Gist`, and we are going to use it inside the loop in the following way:

```
const List = ({ gists }) => (
  gists.fulfilled && (
    <ul>
      {gists.value.map(gist => (
        <Gist key={gist.id} {...gist} />
      ))}
    </ul>
  )
);
```

We just replaced the `<li>` element with the `Gist` component, and we spread the `gist` object to it so that it receives single properties and becomes easier to test and maintain.

The `Gist` component is a stateless functional component because the starring logic is handled by `react-refetch` and we do not need any state or event handlers.

The component receives the description and, for now, the only difference from the previous markup is that it has a +1 button, to which we will add some functionalities soon:

```
const Gist = ({ description }) => (
  <li>
    {description}
    <button>+1</button>
  </li>
);
Gist.propTypes = {
  description: string
};
```

The URL of the endpoint to star a gist is as follows:
https://api.github.com/gists/:id/star?access_token=:access_token.

Here, :id is the ID of the gist that we want to star, and the access token is the authentication token that's required to run the action. There are different ways of getting an access token, and they are well explained in the GitHub documentation.

They are also outside the scope of this book, so we are not going to cover them in this section. The next step is to add a function to the onClick event of the button to make an API call with the ID of the gist.

The connect function of react-refetch accepts a function as the first argument, and the function has to return an object of requests, as we have previously seen. If the values of the requests are strings, then the data is fetched as soon as the props are available.

If the value of a request key is a function instead, it gets passed into the component, and it can be fired lazily. For example, it can be triggered when a particular event occurs.

Let's delve into the code:

```
const token = 'access_token=123';

const connectWithStar = connect(({ id }) => ({
  star: () => ({
    starResponse: {
      url: `https://api.github.com/gists/${id}/star?${token}`,
      method: 'PUT'
    }
  })
}));
```

First, we partially apply the collection function, and we use the id prop to compose the URL.

We then define an object of requests, where the key is star and the value is a function that, again, returns an object of requests. In this case, the value of the starResponse key is not a simple string, but an object with two parameters: URL and method.

This is because, by default, the library fires an HTTP GET, but in this case, we are required to use a PUT to star a gist.

It is now time to enhance our component:

```
const GistWithStar = connectWithStar(Gist);
```

Also, it is time to use the star function inside it to fire the request:

```
const Gist = ({ description, star }) => (
  <li>
```

```
        {description}
        <button onClick={star}>+1</button>
    </li>
);
Gist.propTypes = {
    description: string,
    star: func
};
```

As you can see, it is very simple; the component receives the `star` function, where the star is the name of the request that we defined in the connect function. The function gets fired when the button is clicked on.

This is the final result in the browser window:

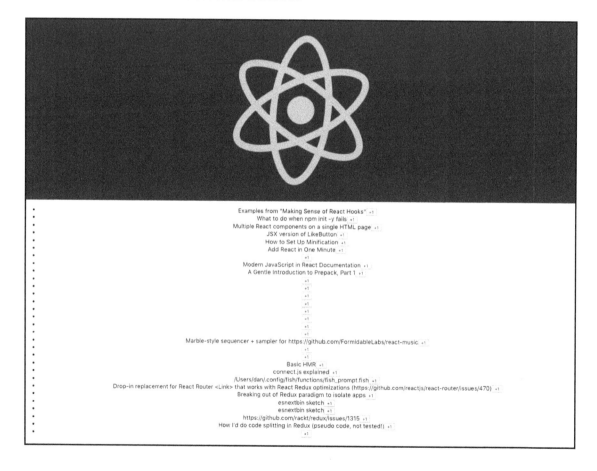

You may have noted that thanks to `react-refetch`, we can keep our components stateless and unaware of the actions that they are firing.

This makes tests easier, and means that we can also change the implementation of the HoC without modifying the subcomponent.

Context API

The new and official Context API was introduced in React 16.3.0. Before, React offered an experimental API for context. Although it was a powerful tool, its use was discouraged because of inherent problems in the API.

React 16.3 introduces a new context API that is more efficient and supports both static type checking and deep updates.

The Context API implementation is really easy. First, you need to create your Context (using `createContext`) and your Provider, which is a React `class` component. Let's create a context for our `List` component to fetch the gists. This file needs to be called `ListContext.jsx`:

```jsx
// Dependencies
import React, { Component, createContext } from 'react';
import { element } from 'prop-types';

// Context
export const ListContext = createContext();

export class ListProvider extends Component {
  static propTypes = {
    children: element
  };

  state = {
    gists: [],
    status: 'initial'
  }

  componentDidMount() {
    // Fetching the gists when the component is mounted
    this.fetchGists();
  }

  fetchGists = async () => {
    this.setState({
```

```
        gists: [],
        status: 'fetching'
    });

    try {
      const data = await
      fetch('https://api.github.com/users/gaearon/gists')
        .then(response => response.json());

      this.setState({
        gists: data,
        status: 'done'
      });
    } catch (error) {
      this.setState({
        status: 'error'
      });
    }
  }

  render() {
    const { children } = this.props;

    return (
      <ListContext.Provider
        value={{
          ...this.state
          // Everything you pass in here will be available in the
             Consumer
        }}
      >
        {children}
      </ListContext.Provider>
    );
  }
}
```

After we have created our `Context` and `Provider`, we need to import it in the component we want to consume it with, like this:

```
// Dependencies
import React from 'react';
import { array } from 'prop-types';

// Providers
import { ListProvider, ListContext } from './ListContext';

const List = () => (
```

```
    <ListProvider>
      <ListContext.Consumer>
        {/* These props are comming from the Provider's value*/}
        {({ gists }) => (
          <ul>
            {gists.map(gist => (
              <li key={gist.id}>{gist.description}</li>
            ))}
          </ul>
        )}
      </ListContext.Consumer>
    </ListProvider>
  );

List.propTypes = {
  data: array
};

export default List;
```

As you can see, everything you add to your Provider's value will be available in your Consumer. If you have used Redux, this is very similar to getting your Redux state by using the `connect` HoC. It is also possible to add functions (similar to Redux actions) and then execute those in your Consumer. Let's try a basic example and create a function that will do a simple `console.log`:

```
myLogAction = () => {
  console.log('This is similar to a Redux action');
}

render() {
  const { children } = this.props;

  return (
    <ListContext.Provider
      value={{
        myLogAction: this.myLogAction, // Here you can pass your actions
        ...this.state
      }}
    >
      {children}
    </ListContext.Provider>
  );
}
```

Then, in your consumer, you can do something like this:

```
const List = () => (
  <ListProvider>
    <ListContext.Consumer>
      {/* These props are comming from the Provider's value*/}
      {({ gists, myLogAction }) => (
        <ul>
          {myLogAction()}
          {gists.map(gist => (
            <li key={gist.id}>{gist.description}</li>
          ))}
        </ul>
      )}
    </ListContext.Consumer>
  </ListProvider>
);
```

Then, in your browser console, you will see the following:

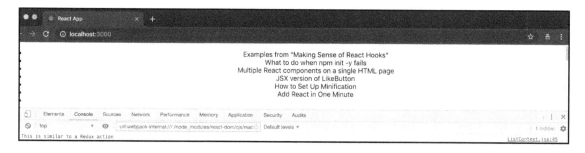

Summary

The journey through data fetching in React has come to an end, and you now know how to send and retrieve data to and from API endpoints. We saw how data flow works in React and why the approach it enforces can make our applications simple and clean.

We went through some of the most common patterns to make children and parents communicate using callbacks. We learned how we could use a common parent to share data across components that are not directly connected.

In the second section, we started with a simple component, which was able to load data from GitHub, and we made it reusable, thanks to HoCs. We have now mastered the techniques that let us abstract the logic away from components so that we can make them as dumb as possible, thus improving their testability.

We learned how we could use `react-refetch` to apply data fetching patterns to our components and avoid reinventing the wheel.

Finally, we learned how to use the new Context API.

In the next chapter, we will see how we can work effectively with React in the browser.

6 Write Code for the Browser

There are some specific operations we can do when we work with React and the browser. For example, we can ask our users to enter some information using forms, and we will look at how, in React, we can apply different techniques to deal with them.

We can implement **uncontrolled components** and let the fields keep their internal states, or we can use controlled ones, where we have full control over the state of the fields.

In this chapter, we will also look at how events in React work and how the library implements some advanced techniques to give us a consistent interface across different browsers. We will also look at some interesting solutions that the React team has implemented to make the event system very performant.

After the events, we will jump into refs to look at how we can access the underlying DOM nodes in our React components. This represents a powerful feature, but it should be used carefully because it breaks some of the conventions that make React easy to work with.

After the refs, we will look at how we can implement animations easily with the React add-ons and third-party libraries such as **react-motion**. Finally, we will learn how easy it is to work with SVGs in React, and how we can create dynamically configurable icons for our applications.

In this chapter, we will go through the following topics:

- Using different techniques to create forms with React
- Listening to DOM events and implementing custom handlers
- A way of performing imperative operations on DOM nodes using refs
- Creating simple animations that work across the different browsers
- The React way of generating SVGs

Forms

As soon as we start building a real application with React, we need to interact with the users. If we want to ask for information from our users within the browser, forms are the most common solution. Due to the way the library works and its declarative nature, dealing with input fields and other form elements is non-trivial with React, but as soon as we understand its logic, it becomes clear.

Uncontrolled components

Let's start with a basic example—displaying a form with an input field and a **Submit** button.

The code is pretty straightforward:

```
const Uncontrolled = () => (
  <form>
    <input type="text" />
    <button>Submit</button>
  </form>
);
```

If we run the preceding snippet in the browser, we can see exactly what we expect—an input field in which we can write something and a clickable button. This is an example of an uncontrolled component, where we do not set the value of the input field, but we let the component manage its own internal state.

Most likely, we want to do something with the value of the element when the **Submit** button is clicked. For example, we may want to send the data to an API endpoint.

We can do this easily by adding an onChange listener (we will talk more about event listeners later in this chapter). Let's look at what it means to add a listener.

First, we have to change the component from stateless to a class because we need to define some functions and a state:

```
class Uncontrolled extends Component
```

The class has a constructor where we bind the event listener:

```
constructor(props) {
  super(props);
  this.handleChange = this.handleChange.bind(this);
}
```

Then, we define the event listener itself:

```
handleChange({ target: { value } }) {
  console.log(value);
}
```

The event listener is receiving an event object, where the target represents the field that generated the event, and we are interested in its value. We start by just logging it because it is important to proceed with small steps, but we will store the value into the state soon.

Finally, we render the form:

```
render() {
  return (
    <form>
      <input type="text" onChange={this.handleChange} />
      <button>Submit</button>
    </form>
  );
}
```

If we render the component inside the browser and type the word React into the form field, we will see something like the following inside the console:

```
R
Re
Rea
Reac
React
```

The handleChange listener is fired every time the value of the input changes. Therefore, our function is called once for each typed character. The next step is to store the value that's entered by the user and make it available when the user clicks the **Submit** button.

We just have to change the implementation of the handler to store it in the state instead of logging it, as follows:

```
handleChange({ target: { value } }) {
  this.setState({
    value
  });
}
```

Getting notified of when the form is submitted is very similar to listening to the change event of the input field; they are both events that are called by the browser when something happens.

So, let's say we add a second event handler inside the `constructor`, as follows:

```
constructor(props) {
  super(props);
  this.state = {
    value: ''
  };
  this.handleChange = this.handleChange.bind(this);
  this.handleSubmit = this.handleSubmit.bind(this);
}
```

We may also want to initialize the value property of the state as an empty string, in case the button gets clicked before any change event is triggered.

Let's define the `handleSubmit` function, where we just log the value. In a real-world scenario, you could send the data to an API endpoint or pass it to another component:

```
handleSubmit(e) {
  e.preventDefault();
  console.log(this.state.value);
}
```

This handler is pretty straightforward—we just log the value currently stored in the state. We also want to overcome the default behavior of the browser when the form is submitted, to perform a custom action.

This seems reasonable, and it works very well for a single field. The question now is, what if we have multiple fields? Suppose we have tens of different fields?

Let's start with a basic example, where we create each field and handler manually and look at how we can improve it by applying different levels of optimization.

Let's create a new form with first and last name fields. We can reuse the `Uncontrolled` class we just created and change the `constructor`, as follows:

```
constructor(props) {
  super(props);
  this.state = {
    firstName: '',
    lastName: ''
  };
  this.handleChangeFirstName = this.handleChangeFirstName.bind(this);
  this.handleChangeLastName = this.handleChangeLastName.bind(this);
  this.handleSubmit = this.handleSubmit.bind(this);
}
```

We initialize the two fields inside the state and we define an event handler for each one of the fields as well. As you may have noticed, this does not scale very well when there are lots of fields, but it is important to understand the problem clearly before moving to a more flexible solution.

Now, we implement the new handlers:

```
handleChangeFirstName({ target: { value } }) {
  this.setState({
    firstName: value
  })
}
handleChangeLastName({ target: { value } }) {
  this.setState({
    lastName: value
  })
}
```

We also have to change the submit handler a little bit so that it displays the first and the last name when it gets clicked:

```
handleSubmit(e) {
  e.preventDefault();
  console.log(`${this.state.firstName} ${this.state.lastName}`);
}
```

Finally, we describe our elements, structure inside the render method:

```
render() {
  return (
    <form onSubmit={this.handleSubmit}>
      <input type="text" onChange={this.handleChangeFirstName} />
      <input type="text" onChange={this.handleChangeLastName} />
      <button>Submit</button>
    </form>
  );
}
```

We are ready to go—if we run the preceding component in the browser, we will see two fields, and if we type Dan into the first one and Abramov into the second one, we will see the full name displayed in the browser console when the form is submitted.

Again, this works fine, and we can do some interesting things in this way, but it does not handle complex scenarios without requiring us to write a lot of boilerplate code.

Let's look at how we can optimize it a little bit. Our goal is to use a single change handler so that we can add an arbitrary number of fields without creating new listeners.

Let's go back to the `constructor` and define a single change handler:

```
constructor(props) {
  super(props);
  this.state = {
    firstName: '',
    lastName: ''
  }
  this.handleChange = this.handleChange.bind(this);
  this.handleSubmit = this.handleSubmit.bind(this);
}
```

We may still want to initialize the values, and later in this section, we will look at how to provide prefilled values for the form.

Now, the interesting bit is the way in which we can modify the `onChange` handler implementation to make it work in different fields:

```
handleChange({ target: { name, value } }) {
  this.setState({
    [name]: value
  });
}
```

As we have seen previously, the `target` property of the event we receive represents the input field that has fired the event, so we can use the name of the field and its value as variables.

We then have to set the name for each field, which we are going to do using the `render` method:

```
render() {
  return (
    <form onSubmit={this.handleSubmit}>
      <input
        type="text"
        name="firstName"
        onChange={this.handleChange}
      />
      <input
        type="text"
        name="lastName"
        onChange={this.handleChange}
      />
```

```
    <button>Submit</button>
  </form>
);
}
```

That's it; we can now add as many fields as we want without creating additional handlers.

Controlled components

The next thing we are going to look at is how we can prefill the form fields with some values, which we may receive from the server or as props from the parent.

To understand this concept fully, we will start again from a very simple stateless function component, and we will improve it step by step.

The first example shows a predefined value inside the input field:

```
const Controlled = () => (
  <form>
    <input type="text" value="Hello React" />
    <button>Submit</button>
  </form>
);
```

If we run this component inside the browser, we realize that it shows the default value as expected, but it does not let us change the value or type anything else inside it.

The reason it does that is because, in React, we declare what we want to see on the screen, and setting a fixed value attribute ends up always rendering that value, no matter what other actions are taken. This is unlikely to be a behavior we want in a real-world application.

If we open the console, React itself is telling us that we are doing something wrong:

```
You provided a `value` prop to a form field without an `onChange` handler.
This will render a read-only field.
```

And that is exactly what happened.

Now, if we just want the input field to have a default value and we want to be able to change it by typing, we can use the defaultValue property:

```
const Controlled = () => (
  <form>
    <input type="text" defaultValue="Hello React" />
    <button>Submit</button>
```

```
      </form>
    );
```

In this way, the field is going to show `Hello React` when it is rendered, but then the user can type anything inside it and change its value. This is OK, and it works, but we want to control the value of the component fully, and to do so we should transform the component from a stateless functional one into a `class`:

```
class Controlled extends Component
```

As usual, we start defining a constructor where we initialize the state, this time with the default values of the fields. We also bind the event handlers that we need to make the form work.

We will use a single handler, which will update the state using the name attribute, as we have seen in the optimized version of the uncontrolled components example:

```
constructor(props) {
  super(props);
  this.state = {
    firstName: 'Dan',
    lastName: 'Abramov'
  };
  this.handleChange = this.handleChange.bind(this);
  this.handleSubmit = this.handleSubmit.bind(this);
}
```

The handlers are the same as the previous ones:

```
handleChange({ target: { name, value } }) {
  this.setState({
    [name]: value
  });
}
handleSubmit(e) {
  e.preventDefault();
  console.log(`${this.state.firstName} ${this.state.lastName}`);
}
```

The important thing to change is inside the `render` method. In fact, we will use the value attributes of the input fields to set their initial values, as well as the updated one:

```
render() {
  return (
    <form onSubmit={this.handleSubmit}>
      <input
        type="text"
```

```
      name="firstName"
      value={this.state.firstName}
      onChange={this.handleChange}
    />
    <input
      type="text"
      name="lastName"
      value={this.state.lastName}
      onChange={this.handleChange}
    />
    <button>Submit</button>
  </form>
  );
}
```

The first time the form is rendered, React uses the initial values from the state as the value of the input fields. When the user types something into the field, the `handleChange` function is called and the new value for the field is stored in the state.

When the state changes, React re-renders the component and uses it again to reflect the current value of the input fields.

We now have full control over the value of the fields, and we call this pattern **controlled components**.

JSON schema

Now that we know how forms work in React, we can move in to something that helps us automate form creation, avoid writing a lot of boilerplate, and keep our code much cleaner.

A popular solution is `react-jsonschema-form`, which is maintained by Mozilla services. First, we must install it using npm:

```
npm install --save react-jsonschema-form
```

Once the library is installed, we import it inside our component:

```
import Form from 'react-jsonschema-form';
```

We define a schema, as follows:

```
const schema = {
  type: 'object',
  properties: {
    firstName: { type: 'string', default: 'Dan' },
    lastName: { type: 'string', default: 'Abramov' },
```

```
    }
  };
```

We will not go into the details of the JSON schema format in this book: the important bit here is that we can describe the fields of our forms using a configuration object instead of creating multiple HTML elements.

As you can see in the preceding example, we set the type of the schema to `object` and then we declare the properties of the form, `firstName`, and `lastName`, each one with a string type and its default value.

If we then pass the schema to the `Form` component we imported from the library, a form will be generated for us automatically.

Once more, let's start with a simple stateless functional component so that we can add features to it iteratively:

```
const JSONSchemaForm = () => (
  <Form schema={schema} />
);
```

Now, if we render this component inside the page, we will see a form with the fields we declared in the schema and a **Submit** button. We now want to be notified when the form is submitted, so that we can do something with the form data.

The first thing we have to do is create an event handler that transforms the stateless functional component into a `class`:

```
class JSONSchemaForm extends Component
```

Inside the `constructor`, we bind the event handler:

```
constructor(props) {
  super(props);
  this.handleSubmit = this.handleSubmit.bind(this);
}
```

In the preceding example, we just log the form data into the console, but in a real-world application, you may want to post the fields to an endpoint.

The `handleSubmit` handler is receiving an object, which has a `formData` attribute that contains the names and the values of the form fields:

```
handleSubmit({ formData }) {
  console.log(formData);
}
```

Finally, our `render` method looks as follows:

```
render() {
  return (
    <Form schema={schema} onSubmit={this.handleSubmit} />
  );
}
```

Here, the schema prop is the schema object we previously defined. It can be defined statically, as in the current example, or it can be received from the server, or composed using props.

We just attach our handler to the `onSubmit` callback of the `Form` component provided by the library and then we have created a working form easily.

There are also different callbacks, such as `onChange`, which is fired every time the value of a field changes, and `onError`, which is fired whenever the form is submitted using invalid data.

Handling events

Events work in a slightly different way across the various browsers. React tries to abstract the way events work and give developers a consistent interface to deal with. This is a great feature of React because we can forget about the browsers we are targeting and write event handlers and functions that are vendor-agnostic.

To offer this feature, React introduced the concept of the **synthetic event**. A synthetic event is an object that wraps the original event object provided by the browser, and it has the same properties, no matter where it is created.

To attach an event listener to a node and get the event object when the event is fired, we can use a simple convention which recalls the way events are attached to the DOM nodes. In fact, we can use the word `on` plus the camelCased event name (for example, `onKeyDown`) to define the callback to be fired when the events happen. A popular convention is to name the event handler functions after the event name and prefix them using `handle` (for example, `handleKeyDown`).

We have seen this pattern in action in the previous examples, where we were listening to the `onChange` event of the form fields.

Let's reiterate a basic event listener example to see how we can organize multiple events inside the same component in a nicer way.

We are going to implement a simple button, and we start, as usual, by creating a class:

```
class Button extends Component
```

We add a `constructor` where we bind the event listener:

```
constructor(props) {
  super(props);
  this.handleClick = this.handleClick.bind(this);
}
```

We define the event handler itself:

```
handleClick(syntheticEvent) {
  console.log(syntheticEvent instanceof MouseEvent);
  console.log(syntheticEvent.nativeEvent instanceof MouseEvent);
}
```

As you can see here, we are doing a very simple thing: we just check the type of the event object we receive from React and the type of native event attached to it. We expect the first to return `false` and the second to return `true`.

You should never need to access the original native event, but it is good to know you can do it if you need to. Finally, in the `render` method, we define the button with the `onClick` attribute to which we attach our event listener:

```
render() {
  return (
    <button onClick={this.handleClick}>Click me!</button>
  );
}
```

Now, suppose we want to attach a second handler to the button that listens to the double-click event. One solution would be to create a new separate handler and attach it to the button using the `onDoubleClick` attribute, as follows:

```
<button
  onClick={this.handleClick}
  onDoubleClick={this.handleDoubleClick}
>
  Click me!
</button>
```

Remember that we always aim to write less boilerplate and avoid duplicating the code. For that reason, a common practice is to write a **single event handler** for each component, which can trigger different actions according to the event type.

This technique is described in a collection of patterns by Michael Chan: `http://reactpatterns.com/#event-switch`.

First, we change the `constructor` of the component, because we now want it to bind the new generic event handler:

```
constructor(props) {
  super(props);
  this.handleEvent = this.handleEvent.bind(this);
}
```

Second, we implement the generic event handler:

```
handleEvent(event) {
  switch (event.type) {
    case 'click':
      console.log('clicked');
      break;
    case 'dblclick':
      console.log('double clicked');
      break;
    default:
      console.log('unhandled', event.type);
  }
}
```

The generic event handler receives the event object and switches on the event type to fire the right action. This is particularly useful if we want to call a function on each event (for example, analytics) or if some events share the same logic.

Finally, we attach the new event listener to the `onClick` and `onDoubleClick` attributes:

```
render() {
  return (
    <button
      onClick={this.handleEvent}
      onDoubleClick={this.handleEvent}
    >
      Click me!
    </button>
  );
}
```

From this point on, whenever we need to create a new event handler for the same component, instead of creating a new method and binding it, we can just add a new case to the switch.

A couple more interesting things to know about events in React are that synthetic events are reused and that there is a **single global handler**. The first concept means that we cannot store a synthetic event and reuse it later because it becomes null right after the action. This technique is very good in terms of performance, but it can be problematic if we want to store the event inside the state of the component for some reason. To solve this problem, React gives us a `persist` method on the synthetic events, which we can call to make the event persistent so that we can store it and retrieve it later.

The second very interesting implementation detail is again about performance, and it regards the way React attaches the event handlers to the DOM.

Whenever we use the `on` attributes, we are describing to React the behavior we want to achieve, but the library does not attach the actual event handler to the underlying DOM nodes.

What it does instead is attach a single event handler to the root element, which listens to all the events, thanks to **event bubbling**. When an event we are interested in is fired by the browser, React calls the handler on the specific components on its behalf. This technique is called **event delegation** and is used for memory and speed optimization.

Refs

One of the reasons people love React is because it is declarative. Being declarative means that you just describe what you want to be displayed on the screen at any given point in time and React takes care of the communications with the browser. This feature makes React very easy to reason about and it is very powerful at the same time.

However, there might be some cases where you need to access the underlying DOM nodes to perform some imperative operations. It should be avoided because, in most cases, there is a more React-compliant solution to achieve the same result, but it is important to know that we have the possibility to do it and to know how it works so that we can make the right decision.

Suppose we want to create a simple form with an input element and a button, and we want it to behave in such a way that when the button is clicked, the input field gets focused.

What we want to do, is call the `focus` method on the input node, the actual DOM instance of the input, inside the browser's window.

Let's create a class called `Focus` with a constructor where we bind the `handleClick` method:

```
class Focus extends Component
```

We will listen to the click events on the button to focus the input field:

```
constructor(props) {
  super(props);
  this.handleClick = this.handleClick.bind(this);
}
```

Then, we implement the actual `handleClick` method:

```
handleClick() {
  this.element.focus();
}
```

As you can see, we are referencing the `element` attribute of the class and calling the `focus` method on it.

To understand where it comes from, you just have to check the implementation of the `render` method:

```
render() {
  return (
    <form>
      <input
        type="text"
        ref={element => (this.element = element)}
      />
      <button onClick={this.handleClick}>Focus</button>
    </form>
  );
}
```

Here comes the core of the logic. We create a form with an input element inside it and we define a function on its `ref` attribute.

The callback we defined is called when the component gets mounted, and the element parameter represents the DOM instance of the input. It is important to know that, when the component gets unmounted, the same callback is called with a `null` parameter to free the memory. What we are doing in the callback is storing the reference of the element to be able to use it in the future (for example, when the `handleClick` method is fired). Then, we have the button with its event handler. Running the preceding code in a browser will show the form with the field and the button, and clicking on the button will focus the input field, as expected.

 As we mentioned previously, in general, we should try to avoid using refs because they force the code to be more imperative, and they become harder to read and maintain.

The scenarios where we might need to use it without any other solutions are the ones where we are integrating our components with other imperative libraries, such as jQuery. It is important to know that when setting the ref callback on a non-native component (a custom component that starts with an uppercase letter), the reference we receive as a parameter of the callback is not a DOM node instance, but the instance of the component itself. This is really powerful because it gives us access to the internal instance of a child component, but it is also dangerous and should be avoided. To see an example of this solution, we are going to create two components:

- The first one is a simple controlled input field, which exposes a reset function that resets the value of the input itself to an empty string
- The second component is a form with the previous input field and a reset button that fires the instance method when clicked

Let's start by creating the input:

```
class Input extends Component
```

We define a constructor with a default state (empty string) and bind the `onChange` method we need to control the component, and the `reset` method, which represents the public API of the component:

```
constructor(props) {
  super(props);
  this.state = {
    value: ''
  };
  this.reset = this.reset.bind(this);
  this.handleChange = this.handleChange.bind(this);
}
```

The `reset` function is very simple, and just brings the state back to empty:

```
reset() {
  this.setState({
    value: ''
  });
}
```

The `handleChange` is pretty simple as well, and it just keeps the state of the component in sync with the current value of the input element:

```
handleChange({ target: { value } }) {
  this.setState({
    value
  });
}
```

Finally, inside the `render` method, we define our `input` field with its controlled value and the event handler:

```
render() {
  return (
    <input
      type="text"
      value={this.state.value}
      onChange={this.handleChange}
    />
  );
}
```

Now, we are going to create the `Reset` component, which uses the preceding component, and call its `reset` method when the button is clicked:

```
class Reset extends Component
```

Inside the `constructor`, we bind the event handler, as usual:

```
constructor(props) {
  super(props);
  this.handleClick = this.handleClick.bind(this);
}
```

The interesting part is the code inside the `handleClick` function because this is where we can call the `reset` method on the instance of the input:

```
handleClick() {
  this.element.reset();
}
```

Finally, we define our `render` method, as follows:

```
render() {
  return (
    <form>
      <Input ref={element => (this.element = element)} />
      <button onClick={this.handleClick}>Reset</button>
    </form>
  );
}
```

As you can see here, referencing node elements or instances is basically the same in terms of ref callback.

This is pretty powerful because we can easily access methods on the components, but we should be careful because it breaks the encapsulation and makes refactoring pretty hard. Suppose, in fact, that you need to rename the `reset` function for some reason; you have to check all the parent components that are using it and change them as well.

React is great because it gives us a declarative API to use in all cases, but we can also access the underlying DOM nodes and component instances in case we need them to create more advanced interactions and complex structures.

Animations

When we think about UIs and the browser, we must surely think about animations as well.

Animated UIs are more pleasant for users, and they are a very important tool to show users that something has happened or is about to occur.

This section does not aim to be an exhaustive guide to creating animations and beautiful UIs; the goal here is to provide you with some basic information about the common solutions we can put in place to animate our React components.

For a UI library such as React, it is crucial to provide an easy way for developers to create and manage animations. React comes with an add-on, called `react-addons-css-transition-group`, which is a component that helps us build animations in a declarative way. Again, being able to perform operations declaratively is incredibly powerful, and it makes the code much easier to reason about and share with the team.

Let's look at how to apply a simple fade-in effect to text with the React add-on, and then we will perform the same operation using `react-motion`, a third-party library that makes creating complex animations even easier.

The first thing we need to do to start building an animated component is to install the add-on:

```
npm install --save react-addons-css-transition-group
```

Once we have done that, we can import the component:

```
import CSSTransitionGroup from 'react-addons-css-transition-group';
```

Then, we just wrap the component to which we want to apply the animation with it:

```
const Transition = () => (
  <CSSTransitionGroup
    transitionName="fade"
    transitionAppear
    transitionAppearTimeout={500}
  >
    <h1>Hello React</h1>
  </CSSTransitionGroup>
);
```

As you can see, there are some props that need explaining.

First, we are declaring a `transitionName`. The `ReactCSSTransitionGroup` applies a class with the name of that property to the child element so that we can then use CSS transitions to create our animations.

With a single class, we cannot easily create a proper animation, and that is why the transition group applies multiple classes according to the state of the animation.

In this case, with the `transitionAppear` prop, we are telling the component that we want to animate the children when they appear on the screen.

So, what the library does is apply the `fade-appear` class (where fade is the value of the `transitionName` prop) to the component as soon as it gets rendered.

On the next tick, the `fade-appear-active` class is applied so that we can fire our animation from the initial state to the new one, using CSS.

We also have to set the `transitionAppearTimeout` property to tell React the length of the animation so that it doesn't remove elements from the DOM before animations are completed.

The CSS to make an element fade in is as follows.

First, we define the opacity of the element in the initial state:

```
.fade-appear {
  opacity: 0.01;
}
```

Then, we define our transition using the second class, which starts as soon as it gets applied to the element:

```
.fade-appear.fade-appear-active {
  opacity: 1;
  transition: opacity .5s ease-in;
}
```

We are transitioning the opacity from `0.01` to `1` in `500ms` using the `ease-in` function.

This is pretty easy, but we can create more complex animations, and we can also animate different states of the component.

For example, the `*-enter` and `*-enter-active` classes are applied when a new element is added as a child of the transition group.

A similar thing applies to remove elements.

React motion

As soon as the complexity of the animations grows, or when we need animations that depend on other animations, or, which is more advanced, when we need to apply some physics-based behavior to our components, we realize that the transition group is not helping us enough, so we may consider using a third-party library.

The most popular library to create animations in React is `react-motion`, which is maintained by Cheng Lou. It provides a very clean and easy API that gives us a very powerful tool to create any animations.

To use it, we first have to install it:

```
npm install --save react-motion
```

Once the installation is successfully completed, we need to import the **motion** component and the `spring` function. Motion is the component we will use to wrap the elements we want to animate, while the function is a utility that can interpolate a value from its initial state to the final one:

```
import { Motion, spring } from 'react-motion';
```

Let's look at the code:

```
const Transition = () => (
  <Motion
    defaultStyle={{ opacity: 0.01 }}
    style={{ opacity: spring(1) }}
  >
    {interpolatingStyle => (
      <h1 style={interpolatingStyle}>Hello React</h1>
    )}
  </Motion>
);
```

There are a lot of interesting things here.

First, you may have noticed that this component uses the function as a child pattern (see `Chapter 4`, *Compose All the Things*), which is a pretty powerful technique to define children that receive values at runtime.

Then, we can see that the `Motion` component has two attributes: the first one is `defaultStyle`, which represents the initial style.

Again, we set the opacity to `0.0.1` to hide the element and start the fade.

The style attribute represents the final style instead, but we do not set the value directly; instead we use the `spring` function so that the value is interpolated from the initial state to the final one.

On each iteration of the `spring` function, the child function receives the interpolated style for the given point in time and, just by applying the received object to the style attribute of the component, we can see the transition of the opacity.

This library can do some more cool stuff, but the first things to learn about are the basic concepts, and this example should clarify them.

It is also interesting to compare the two different approaches of the transition group and `react-motion` to be able to choose the right one for the project you are working on.

Scalable Vector Graphics

Last but not least, one of the most interesting techniques we can apply in the browser to draw icons and graphs is **Scalable Vector Graphics** (**SVG**).

SVG is great because it is a declarative way of describing vectors and it fits perfectly with the purposes of React.

We used to use icon fonts to create icons, but they have well-known problems, with the first being that they are not accessible. It is also pretty hard to position icon fonts with CSS, and they do not always look beautiful in all browsers. These are the reasons we should prefer SVG for our web applications.

From a React point of view, it does not make any difference if we output a `div` or an SVG element from the render method, and this is what makes it so powerful.

We tend also to choose SVGs because we can easily modify them at runtime using CSS and JavaScript, which makes them an excellent candidate for the functional approach of React.

So, if we think about our components as a function of their props, we can easily imagine how we can create self-contained SVG icons that we can manipulate by passing different props to them.

A common way to create SVGs in a web app with React is to wrap our vectors into a React component and use the props to define their dynamic values.

Let's look at a simple example where we draw a blue circle, thus creating a React component that wraps an SVG element:

```
const Circle = ({ x, y, radius, fill }) => (
  <svg>
    <circle cx={x} cy={y} r={radius} fill={fill} />
  </svg>
);
```

As you can see, we can easily use a stateless functional component that wraps the SVG markup, and it accepts the same props as the SVG does.

So, the SVG is just a template, and we can use the same `Circle` multiple times in our application with various props.

The props are defined in the following way:

```
import { number, string } from 'prop-types';
...
Circle.propTypes = {
  x: number,
  y: number,
  radius: number,
  fill: string
};
```

This is great because it makes working with SVGs and their properties more explicit so that the interface is clear and we know exactly how to configure our icons.

An example usage is as follows:

```
<Circle x={20} y={20} radius={20} fill="blue" />
```

We can obviously use the full power of React and set some default parameters so that, if the Circle icon is rendered without props, we still show something.

For example, we can define the default color:

```
Circle.defaultProps = {
  fill: 'red'
};
```

This is pretty powerful when we build UIs, especially in a team where we share our icon set and we want to have some default values in it, but we also want to let other teams decide their settings without having to recreate the same SVG shapes.

However, in some cases, we prefer to be more strict and fix some values to keep consistency. With React, this is a super simple task.

For example, we can wrap the base circle component into a `RedCircle`, as follows:

```
const RedCircle = ({ x, y, radius }) => (
  <Circle x={x} y={y} radius={radius} fill="red" />
);
```

Here, the color is set by default and it cannot be changed, while the other props are transparently passed to the original circle.

The prop types are the same without the fill:

```
RedCircle.propTypes = {
  x: number,
  y: number,
  radius: number
};
```

The following screenshot shows two circles, blue and red, that are generated by React using SVG:

We can apply this technique and create different variations of the circle, such as SmallCircle and RightCircle, and everything else we need to build our UIs.

Summary

In this chapter, we looked at the different things we can do when we target the browser with React, from form creation to events, and from animations to SVGs.

React gives us a declarative way to manage all the aspects we need to deal with when we create a web application.

In case we need it, React gives us access to the actual DOM nodes in a way that we can perform imperative operations with them, which is useful if we need to integrate React with an existing imperative library.

The next chapter will be about CSS and inline styles, and it will clarify what it means to write CSS in JavaScript.

Section 3: Performance, Improvements and Production!

We will begin this section by learning how to make our components beautiful, and come to understand the concept of server-side rendering in React for both fun and profit. We will then learn how to improve the performance of our applications by testing and debugging them. We will also dip into a quick chapter about React Router. Finally, we will end this section and the book itself by learning how to deploy our application to production and see what steps you can take next.

In this section, we will cover the following chapters:

- Chapter 7, *Make Your Components Look Beautiful*
- Chapter 8, *Server-Side Rendering for Fun and Profit*
- Chapter 9, *Improve the Performance of Your Applications*
- Chapter 10, *About Testing and Debugging*
- Chapter 11, *React Router*
- Chapter 12, *Anti-Patterns to be Avoided*
- Chapter 13, *Deploying to Production*
- Chapter 14, *Next Steps*

Make Your Components Look Beautiful

Our journey into React best practices and design patterns has now reached the point where we want to make our components look beautiful. To do that, we will go through all the reasons why regular CSS may not be the best approach for styling components, and we will check out various alternative solutions.

Starting with inline styles, then Radium, CSS modules, and styled components, this chapter will guide you into the magical world of CSS in JavaScript.

This topic is very hot and highly controversial, so this chapter requires an open mind to be understood and followed.

In this chapter, we will cover the following topics:

- Common problems with regular CSS at scale
- What it means to use inline styles in React and the downsides
- How the Radium library can help fix issues of inline styles
- How to set up a project from scratch using webpack and CSS modules
- Features of CSS modules and why they represent a great solution to avoid global CSS
- Styled components, a new library that offers a modern approach to styling React components

CSS in JavaScript

In the community, everyone agrees that a revolution took place in the styling of React components in November 2014, when Christopher Chedeau gave a talk at the NationJS conference.

Also known as vjeux on the internet, Christopher works at Facebook and contributes to React. In his talk, he went through all the problems related to CSS on the scale that they were facing them at Facebook.

It is worth understanding all of them because some are pretty common and they will help us introduce concepts such as inline styles and locally scoped class names.

The following is the list of issues with CSS, basically problems with CSS at scale:

- Global Namespace
- Dependencies
- Dead Code Elimination
- Minification
- Sharing Constants
- Non-deterministic Resoulution
- Isolation

The first well-known problem of CSS is that all the selectors are global. No matter how we organize our styles, using namespaces or a procedure like the **Block, Element, Modifier** (**BEM**) methodology, in the end, we are always polluting the global namespace, which we all know is wrong. It is not only wrong in principle, but it also leads to many errors in big codebases, and it makes maintainability very hard in the long term. Working with big teams, it is nontrivial to know if a particular class or element has already been styled, and most of the time we tend to add more classes instead of reusing existing ones.

The second problem with CSS regards the definition of the dependencies. It is very hard, in fact, to state clearly that a particular component depends on a specific CSS and that the CSS has to be loaded for the style to be applied. Since styles are global, any style from any file can be applied to any element, and losing control is very easy.

Frontend developers tend to use preprocessors to be able to split their CSS into submodules, but in the end, a big, global CSS bundle is generated for the browser. Since CSS codebases tend to become huge quickly, we lose control over them, and the third problem is to do with **dead code elimination**. It is not easy to identify quickly which styles belong to which component, and this makes deleting code incredibly hard. In fact, due to the cascading nature of CSS, removing a selector or a rule can result in an unintended result within the browser.

Another pain of working with CSS concerns the minification of the selectors and the class names, both in the CSS and in the JavaScript application. It would seem an easy task, but it is not, especially when classes are applied on the fly or concatenated in the client.

Not being able to minify and optimize class names is pretty bad for performance, and it can make a huge difference to the size of the CSS.

Another pretty common operation that is non-trivial with regular CSS is sharing constants between the styles and the client application. We often need to know the height of a header, for example, to recalculate the position of other elements that depend on it.

Usually, we read the value in the client using the JavaScript APIs, but the optimal solution would be to share constants and avoid doing expensive calculations at runtime. This represents the fifth problem that vjeux and the other developers at Facebook tried to solve.

The sixth issue concerns the nondeterministic resolution of CSS. In fact, in CSS, the order matters and if the CSS is loaded on demand, the order is not guaranteed, which leads to the wrong styles being applied to the elements.

Suppose, for example, that we want to optimize the way we request CSS, loading the CSS related to a particular page only when the users navigate to it. If the CSS related to this last page has some rules that also apply to the elements of different pages, the fact that it has been loaded last could affect the styling of the rest of the app. For example, if the user goes back to the previous page, they might see a page with a UI that is slightly different than the first time they visited it.

It is incredibly hard to control all the various combinations of styles, rules, and navigation paths, but again, being able to load the CSS when needed could have a critical impact on the performance of a web application.

Last but not least, the seventh problem of CSS, according to Christopher Chedeau, is related to isolation. In CSS, it is almost impossible to achieve proper isolation between files or components. Selectors are global, and they can easily be overwritten. It is tricky to predict the final style of an element just by knowing the class names applied to it because styles are not isolated and other rules in other parts of the application can affect unrelated elements.

In the following section, we will look at what it means to use inline styles with React and the benefits and downsides of it.

Inline styles

The official React documentation suggests developers use inline styles to style their React components. This seems odd because we all learned in past years that separating the concerns is important and we should not mix markup and CSS.

React tries to change the concept of separation of concerns by moving it from the separation of technologies to the separation of components. Separating markup, styling, and logic into different files when they are tightly coupled and where one cannot work without the other is just an illusion. Even if it helps keep the project structure cleaner, it does not give any real benefit.

In React, we compose components to create applications where components are a fundamental unit of our structure. We should be able to move components across the application, and they should provide the same result regarding both logic and UI, no matter where they get rendered.

This is one of the reasons why collocating the styles within our components and applying them using inline styles on the elements could make sense in React.

First, let's look at an example of what it means to use the style attribute of the nodes to apply the styling to our components in React.

We are going to create a button with the text **Click me!**, and we are going to apply a color and a background color to it:

```
const style = {
  color: 'palevioletred',
  backgroundColor: 'papayawhip'
};
const Button = () => <button style={style}>Click me!</button>;
```

As you can see, it is pretty easy to style elements with inline styles in React. We just have to create an object where the attributes are the CSS rules, and the values are the values we would use in a regular CSS file.

The only differences are that the hyphenated CSS rules must be camelCased to be JavaScript-compliant, and the values are strings, so they have to be wrapped in quote marks.

There are some exceptions regarding the vendor prefixes. For example, if we want to define a transition on **webkit**, we should use the `WebkitTransition` attribute, where the webkit prefix begins with a capital letter. This rule applies to all the vendor prefixes, except for **ms**, which is lowercase.

Other use cases are numbers—they can be written without quotes or units of measurement and, by default, they are treated as pixels.

The following rule applies a height of `100` px:

```
const style = {
  height: 100
};
```

By using inline styles works, we can also do things that are hard to implement with regular CSS. For example, we can recalculate some CSS values on the client at runtime, which is a very powerful concept, as you will see in the following example.

Suppose you want to create a form field in which the font size changes according to its value. So, if the value of the field is `24`, the font size is going to be 24 pixels. With normal CSS, this behavior is almost impossible to reproduce without putting in a huge effort and duplicated code.

Let's look at how easy it is to use inline styles instead.

We create a class because we have to store the state, and we need an event handler:

```
class FontSize extends Component {

}
```

The class has a `constructor`, where we set the default value for the state, and we bind the `handleChange` handler, which listens to the `onChange` event of the input field:

```
constructor(props) {
  super(props);
  this.state = {
    value: 16
```

```
    };
    this.handleChange = this.handleChange.bind(this);
  }
```

We implement a simple change handler, where we use the target attribute of the event to retrieve the current value of the field:

```
handleChange({ target: { value } }) {
  this.setState({
    value: Number(value)
  });
}
```

Finally, we render the input file of type number, which is a controlled component because we keep its value updated by using the state. It also has an event handler, which is fired every time the value of the field changes.

Last but not least, we use the style attribute of the field to set its font-size. As you can see, we are using the camelCased version of the CSS rule to follow the React convention:

```
render() {
  return (
    <input
      type="number"
      value={this.state.value}
      onChange={this.handleChange}
      style={{ fontSize: this.state.value }}
    />
  );
}
```

Rendering the preceding component, we can see an input field, which changes its font size according to its value. The way it works is that when the value changes, we store the new value of the field inside the state. Modifying the state forces the component to re-render, and we use the new state value to set the display value of the field and its font size: it's easy and powerful.

Every solution in computer science has its downsides, and it always represents a trade-off. In the case of inline styles, unfortunately, the problems are many.

For example, with inline styles, it is not possible to use pseudo-selectors (for example, :hover) and pseudo-elements, which is a pretty significant limitation if you are creating a UI with interactions and animations.

There are some workarounds, and for example, you can always create real elements instead of pseudo ones, but for the pseudo-classes, it is necessary to use JavaScript to simulate the CSS behavior, which is not optimal.

The same applies to **media queries**, which cannot be defined using inline styles, and it makes it harder to create responsive web applications. Since styles are declared using JavaScript objects, it is also not possible to use style fallbacks:

```
display: -webkit-flex;
display: flex;
```

JavaScript objects cannot have two attributes with the same name. Style fallbacks should be avoided, but it is always good to have the ability to use them if needed.

Another feature of CSS that it is not possible to emulate using inline styles is **animations**. The workaround here is to define animations globally and use them inside the style attribute of the elements.

With inline styles, whenever we need to override a style with regular CSS, we are always forced to use the !important keyword, which is bad practice because it prevents any other style being applied to the element.

The most difficult thing that happens working with inline styles is debugging. We tend to use class names to find elements in the browser DevTools to debug and check which styles have been applied.

With inline styles, all the styles of the items are listed in their style attribute, which makes it very hard to check and debug the result.

For example, the button that we created earlier in this section is rendered in the following way:

```
<button style="color:palevioletred;background-
color:papayawhip;">Click me!</button>
```

By itself, it does not seem very hard to read, but if you imagine you have hundreds of elements and hundreds of styles, you realize that the problem becomes very complicated.

Also, if you are debugging a list where every single item has the same style attribute, and if you modify one on the fly to check the result in the browser, you will see that you are applying the styles only to it and not to all the other siblings, even if they share the same style.

Last but not least, if we render our application on the server side (we will cover this topic in `Chapter 8`, *Server-Side Rendering for Fun and Profit*), the size of the page is bigger when using inline styles.

With inline styles, we are putting all the content of the CSS into the markup, which adds an extra number of bytes to the file that we send to the clients and makes the web application appear slower.

Compression algorithms can help with that because they can easily compress similar patterns, and, in some cases, loading the critical path CSS is a good solution, but in general, we should try to avoid it.

It turns out that inline styles give more problems than the problems they try to solve.

For this reason, the community created different tools to solve the problems of inline styles but keeping the styles inside the components, or local to the components, to get the best of both worlds.

After Christopher Chedeau's talk, a lot of developers started talking about inline styles, and many solutions and experiments have been made to find new ways of writing CSS in JavaScript.

In the beginning, there were two or three, while today there are more than forty.

In the following sections, we will go through the most popular ones.

Radium

One of the first libraries that was created to solve the problems of inline styles we encountered in the previous section is **Radium**. It is maintained by the great developers at Formidable Labs, and it is still one of the most popular solutions.

In this section, we will look at how Radium works, which problems it solves, and why it is a great library to use in conjunction with React for styling components.

We are going to create a very simple button, similar to the one we built in the example earlier in this chapter.

We will start with a basic button without styling, and we will add some basic styling, as well as pseudo-classes and media queries so that we can learn about the main features of the library.

The button we will start with is created as follows:

```
const Button = () => <button>Click me!</button>;
```

First, we have to install Radium using npm:

```
npm install --save radium
```

Once the installation is complete, we can import the library and wrap the button into it:

```
import radium from 'radium';
const Button = () => <button>Click me!</button>;
export default radium(Button);
```

The `radium` function is an HoC (see `Chapter 4`, *Compose All the Things*), which extends the functionalities of our `Button`, returning a new enhanced component.

If we render the button inside the browser, we will not see anything in particular at the moment, because we are not applying any styles to it.

Let's start with a simple style object, where we set the background color, the padding, the size, and a couple of other CSS properties.

As we saw in the previous section, inline styles in React are defined using JavaScript objects with camelCased CSS properties:

```
const styles = {
  backgroundColor: '#ff0000',
  width: 320,
  padding: 20,
  borderRadius: 5,
  border: 'none',
  outline: 'none'
};
```

The preceding snippet is no different from plain inline styles with React, and if we pass it to our button as follows, we can see all the styles applied to the button inside the browser:

```
const Button = () => <button style={styles}>Click me!</button>;
```

The result is the following markup:

```
<button data-radium="true" style="background-color: rgb(255, 0, 0); width:
320px; padding: 20px; border-radius: 5px; border: none; outline:
none;">Click me!</button>
```

The only difference you can see here is that there is a `data-radium` attribute set to `true` attached to the element.

Now, we have seen that inline styles do not let us define any pseudo-classes; let's take a look at how to solve the problem using Radium.

Using pseudo-classes, such as :hover, with Radium is pretty straightforward.

We have to create a :hover property inside our style object, and Radium will do the rest:

```
const styles = {
  backgroundColor: '#ff0000',
  width: 320,
  padding: 20,
  borderRadius: 5,
  border: 'none',
  outline: 'none',
  ':hover': {
    color: '#fff'
  }
};
```

If you apply this style object to your button and render it on the screen, you can see that passing the mouse over the button results in a button with white text, as opposed to the default black one.

That is great—we can use pseudo-classes and inline styles together.

However, if you open your DevTools and try to force the :hover status in the **Styles** panel, you will see that nothing happens.

The reason you can see the hover effect but you cannot simulate it with CSS is that Radium uses JavaScript to apply and remove the hover state defined in the style object.

If you hover over the element with the DevTools open, you can see that the style string changes and the color gets added to it dynamically:

```
<button data-radium="true" style="background-color: rgb(255, 0, 0); width:
320px; padding: 20px; border-radius: 5px; border: none; outline: none;
color: rgb(255, 255, 255);">Click me!</button>
```

The way Radium works is by adding an event handler for each one of the events that can trigger the behavior of pseudo-classes and listening to them.

As soon as one of the events gets fired, Radium changes the state of the component, which re-renders with the right style for the state. This might seem weird in the beginning, but there are no real downsides to this approach, and the difference regarding performance is not perceivable.

We can add new pseudo-classes, for example, `:active`, and they will work as well:

```
const styles = {
  backgroundColor: '#ff0000',
  width: 320,
  padding: 20,
  borderRadius: 5,
  border: 'none',
  outline: 'none',
  ':hover': {
    color: '#fff'
  },
  ':active': {
    position: 'relative',
    top: 2
  }
};
```

Another critical feature that Radium enables is media queries. Media queries are crucial for creating responsive applications, and Radium again uses JavaScript to enable that CSS feature in our application.

Let's look at how it works—the API is pretty similar; we have to create a new attribute on our style object and nest the styles that must be applied when the media query matches inside it:

```
const styles = {
  backgroundColor: '#ff0000',
  width: 320,
  padding: 20,
  borderRadius: 5,
  border: 'none',
  outline: 'none',
  ':hover': {
    color: '#fff'
  },
  ':active': {
    position: 'relative',
    top: 2
  },
  '@media (max-width: 480px)': {
    width: 160
  }
};
```

There is one thing we must do to make media queries work, and that is wrapping our application into the `StyleRoot` component provided by Radium.

For the media queries to work properly, especially with server-side rendering, Radium will inject the rules related to the media query in a style element inside the DOM, with all the properties set as `!important`.

This is to avoid flickering between the different styles that are applied to the document before the library figures out which is the matching query. Implementing the styles inside a style element prevents this by letting the browser do its regular job.

So, the idea is to import the `StyleRoot` component:

```
import { StyleRoot } from 'radium';
```

Then, we can wrap our entire application inside it:

```
class App extends Component {
  render() {
    return (
      <StyleRoot>
        ...
      </StyleRoot>
    )
  }
}
```

As a result of this, if you open the DevTools, you can see that Radium injected the following style into the DOM:

```
<style>@media (max-width: 480px) { .rmq-1d8d7428{width: 160px
!important;}}</style>
```

The `rmq-1d8d7428` class has been applied to the button automatically, as well:

```
<button class="rmq-1d8d7428" data-radium="true" style="background-color:
rgb(255, 0, 0); width: 320px; padding: 20px; border-radius: 5px; border:
none; outline: none;">Click me!</button>
```

If you now resize the browser window, you can see that the button becomes smaller for small screens, as expected.

CSS modules

If you feel that inline styles are not a suitable solution for your project and your team, but you still want to keep the styles as close as possible to your components, there is a solution for you, called **CSS modules**.

Webpack 4

Before diving into CSS modules and learning how it works, it is important to understand how it was created and the tools that support it.

In Chapter 2, *Clean Up Your Code*, we looked at how we can write ES6 code and transpile it using Babel and its presets. As soon as the application grows, you may want to split your code base into modules as well.

You can use webpack or Browserify to divide the application into small modules that you can import whenever you need them, while still creating a big bundle for the browser. These tools are called **module bundlers**, and what they do is load all the dependencies of your application into a single bundle that can be executed in the browser, which does not have any concept of modules (yet).

In the React world, webpack is especially popular because it offers many interesting and useful features, with the first one being the concept of loaders. With webpack, you can potentially load any dependencies other than JavaScript, if there is a loader for it. For example, you can load JSON files, as well as images and other assets, inside the bundle.

In May 2015, Mark Dalgleish, one of the creators of CSS Modules, figured out that you could import CSS inside a webpack bundle as well, and he pushed the concept forward.

He thought that, since the CSS could be imported locally into a component, all the imported class names could be locally scoped as well.

Setting up a project

In this section, we will look at how to set up a very simple webpack application, using Babel to transpile the JavaScript and the CSS modules to load our locally scoped CSS into the bundle. We will also go through all the features of CSS modules and look at the problems they can solve. The first thing to do is move to an empty folder and run the following code:

```
npm init
```

This will create a package.json with some defaults.

Now, it is time to install the dependencies, with the first one being webpack and the second being webpack-dev-server, which we will use to run the application locally and to create the bundle on the fly:

```
npm install webpack webpack-dev-server webpack-cli
```

Once webpack is installed, it is time to install Babel and its loader. Since we are using webpack to create the bundle, we will use the Babel loader to transpile our ES6 code within webpack itself:

```
npm install @babel/core @babel/preset-env @babel/preset-react babel-loader
```

Finally, we install the style loader and the CSS loader, which are the two loaders we need to enable the CSS modules:

```
npm install style-loader css-loader
```

There is one more thing to do to make things easier, and that is to install the `html-webpack-plugin`, which is a plugin that can create an HTML page to host our JavaScript application on the fly, just by looking into the webpack configuration and without us needing to create a regular file:

```
npm install html-webpack-plugin
```

Last but not least, we install `react` and `react-dom` to use them in our simple example:

```
npm install react react-dom
```

Now that all the dependencies are installed, it is time to configure everything to make it work.

The first thing to do is add an `npm` script in `package.json` to run the `webpack-dev-server`, which will serve the application in development:

```
"scripts": {
  "start": "webpack-dev-server"
}
```

The webpack needs a configuration file to know how to handle the different types of dependencies we are using in our application, and to do so we must create a file called `webpack.config.js`, which exports an object:

```
module.exports = {};
```

The object we export represents the configuration object used by webpack to create the bundle, and it can have different properties depending on the size and the features of the project.

We want to keep our example very simple, so we are going to add three attributes.

The first one is the entry, which tells webpack where the main file of our application is:

```
entry: './index.js'
```

The second one is module, which is where we tell webpack how to load the external dependencies. It has an attribute called `rules`, where we set a specific loader for each one of the file types:

```
module: {
  rules: [
    {
      test: /\.(jsx|js)$/,
      exclude: /node_modules/,
      use: {
        loader: 'babel-loader',
        options: {
          presets: [
            '@babel/preset-env',
            '@babel/preset-react'
          ]
        }
      }
    },
    {
      test: /\.css/,
      use: [
        'style-loader',
        'css-loader?modules=true'
      ]
    }
  ]
},
```

We are saying that the files that match the `.js` or `.jsx` regex are loaded using the `babel-loader` so that they get transpiled and loaded into the bundle.

You may also have noticed that we are setting the presets in there as well. As we saw in `Chapter 2`, *Clean Up Your Code*, the presets are sets of configuration options that instruct Babel on how to deal with the different types of syntax (for example, JSX).

The second entry in the `rules` array tells webpack what to do when a CSS file is imported, and it uses the `css-loader` with the `modules` flag enabled to activate CSS modules. The result of the transformation is then passed to the style loader, which injects the styles into the header of the page.

Finally, we enable the HTML plugin to generate the page for us, adding the script tag automatically using the entry path we specified earlier:

```
const HtmlWebpackPlugin = require('html-webpack-plugin');
...
plugins: [new HtmlWebpackPlugin()]
```

The complete `webpack.config.js` should be like this:

```
const HtmlWebpackPlugin = require('html-webpack-plugin');

module.exports = {
  entry: './index.js',
  module: {
    rules: [
      {
        test: /\.(jsx|js)$/,
        exclude: /node_modules/,
        use: {
          loader: 'babel-loader',
          options: {
            presets: [
              '@babel/preset-env',
              '@babel/preset-react'
            ]
          }
        }
      },
      {
        test: /\.css/,
        use: [
          'style-loader',
          'css-loader?modules=true'
        ]
      }
    ]
  },
  plugins: [new HtmlWebpackPlugin()]
};
```

We are done, and if we run the `npm start` command in the Terminal and point the browser to `http://localhost:8080`, we should be able to see the following markup being served:

```
<!DOCTYPE html>
<html>
  <head>
    <meta charset="UTF-8">
```

```
    <title>Webpack App</title>
  </head>
  <body>
    <script type="text/javascript" src="bundle.js"></script>
  </body>
</html>
```

Locally scoped CSS

Now, it is time to create our app, which will consist of a **Simple** button, of the same sort we used in previous examples. We will use it to show all the features of the CSS modules.

Let's create an index.js file, which is the entry we specified in the webpack configuration, and let's import React and ReactDOM as well:

```
import React from 'react';
import { render } from 'react-dom';
```

We can then create a **Simple** button. As usual, we are going to start with a nonstyled button, and we will add the styles step by step:

```
const Button = () => <button>Click me!</button>;
```

Finally, we can render the button into the DOM:

```
render(<Button />, document.body);
```

Please note that rendering a React component into the body is bad practice, but in this case, we are doing it for simplicity.

Now, suppose we want to apply some styles to the button—a background color, the size, and so on.

We create a regular CSS file, called index.css, and we put the following class into it:

```
.button {
  background-color: #ff0000;
  width: 320px;
  padding: 20px;
  border-radius: 5px;
  border: none;
  outline: none;
}
```

Now, we said that with CSS modules, we could import the CSS files into the JavaScript; let's look at how it works.

Inside our `index.js` where we defined the button component, we can add the following line:

```
import styles from './index.css';
```

The result of this `import` statement is a `styles` object, where all the attributes are the classes defined in the `index.css`.

If we run `console.log(styles)`, we can see the following object in DevTools:

```
{
    button: "_2wpxM3yizfwbWee6k0UlD4"
}
```

So, we have an object where the attributes are the class names and the values are (apparently) random strings. We will see later that they are nonrandom, but let's check what we can do with that object first.

We can use the object to set the class name attribute of our button, as follows:

```
const Button = () => (
    <button className={styles.button}>Click me!</button>
);
```

If we go back to the browser, we can now see that the styles we defined in `index.css` have been applied to the button.

And that is not magic, because if we check in DevTools, the class that has been applied to the element is the same string that's attached to the style object we imported inside our code:

```
<button class="_2wpxM3yizfwbWee6k0UlD4">Click me!</button>
```

If we look at the header section of the page, we can now see that the same class name has also been injected into the page:

```
<style type="text/css">
  ._2wpxM3yizfwbWee6k0UlD4 {
    background-color: #ff0000;
    width: 320px;
    padding: 20px;
    border-radius: 5px;
    border: none;
    outline: none;
  }
</style>
```

This is how the CSS and the style loaders work.

The CSS loader lets you import the CSS files into your JavaScript modules and, when the modules flag is activated, all the class names are locally scoped to the module they are imported into.

As we mentioned previously, the string we imported was nonrandom, but it is generated using the hash of the file and some other parameters in a way that is unique within the codebase.

Finally, the style loader takes the result of the CSS module's transformation and it injects the styles inside the header section of the page.

This is very powerful because we have the full power and expressiveness of the CSS, combined with the advantages of having locally scoped class names and explicit dependencies.

As mentioned at the beginning of this chapter, CSS is global, and that makes it very hard to maintain in large applications. With CSS modules, class names are locally scoped and they cannot clash with other class names in different parts of the application, enforcing a deterministic result.

Moreover, explicitly importing the CSS dependencies inside our components helps us see clearly which components need which CSS. It is also very useful for eliminating dead code because when we delete a component for any reason, we can tell exactly which CSS it was using.

CSS modules are regular CSS, so we can use pseudo-classes, media queries, and animations.

For example, we can add CSS rules like the following:

```css
.button:hover {
  color: #fff;
}
.button:active {
  position: relative;
  top: 2px;
}
@media (max-width: 480px) {
  .button {
    width: 160px
  }
}
```

This will be transformed into the following code and injected into the document:

```
._2wpxM3yizfwbWee6k0UlD4:hover {
  color: #fff;
}
._2wpxM3yizfwbWee6k0UlD4:active {
  position: relative;
  top: 2px;
}
@media (max-width: 480px) {
  ._2wpxM3yizfwbWee6k0UlD4 {
    width: 160px
  }
}
```

The class names get created and they get replaced everywhere the button is used, making it reliable and local, as expected.

As you may have noticed, those class names are great, but they make debugging pretty hard because we cannot easily tell which classes generated the hash.

What we can do in development mode is add a special configuration parameter, with which we can choose the pattern that's used to produce the scoped class names.

For example, we can change the value of the loader as follows:

```
{
  test: /\.css/,
  use: [
    'style-loader',
    'css-loader?modules=true&localIdentName=[local]--[hash:base64:5]'
  ]
}
```

Here, `localIdentName` is the parameter and `[local]` and `[hash:base64:5]` are placeholders for the original class name value and a five-character hash.

Other available placeholders are `[path]`, which represents the path of the CSS file, and `[name]`, which is the name of the source CSS file.

Activating the previous configuration option, the result we have in the browser is as follows:

```
<button class="button--2wpxM">Click me!</button>
```

This is way more readable and easier to debug.

In production, we do not need class names like this, and we are more interested in performance, so we may want shorter class names and hashes.

With webpack, it is pretty straightforward because we can have multiple configuration files that can be used in the different stages of our application life cycle. Also, in production, we may want to extract the CSS file instead of injecting it into the browser from the bundle so that we can have a lighter bundle and cache the CSS on a CDN for better performance.

To do that, you need to install another webpack plugin, called `mini-css-extract-plugin`, which can write an actual CSS file, putting in all the scoped classes that were generated from CSS modules.

There are a couple of features of CSS modules that are worth mentioning.

The first one is the `global` keyword. Prefixing any class with `:global`, in fact, means asking CSS modules not to scope the current selector locally.

For example, let's say we change our CSS as follows:

```
:global .button {
  . . .
}
```

The output will be as follows:

```
.button {
  . . .
}
```

This is good if you want to apply styles that cannot be scoped locally, such as third-party widgets.

My favorite feature of CSS modules is **composition**. With composition, we can classes from the same file or external dependencies and get all the styles applied to the element.

For example, extract the rule to set the background to red from the rules for the button into a separate block, as follows:

```
.background-red {
  background-color: #ff0000;
}
```

We can then compose it inside our button in the following way:

```
.button {
  composes: background-red;
  width: 320px;
```

```
    padding: 20px;
    border-radius: 5px;
    border: none;
    outline: none;
}
```

The result is that all the rules of the button and all the rules of the `composes` declaration are applied to the element.

This is a very powerful feature and it works in a fascinating way. You might expect that all the composed classes are duplicated inside the classes where they are referenced as SASS `@extend` does, but that is not the case. Simply put, all the composed class names are applied one after the other on the component in the DOM.

In our specific case, we would have the following:

```
<button class="_2wpxM3yizfwbWee6k0UlD4 Sf8w9cFdQXdRV_i9dgcOq">Click
me!</button>
```

Here, the CSS that is injected into the page is as follows:

```
.Sf8w9cFdQXdRV_i9dgcOq {
    background-color: #ff0000;
}
._2wpxM3yizfwbWee6k0UlD4 {
    width: 320px;
    padding: 20px;
    border-radius: 5px;
    border: none;
    outline: none;
}
```

Atomic CSS modules

It should be clear how composition works and why it is a very powerful feature of CSS modules. At YPlan, the company where I worked when I started writing this book, we tried to push it a step further, combining the power of `composes` with the flexibility of **Atomic CSS** (also known as **Functional CSS**).

Atomic CSS is a way to use CSS where every class has a single rule.

For example, we can create a class to set the margin-bottom to zero:

```
.mb0 {
    margin-bottom: 0;
}
```

We can use another one to set the font-weight to `600`:

```
.fw6 {
    font-weight: 600;
}
```

Then, we can apply all those atomic classes to the elements:

```
<h2 class="mb0 fw6">Hello React</h2>
```

This technique is controversial, and particularly efficient at the same time. It is hard to start using it because you end up having too many classes in your markup, which makes it hard to predict the final result. If you think about it, it is pretty similar to inline styles, because you apply one class per rule, apart from the fact that you are using a shorter class name as a proxy.

The biggest argument against Atomic CSS is usually that you are moving the styling logic from the CSS to the markup, which is wrong. Classes are defined in CSS files, but they are composed in the views, and every time you have to modify the style of an element, you end up editing the markup.

On the other hand, we tried using Atomic CSS for a bit and we found that it makes prototyping incredibly fast.

In fact, when all the base rules have been generated, applying those classes to the elements and creating new styles is a very quick process, which is good. Second, using Atomic CSS, we can control the size of the CSS file, because as soon as we create new components with their styles, we are using existing classes and we do not need to create new ones, which is great for performance.

So, we tried to solve the problems of Atomic CSS using CSS modules and we called the technique **Atomic CSS modules**.

In essence, you start creating your base CSS classes (for example, `mb0`) and then, instead of applying the class names one by one in the markup, you compose them into placeholder classes using CSS modules.

Let's look at an example:

```css
.title {
  composes: mb0 fw6;
}
```

Here's another example:

```
<h2 className={styles.title}>Hello React</h2>
```

This is great because you still keep the styling logic inside the CSS, and the CSS module's `composes` does the job for you by applying all the single classes into the markup.

The result of the preceding code is as follows:

```
<h2 class="title--3JCJR mb0--21SyP fw6--1JRhZ">Hello React</h2>
```

Here, `title`, `mb0`, and `fw6` are all applied automatically to the element. They are scoped locally as well, so we have all the advantages of CSS modules.

React CSS modules

Last but not least, there is a great library that can help us work with CSS modules. You may have noticed how we were using a style object to load all the classes of the CSS, and because JavaScript does not support hyphenated attributes, we are forced to use a camelCased class name.

Also, if we are referencing a class name that does not exist in the CSS file, there is no way to know it, and `undefined` is added to the list of classes.

For these and other useful features, we may want to try a package that makes working with CSS modules even smoother.

Let's look at what it means to go back to the `index.js` we were using previously in this section with plain CSS modules, and change it to use React CSS modules instead.

The package is called `react-css-modules`, and the first thing we must do is install it:

```
npm install react-css-modules
```

Once the package is installed, we import it inside our `index.js` file:

```
import cssModules from 'react-css-modules';
```

We use it as an HoC, passing to it the `Button` component we want to enhance and the styles object we imported from the CSS:

```
const EnhancedButton = cssModules(Button, styles);
```

Now, we have to change the implementation of the button to avoid using the `styles` object. With React CSS modules, we use the `styleName` property, which is transformed into a regular class.

The great thing about this is that we can use the class name as a string (for example, `"button"`):

```
const Button = () => <button styleName="button">Click me!</button>;
```

If we now render the `EnhancedButton` into the DOM, we will see that nothing has really changed from before, which means that the library works.

Let's say we try to change the `styleName` property to reference a nonexisting class name, as follows:

```
import React from 'react';
import { render } from 'react-dom';
import styles from './index.css';
import cssModules from 'react-css-modules';

const Button = () => <button styleName="button1">Click me!</button>;

const EnhancedButton = cssModules(Button, styles);

render(<EnhancedButton />, document.body);
```

We will see the following error in the console of the browser by doing so:

```
Uncaught Error: "button1" CSS module is undefined.
```

This is particularly helpful when the codebase grows and we have multiple developers working on different components and styles.

Styled components

There is a library that is very promising because it takes into account all the problems the other libraries have encountered in styling components.

Different paths have been followed for writing CSS in JavaScript, and many solutions have been tried, so now the time is ripe for a library that takes all the learning and then builds something on top of it.

The library is conceived and maintained by two popular developers in the JavaScript community: Glenn Maddern and Max Stoiberg.

It represents a very modern approach to the problem, and it uses edge features of ES2015 and some advanced techniques that have been applied to React to provide a complete solution for styling.

Let's look at how it is possible to create the same button we saw in the previous sections, and check if all the CSS features we are interested in (for example, pseudo-classes and media queries) work with styled components.

First, we have to install the library by running the following command:

```
npm install styled-components
```

Once the library is installed, we have to import it inside our component's file:

```
import styled from 'styled-components';
```

At that point, we can use the `styled` function to create any element by using `styled.elementName`, where `elementName` can be a `div`, a button, or any other valid DOM element.

The second thing to do is to define the style of the element we are creating, and to do so, we use an ES6 feature called **tagged template literals**, which is a way of passing template strings to a function without them being interpolated beforehand.

This means that the function receives the actual template with all the JavaScript expressions, and this makes the library able to use the full power of JavaScript to apply the styles to the elements.

Let's start by creating a simple button with a basic styling:

```
const Button = styled.button`
  backgroundColor: #ff0000;
  width: 320px;
```

```
  padding: 20px;
  borderRadius: 5px;
  border: none;
  outline: none;
`;
```

This kind-of-weird syntax returns a proper React component called `Button`, which renders a button element and applies to it all the styles defined in the template. The way the styles are applied is by creating a unique class name, adding it to the element, and then injecting the corresponding style in the head of the document.

The following is the component that gets rendered:

```
<button class="kYvFOg">Click me!</button>
```

The style that gets added to the page is as follows:

```
.kYvFOg {
  background-color: #ff0000;
  width: 320px;
  padding: 20px;
  border-radius: 5px;
  border: none;
  outline: none;
}
```

The good thing about styled components is that it supports almost all the features of CSS, which makes it a good candidate to be used in a real-world application.

For example, it supports pseudo-classes using a SASS-like syntax:

```
const Button = styled.button`
  background-color: #ff0000;
  width: 320px;
  padding: 20px;
  border-radius: 5px;
  border: none;
  outline: none;
  &:hover {
    color: #fff;
  }
  &:active {
    position: relative;
    top: 2px;
  }
`;
```

It also supports media queries:

```
const Button = styled.button`
  background-color: #ff0000;
  width: 320px;
  padding: 20px;
  border-radius: 5px;
  border: none;
  outline: none;
  &:hover {
    color: #fff;
  }
  &:active {
    position: relative;
    top: 2px;
  }
  @media (max-width: 480px) {
    width: 160px;
  }
`;
```

There are many other features that this library can bring to your project.

For example, once you have created the button, you can easily override its styles and use it multiple times with different properties.

Inside the templates, it is also possible to use the props that the component received and change the style accordingly.

Another great feature is **theming**. Wrapping your components into a `ThemeProvider` component, you can inject a theme property down to the three, which makes it extremely easy to create UIs where part of the style is shared between components and some other properties depend on the currently selected theme.

Summary

In this chapter, we looked at a lot of interesting topics. We started by going through the problems of CSS at scale, specifically, the problems that they had at Facebook while dealing with CSS.

We learned how inline styles work in React and why it is good to colocate the styles within components. We also looked at the limitations of inline styles.

Then, we moved on to Radium, which solves the main problems of inline styles, giving us a clear interface to write our CSS in JavaScript. For those who think that inline styles are a bad solution, we moved into the world of CSS modules, setting up a simple project from scratch.

Importing the CSS files into our components makes the dependencies clear, and scoping the class names locally avoids clashes. We looked at how CSS module's `composes` is a great feature, and how we can use it in conjunction with Atomic CSS to create a framework for quick prototyping.

Finally, we had a quick look at `styled` components, which is a very promising library and is meant to change the way we approach the styling of components completely.

8
Server-Side Rendering for Fun and Profit

The next step to building React applications is about learning how the server-side rendering works and what benefits it can give us. The **universal applications** are better for SEO, and they enable knowledge sharing between the frontend and the backend. They can also improve the perceived speed of a web application, which usually leads to increased conversions. However, applying server-side rendering to a React application comes with a cost, and we should think carefully about whether we need it or not.

In this chapter, you will see how to set up a server-side rendered application, and by the end of the relevant sections, you will be able to build a universal application and understand the pros and the cons of the technique.

In this chapter, we will cover the following:

- Understanding what a universal application is
- Figuring out the reasons why we may want to enable server-side rendering
- Creating a simple static server-side rendered application with React
- Adding data fetching to server-side rendering and understanding concepts such as dehydration/hydration
- Using **Next.js** by Zeith to easily create a React application that runs on both the server and the client

Universal applications

When we talk about JavaScript web applications, we usually think of client-side code that lives in the browser.

The way they usually work is that the server returns an empty HTML page with a script tag to load the application. When the application is ready, it manipulates the DOM inside the browser to show the UI and to interact with users. This has been the case for the last few years, and it is still the way to go for a huge number of applications.

In this book, we have seen how easy it is to create applications using React components and how they work within the browser. What we have not seen yet is how React can render the same components on the server, giving us a powerful feature called **server-side rendering (SSR)**.

Before going into the details, let's try to understand what it means to create applications that render both on the server and the client. For years, we used to have completely different applications for the server and client: for example, a Django application to render the views on the server, and some JavaScript frameworks, such as Backbone or jQuery, on the client. Those separate apps usually had to be maintained by two teams of developers with different skill sets. If you needed to share data between the server-side rendered pages and the client-side application, you could inject some variables inside a script tag. Using two different languages and platforms, there was no way to share common information, such as models or views, between the different sides of the application.

Since Node.js was released in 2009, JavaScript has gained a lot of attention and popularity on the server-side as well, thanks to web-application frameworks, such as **Express**.

Using the same language on both sides not only makes it easy for developers to reuse their knowledge, but it also enables different ways of sharing code between the server and the client.

With React, in particular, the concept of isomorphic web applications became very popular within the JavaScript community. Writing an **isomorphic application** means building an application that looks the same on the server and the client.

The fact that the same language is used to write the two applications means that a big part of the logic can be shared, which opens many possibilities. This makes the code base easier to reason about and avoids unnecessary duplication.

React brings the concept a step forward, giving us a simple API to render our components on the server and transparently applying all the logic needed to make the page interactive (for example, event handlers) on the browser.

The term isomorphic does not fit in this scenario, because, in the case of React, the applications are the same, and that is why one of the creators of React Router, Michael Jackson, proposed a more meaningful name for this pattern: universal.

A Universal application is an application that can run both on the server- and the client-side with the same code.

In this chapter, we will look at the reasons why we should consider making our applications Universal, and we will learn how React components can be easily rendered on the server-side.

Reasons to implement SSR

SSR is a great feature, but we should not jump into it just for the sake of it; we should have a real and solid reason to start using it. In this section, we will look at how server-side rendering can help our application and what problems it can solve for us.

SEO

One of the main reasons we may want to render our applications on the server-side is **search engine optimization (SEO)**.

If we serve an empty HTML skeleton to the crawlers of the main search engines, they are not able to extract any meaningful information from it. Nowadays, Google seems to be able to run JavaScript, but there are some limitations, and SEO is often a critical aspect of our businesses.

For years, we used to write two applications: an SSR one for the crawlers and another one to be used on the client side by the users.

We used to do that because SSR applications could not give us the level of interactivity users expect, while client-side applications did not get indexed by search engines.

Maintaining and supporting two applications is difficult, and makes the code base less flexible and less prone to changes.

Luckily with React, we can render our components on the server side and serve the content of our applications to the crawlers in such a way that it is easy for them to understand and index the content.

This is great, not only for SEO, but also for social sharing services. Platforms such as Facebook or Twitter give us a way of defining the content of the snippets that are shown when our pages are shared.

For example, using Open Graph, we can tell Facebook that, for a particular page, we want a certain image to be shown and a particular title to be used as the title of the post.

It is almost impossible to do that using client-side-only applications because the engine that extracts the information from the pages uses the markup returned by the server.

If our server returns an empty HTML structure for all the URLs, the result is that when the pages are shared on the social networks, the snippets of our web application are empty as well, which affects their virality.

A common code base

We do not have many options on the client side; our applications have to be written in JavaScript. There are some languages that can be converted into JavaScript at build time, but the concept does not change.

The ability to use the same language on the server represents a significant win regarding maintainability and knowledge sharing across the company.

Being able to share the logic between the client and the server makes it easy to apply any changes on both sides without doing the work twice, which most of the time leads to fewer errors and fewer problems.

The effort of maintaining a single code base is less than the work required to keep two different applications up to date.

Another reason you might consider introducing JavaScript on the server side in your team is sharing knowledge between frontend and backend developers.

The ability to reuse the code on both sides makes collaboration easier, and the teams speak a common language, which helps with making faster decisions and changes.

Better performance

Last, but not least, we all love client-side applications, because they are fast and responsive, but there is a problem—the bundle has to be loaded and run before users can take any action on the application.

This might not be a problem using a modern laptop or a desktop computer on a fast internet connection. However, if we load a huge JavaScript bundle using a mobile device with a 3G connection, users have to wait for a little while before interacting with the application. This is not only bad for the UX in general, but it also affects conversions. It has been proven by the major e-commerce websites that a few milliseconds added to the page load can have an enormous impact on revenues.

For example, if we serve our application with an empty HTML page and a `script` tag on the server and we show a spinner to our users until they can click on anything, the perception of the speed of the website is highly affected.

If we render our website on the server-side instead and the users start seeing some of the content as soon as they hit the page, they are more likely to stay, even if they have to wait the same amount of time before doing anything for real, because the client-side bundle has to be loaded regardless of the SSR.

This perceived performance is something we can greatly improve using server-side rendering because we can output our components on the server and return some information to the users straight-away.

Don't underestimate the complexity

Even if React provides an easy API to render components on the server, creating a Universal application has a cost. So, we should consider carefully before enabling it for one of the preceding reasons and check if our team is ready to support and maintain a Universal application.

As we will see in the coming sections, rendering components it is not the only task that needs to be done to create server-side rendered applications.

We have to set up and maintain a server with its routes and its logic, manage the server data flow, and so on. Potentially, we want to cache the content to serve the pages faster and carry out many other tasks that are required to maintain a fully functional Universal application.

For this reason, my suggestion is to build the client-side version first, and only when the web application is fully working on the server should you think about improving the experience by enabling SSR.

SSR should be enabled only when strictly needed. For example, if you need SEO or if you need to customize the social sharing information, you should start thinking about it.

If you realize that your application takes a lot of time to load fully and you have already done all the optimization (see the following chapter for more about this topic), you can consider using server-side rendering to offer a better experience to your users and improve the perceived speed.

A basic example

We will now create a very simple server-side application to look at the steps that are needed to build a basic Universal setup.

It is going to be a minimal and simple setup on purpose because the goal here is to show how SSR works rather than providing a comprehensive solution or a boilerplate, even though you could use the example application as a starting point for a real-world application.

 This section assumes that all the concepts regarding JavaScript build tools, such as webpack and its loaders, are clear, and it requires a little bit of knowledge of Node.js. As a JavaScript developer, it should be easy for you to follow this section, even if you have never seen a Node.js application before.

The application will consist of two parts:

- The server side, where we will use **Express** to create a basic web server and serve an HTML page with the server-side rendered React application

- The client side, where we will render the application, as usual, using `react-dom`

Both sides of the application will be transpiled with Babel and bundled with webpack before being run, which will let us use the full power of ES6 and the modules both on Node.js and on the browser.

Let's start by moving into an empty folder and running the following to create a new package:

```
npm init
```

When `package.json` has been created, it is time to install the dependencies. We can start with `webpack`:

```
npm install webpack
```

After it is done, it is time to install the Babel loader and the presets that we need to write an ES6 application using React and JSX:

```
npm install @babel/core @babel/preset-env @babel/preset-react babel-loader
```

We also have to install a dependency, which we will need to create the server bundle. The webpack lets us define a set of externals, which are dependencies that we do not want to add to the bundle. When creating a build for the server, in fact, we do not want to add to the bundle of all the node packages that we use; we just want to bundle our server code. There's a package that helps with that, and we can simply apply it to the external entry in our webpack configuration to exclude all the modules:

```
npm install webpack-node-externals
```

Great, it is now time to create an entry in the npm `scripts` section of `package.json` so that we can easily run the build command from the terminal:

```
"scripts": {
  "build": "webpack"
}
```

We now have to create the configuration file, called `webpack.config.js`, to tell webpack how we want our files to be bundled.

Let's start importing the library we will use to set our node externals. We will also define the configuration for the Babel loader, which we will use for both the client and the server:

```
const nodeExternals = require('webpack-node-externals');

const rules = [
  {
    test: /\.(js?|jsx)$/,
    exclude: /node_modules/,
    use: {
      loader: 'babel-loader',
      options: {
```

```
    presets: [
      '@babel/preset-env',
      '@babel/preset-react'
    ]
  }
}
}
];
```

In `Chapter 7`, *Make Your Components Look Beautiful*, we looked at how we had to export a configuration object from the configuration file. There is one cool feature in webpack that lets us export an array of configurations as well so that we can define both client and server configurations in the same place and use both in one go.

The client configuration should be very familiar:

```
const client = {
  entry: './src/client.js',
  output: {
    path: './dist/public',
    filename: 'bundle.js'
  },
  module: {
    rules
  }
};
```

We are telling webpack that the source code of the client application is inside the `src` folder, and we want the output bundle to be generated in the `dist` folder.

We also set the module loaders using the previous object we created with `babel-loader`. It was done as simple as possible.

The server configuration is slightly different, but it should be very easy for you to follow and understand:

```
const server = {
  entry: './src/server.js',
  output: {
    path: './dist',
    filename: 'server.js'
  },
  module: {
    rules
  },
```

```
    target: 'node',
    externals: [nodeExternals()]
};
```

As you can see, entry, output, and module are the same, except for the file names.

The new parameters are the target, where we specify the node to tell webpack to ignore all the built-in system packages of Node.js, such as `fs` and `externals`, where we use the library we imported earlier to tell webpack to ignore the dependencies.

Last, but not least, we have to export the configurations as an array:

```
module.exports = [client, server];
```

The configuration is done. We are now ready to write some code, and we will start from the React application, which we are more familiar with.

Let's create an `src` folder and an `app.js` file inside it.

The `app.js` file should have the following content:

```
import React from 'react';

const App = () => <div>Hello React</div>;

export default App;
```

Nothing complex here: we import React, we create an `App` component, which renders the **Hello React** message, and we export it.

Let's now create `client.js`, which is responsible for rendering the `App` component inside the DOM:

```
import React from 'react';
import { render } from 'react-dom';
import App from './app';

render(<App />, document.getElementById('app'));
```

Again, this should sound familiar, since we import React, ReactDOM, and the `App` component we created earlier, and we use ReactDOM to render it in a DOM element with the appID.

Let's now move to the server.

The first thing to do is create a `template.js` file, which exports a function that we will use to return the markup of the page that our server will give back to the browser:

```
export default body => `
  <!DOCTYPE html>
  <html>
    <head>
      <meta charset="UTF-8">
    </head>
    <body>
      <div id="app">${body}</div>
      <script src="/bundle.js"></script>
    </body>
  </html>`;
```

It should be pretty straightforward, the function accepts `body`, which we will later see contains the React app, and it returns the skeleton of the page.

It is worth noting that we load the bundle on the client side even if the app is rendered server side. SSR is only half of the job that React does to render our application. We still want our application to be a client-side application with all the features we can use in the browser, such as event handlers, for example.

After this, you need to install `express`, `react`, and `react-dom`:

```
npm install express react react-dom
```

Now it is time to create `server.js`, which has more dependencies and is worth exploring in detail:

```
import express from 'express';
import React from 'react';
import { renderToString } from 'react-dom/server';
import path from 'path';
import App from './app';
import template from './template';
```

The first thing that we import is `express`, the library that allows us to create a web server with some routes easily, and which is also able to serve static files.

Secondly, we import React and ReactDOM to render `App`, which we import as well. Notice the `/server` path in the `import` statement of ReactDOM. The last thing we import is the template we defined earlier.

Now we create an Express application:

```
const app = express();
```

We tell the application where our static assets are stored:

```
app.use(express.static(path.resolve(__dirname, './dist/public')));
```

As you may have noticed, the path is the same that we used in the client configuration of webpack as the output destination of the client bundle.

Then, here comes the logic of SSR with React:

```
app.get('/', (req, res) => {
  const body = renderToString(<App />);
  const html = template(body);
  res.send(html);
});
```

We are telling Express that we want to listen to the route, /, and when it gets hit by a client, we render App to a string using the ReactDOM library. Here come the magic and the simplicity of the server-side rendering of React.

What renderToString does is it returns a string representation of the DOM elements generated by our App component; the same tree that it would render in the DOM if we were using the ReactDOM render method.

The value of the body variable is something like the following:

```
<div data-reactroot="" data-reactid="1" data-react-
checksum="982061917">Hello React</div>
```

As you can see, it represents what we defined in the render method of our App, except for a couple of data attributes that React uses on the client to attach the client-side application to the server-side rendered string.

Now that we have the SSR representation of our app, we can use the template function to apply it to the HTML template and send it back to the browser within the Express response.

Last, but not least, we have to start the Express application:

```
app.listen(3000, () => {
  console.log('Listening on port 3000');
});
```

We are now ready to go; there are only a few operations left.

The first one is defining the start script of npm and setting it to run the node server:

```
"scripts": {
  "build": "webpack",
```

```
    "start": "node ./dist/server"
  }
```

The scripts are ready, so we can first build the application with the following:

```
npm run build
```

When the bundles are created, we can run the following command:

```
npm start
```

Point the browser to `http://localhost:3000` and see the result.

There are two important things to note here. First, we use the **View Page Source** feature of the browser, we can see the source code of the application being rendered and returned from the server, which we would not see if SSR was not enabled.

Second, if we open DevTools and we have the React extension installed, we can see that the App component has been booted on the client as well.

The following screenshot shows the source of the page:

A data fetching example

The example in the previous section should explain clearly how to set up a universal application in React.

It is pretty straightforward, and the main focus is on getting things done.

However, in a real-world application, we will likely want to load some data instead of a static React component, such as App in the example. Suppose we want to load Dan Abramov's gists on the server and return the list of items from the Express app we just created.

In the data fetching examples in Chapter 5, *Proper Data Fetching*, we looked at how we can use componentDidMount to fire the data loading. That wouldn't work on the server because components do not get mounted on the DOM and the life cycle hook never gets fired.

Using hooks that are executed earlier, such as componentWillMount, will not work either, because the data fetching operation is async while renderToString is not. For that reason, we have to find a way to load the data beforehand and pass it to the component as props.

Let's look at how we can take the application from the previous section and change it a bit to make it load the gists during the server-side rendering phase.

The first thing to do is to change app.js to accept a list of gists as prop, and loop through it in the render method to display their descriptions:

```
import React from 'react';
import { array } from 'prop-types';

const App = ({ gists }) => (
  <ul>
    {gists.map(gist => (
      <li key={gist.id}>{gist.description}</li>
    ))}
  </ul>
);
App.propTypes = {
  gists: array
};

export default App;
```

Applying the concept that we learned in the previous chapter, we define a stateless functional component, which receives gists as a prop and loops through the elements to render a list of items.

Now, we have to change the server to retrieve gists and pass them to the component.

To use the **fetch** API on the server side, we have to install a library called `isomorphic-fetch`, which implements the fetch standards. It can be used in Node.js and the browser:

```
npm install isomorphic-fetch
```

We first import the library in `server.js`:

```
import fetch from 'isomorphic-fetch';
```

The API call we want to make looks as follows:

```
fetch('https://api.github.com/users/gaearon/gists')
  .then(response => response.json())
  .then(gists => {

  });
```

Here, the `gists` are available to be used inside the last `then` function. In our case, we want to pass them down to `App`.

So, we can change the / route as follows:

```
app.get('/', (req, res) => {
  fetch('https://api.github.com/users/gaearon/gists')
    .then(response => response.json())
    .then(gists => {
      const body = renderToString(<App gists={gists} />);
      const html = template(body);
      res.send(html);
    });
});
```

Here, we first fetch `gists` and then we render `App` to a string, passing the property.

Once `App` is rendered, and we have its markup, we use the template we used in the previous section, and we return it to the browser.

Run the following command in the console and point the browser to `http://localhost:3000`. You should be able to see a server-side render list of `gists`:

```
npm run build && npm start
```

To make sure that the list is rendered from the Express app you can navigate here:

```
view-source:http://localhost:3000/
```

You will see the markup and the descriptions of `gists`.

That is great, and it looks easy, but if we check the DevTools console, we can see the following error:

Cannot read property 'map' of undefined

The reason we see the error is that, on the client, we are rendering App again but without passing any gists to it.

This could sound counterintuitive in the beginning because we might think that React is smart enough to use the gists rendered within the server-side string on the client. But that is not what happens, so we have to find a way to make the gists available on the client side as well.

You may consider that you can execute the fetch again on the client. That would work, but it is not optimal because you would end up firing two HTTP calls, one on the Express server and one in the browser.

If we think about it, we already made the call on the server, and we have all the data we need. A typical solution to share data between the server and the client is dehydrating the data in the HTML markup and hydrating it back in the browser.

This seems like a complex concept, but it is not. We will look at how easy it is to implement now.

The first thing we must do is to inject the gists in the template after we fetched them on the client. To do this, we have to change the template a bit:

```
export default (body, gists) => `
  <!DOCTYPE html>
  <html>
    <head>
      <meta charset="UTF-8">
    </head>
    <body>
      <div id="app">${body}</div>
      <script>window.gists = ${JSON.stringify(gists)}</script>
      <script src="/bundle.js"></script>
    </body>
  </html>
`;
```

The template function now accepts two parameters—the body of the app and the collection of gists.

The first one is inserted inside the app element, while the second is used to define a global gists variable attached to the window object so that we can use it in the client.

Inside the Express route (server.js), we just have to change the line where we generate the template passing the body, as follows:

```
const html = template(body, gists);
```

Last, but not least, we have to use the gists attached to a window inside client.js, which is pretty easy:

```
ReactDOM.hydrate(
  <App gists={window.gists} />,
  document.getElementById('app')
);
```

Hydrate was introduced in React 16 and works similar to render on the client side, whether the HTML has server rendered markup or not. If there is no markup previously using SSR, then the hydrate method will fire a warning that you can silence it by using the new suppressHydrationWarning attribute.

We read gists directly, and we pass them to the App component that gets rendered on the client.

Now, run the following command again:

```
npm run build && npm start
```

If we point the browser window to http://localhost:3000, the error is gone, and if we inspect the App component using React DevTools, we can see how the client-side App component receives the collection of gists.

Next.js

You have looked at the basics of server-side rendering with React, and you can use the project we created as a starting point for a real app.

However, you may think that there is too much boilerplate and that you are required to know too many different tools to run a simple Universal application with React.

This is a common feeling called **JavaScript fatigue**, as described in the introduction to this book.

Luckily, Facebook developers and other companies in the React community, are working very hard to improve the DX and make the life of developers easier. You might have used `create-react-app` at this point to try out the examples in the previous chapters, and you should understand how it makes it very simple to create React applications without requiring developers to learn many technologies and tools.

Now, `create-react-app` does not support SSR yet, but there's a company called Zeit who created a tool called Next.js, which makes it incredibly easy to generate Universal applications without worrying about configuration files. It also reduces the boilerplate a lot.

It is important to say that using abstractions is always very good for building applications quickly. However, it is crucial to know how the internals works before adding too many layers, and that is why we started with the manual process before learning Next.js.

We have looked at how SSR works and how we can pass the state from the server to the client. Now that the base concepts are clear, we can move to a tool that hides a little bit of complexity and makes us write less code to achieve the same results.

We will create the same app where all the gists from Dan Abramov are loaded, and you will see how clean and simple the code is thanks to Next.js.

First of all, let's move into an empty folder and create a new project:

```
npm init
```

When this is done, we can install the Next.js library and React:

```
npm install next react react-dom
```

Now that the project is created, we have to add an `npm` script to run the binary:

```
"scripts": {
  "dev": "next"
}
```

Perfect, it is now time to generate our `App` component.

Next.js is based on conventions, with the most important one being that you can create pages to match the browser URLs. The default page is `index`, so we can create a folder called `pages` and put an `index.js` file inside it.

We start importing the dependencies:

```
import React from 'react';
import fetch from 'isomorphic-fetch';
```

Again, we import `isomorphic-fetch` because we want to be able to use the `fetch` function on the server side.

We then define a class called `App`, which inherits from `React.Component`:

```
class App extends Component
```

Inside the class, we define a `static async` function, called `getInitialProps`, which is where we tell Next.js which data we want to load, both on the server and on the client. The library will make the object returned from the function available as props inside the component.

The `static` and `async` keywords applied to a class method mean that the function can be accessed outside the instance of the class and that the function yields the execution of the `wait` instructions inside its body.

These concepts are pretty advanced, and they are not part of the scope of this chapter, but if you are interested in them, you should check out the ECMAScript proposals (`https://github.com/tc39/proposals`).

The implementation of the method we just described is as follows:

```
static async getInitialProps() {
  const url = 'https://api.github.com/users/gaearon/gists';
  const response = await fetch(url);
  const gists = await response.json();
  return {
    gists
  };
};
```

We are telling the function to fire the fetch and wait for the response; then we are transforming the response into JSON, which returns a promise. When the promise is resolved, we can return the `props` object with the `gists`.

The `render` method of the component looks pretty similar to the preceding one:

```
render() {
  return (
    <ul>
      {this.props.gists.map(gist => (
```

```
          <li key={gist.id}>{gist.description}</li>
        )))}
      </ul>
    );
}
```

However, it uses `this.props.gists` because we are inside a class instance.

Finally, we define `PropTypes`, as you should always do when creating components:

```
App.propTypes = {
  gists: array
};
```

Then we export the component:

```
export default App;
```

Now, open the console and run the following:

```
npm run dev
```

We will see the following output:

```
> Ready on http://localhost:3000
```

If we point the browser to that URL, we can see the Universal application in action.

It is really impressive how easy it is to set up a Universal application with a few lines of code and zero configuration, thanks to Next.js.

You may also notice that if you edit the application inside your editor, you will be able to see the results within the browser instantly without needing to refresh the page. That is another feature of Next.js, which enables hot module replacement. It is incredibly useful in development mode.

If you liked this chapter, go and give them a star on GitHub: `https://github.com/zeit/next.js`.

Summary

The journey through server-side rendering has come to an end. You are now able to create a server-side rendered application with React, and it should be clear why it can be useful for you. SEO is certainly one of the main reasons, but social sharing and performance are important factors as well.

You learned how it is possible to load the data on the server and dehydrate it in the HTML template to make it available for the client-side application when it boots on the browser.

Finally, you have looked at how tools such as Next.js can help you reduce the boilerplate and hide some of the complexity that setting up a server-side render React application usually brings to the code base.

In the next chapter, we will talk about how to improve the performance in our React applications.

Improve the Performance of Your Applications **9**

The effective performance of a web application is critical to providing a good user experience and improving conversions. The React library implements different techniques to render our components fast and to touch the **Document Object Model** (**DOM**) as little as possible. Applying changes to the DOM is usually expensive and so minimizing the number of operations is crucial.

However, there are some particular scenarios where React cannot optimize the process, and it's up to the developer to implement specific solutions to make the application run smoothly.

In this chapter, we will go through the basic concepts of React and we will learn how to use some APIs to help the library find the optimal path to update the DOM without degrading the user experience. We will also see some common mistakes that can harm our applications and make them slower.

Through the simple examples in this chapter, you will learn about the tools that we can import into our code base to monitor performance and find bottlenecks. We will also see how immutability and `PureComponent` are the perfect tools to build fast React applications.

We should avoid optimizing our components for the sake of it, and it is important to apply the techniques that we will see in the following sections only when they are needed.

In this chapter, we will cover the following topics:

- How reconciliation works and how we can help React do a better job using the keys
- How using the production version of React makes the library faster
- What `shouldComponentUpdate` and `PureComponent` can do for us and how to use them

- Common optimization techniques and common performance-related mistakes
- What it means to use immutable data and how to do it
- Useful tools and libraries to make our applications run faster

Reconciliation

Most of the time, React is fast enough by default and you do not need to do anything more to improve the performance of your application. React utilizes different techniques to optimize the rendering of the components on the screen.

When React has to display a component, it calls its `render` method and the `render` methods of its children recursively. The `render` method of a component returns a tree of React elements, which React uses to decide which DOM operations have to be done to update the UI.

Whenever a component state changes, React calls the `render` method on the nodes again, and it compares the result with the previous tree of React elements. The library is smart enough to figure out the minimum set of operations required to apply the expected changes on the screen. This process is called **reconciliation,** and it is managed transparently by React. Thanks to that, we can easily describe how our components have to look at a given point in time in a declarative way and let the library do the rest.

React tries to apply the smallest possible number of operations on the DOM because touching the DOM is an expensive operation.

However, comparing two trees of elements is not free either, and React makes two assumptions to reduce its complexity:

- If two elements have a different type, they render a different tree.
- Developers can use keys to mark children as stable across different render calls.

The second point is interesting from a developer perspective because it gives us a tool to help React render our views faster.

By default, when coming back on the children of a DOM node, both the lists of children are iterated by React at the same time. And whenever there is a difference it creates a mutation.

Let's see some examples. Converting between the following two trees will work well, when adding an element at the end of the children.

```
<ul>
  <li>Carlos</li>
  <li>Javier</li>
</ul>

<ul>
  <li>Carlos</li>
  <li>Javier</li>
  <li>Jona</li>
</ul>
```

The two `<li>Carlos</li>` trees, match the two `<li>Javier</li>` trees, by React and then it will insert the `<li>Jona</li>` tree.

Inserting an element at the beginning has worse performance, if implemented naively. If we look at the example, it works very poorly when converting between those two trees.

```
<ul>
  <li>Carlos</li>
  <li>Javier</li>
</ul>

<ul>
  <li>Jona</li>
  <li>Carlos</li>
  <li>Javier</li>
</ul>
```

Every child will be mutated by React, instead of it realizing that it can keep the subtrees line `<li>Carlos</li>` and `<li>Javier</li>` intact. This can possibly be an issue

Keys

This problem can of course be solved and the way for this is the `key` attribute which is supported by React. Children posses keys and these keys are used by React to match children between the subsequent tree and the original tree. The tree conversion can be made efficient by adding a key to our previous example:

```
<ul>
  <li key="2018">Carlos</li>
  <li key="2019">Javier</li>
</ul>
```

```
<ul>
  <li key="2017">Jona</li>
  <li key="2018">Carlos</li>
  <li key="2019">Javier</li>
</ul>
```

React now knows that 2017 key is the new one and the 2018 and 2019 keys have just moved.

Finding a key is not hard. The element that you will be displaying might already have a unique ID. So the key can just come from your data:

```
<li key={element.id}>{element.title}</li>
```

A new ID can be added to your model by you or the key can be generated by some parts of the content. The key has to only be unique among its siblings, it does not have to be unique globally.

An item index in the array can be passed as a key, but it is now considered as a bad practice. But if the items are never recorded this can work well. The reorders will seriously affect the performance.

If you are rendering multiple items using a map function and you don't specify the key property, you will get this message **Warning: Each child in an array or iterator should have a unique "key" prop.**

Optimization techniques

It is important to notice that, in all the examples in this book, we are using apps that have either been created with create-react-app or have been created from scratch, but always with the development version of React.

Using the development version of React is very useful for coding and debugging as it gives you all the necessary information to fix the various issues. However, all the checks and warnings come with a cost, which we want to avoid in production.

So, the very first optimization that we should do to our applications is to build the bundle, setting the NODE_ENV environment variable to production. This is pretty easy with webpack and it is just a matter of using DefinePlugin in the following way:

```
new webpack.DefinePlugin({
  'process.env': {
    NODE_ENV: JSON.stringify('production')
```

```
      }
})
```

To achieve the best performance, we not only want to create the bundle with the production flag activated, but we also want to split our bundles: one for our application and one for our `node_modules`. To do so, you need to use the new optimization node in webpack 4:

```
optimization: {
  splitChunks: {
    cacheGroups: {
      default: false,
      commons: {
        test: /node_modules/,
        name: 'vendor',
        chunks: 'all'
      }
    }
  }
}
```

Now, webpack 4 has two modes—development and production. By default, the production mode is enabled, meaning the code will be minified and compressed when you compile your bundles using the production mode; you can specify it with this:

```
{
  mode: process.env.NODE_ENV === 'production' ? 'production' :
'development',
}
```

Your `webpack.config.js` file should look like this:

```
module.exports = {
  entry: './index.js',
  optimization: {
    splitChunks: {
      cacheGroups: {
        default: false,
        commons: {
          test: /node_modules/,
          name: 'vendor',
          chunks: 'all'
        }
      }
    }
  },
  plugins: [
    new webpack.DefinePlugin({
```

```
      'process.env': {
        NODE_ENV: JSON.stringify('production')
      }
    })
  ],
  mode: process.env.NODE_ENV === 'production' ? 'production' :
'development'
}
```

shouldComponentUpdate

For many developers, the way the reconciler algorithm works is confusing. They often think that since React is smart enough to find out the shortest path to apply the changes to the DOM, the render methods of the components that are not changed do not ever get called. That's unfortunately far from being true.

In fact, to find out the necessary steps to reduce the DOM operations, React has to fire the render methods of all the components and compare the results with the previous ones.

If nothing changes, no changes will be made in the DOM, which is great. But if our render methods do complex operations, React will take some time to figure out that no operations have to be done, which is not optimal.

We surely want our components to be simple, and we should avoid doing expensive operations inside the renderer. However, sometimes we simply cannot manage this and our applications become slow, even if the DOM is not touched at all.

React is not able to figure out which components do not need to be updated, but we have a function that we can implement to tell the library whether to update a component or not.

The method is called shouldComponentUpdate, and if it returns false, the component and all its children's render methods are not called during an update of its parents.

Let's create a List component to understand this method:

```
class List extends Component
```

The List component has a constructor where we initialize the list and we bind the event handler:

```
constructor(props) {
  super(props);
  this.state = {
    items: ['foo', 'bar']
```

```
  };
  this.handleClick = this.handleClick.bind(this);
}
```

We then define the event handler that appends a new item to the list and stores the resulting array into the state:

```
handleClick() {
  const items = this.state.items.slice();
  items.unshift('baz');
  this.setState({
    items
  });
}
```

Finally, we specify the render method where we loop through the items displaying every single element of the list and declaring button with its onClick event handler:

```
render() {
  return (
    <div>
      <ul>
        {this.state.items.map(item => <li key={item}>{item}</li>)}
      </ul>

      <button onClick={this.handleClick}>+</button>
    </div>
  );
}
```

Now, try to add the following code to the previously created list:

```
shouldComponentUpdate() {
  return false;
}
```

You can see that clicking on the + button has no effect whatsoever on the application inside the browser, even though the state changes. That is because we are telling React that the component does not need to be updated.

Returning false all the time is far from useful, and so developers usually check if the props or the state are changed inside that method.

In the case of `List`, for example, we should check if the `items` array has been modified or not, and return a value accordingly.

The `shouldComponentUpdate` method passes two parameters that we can use to implement those checks, the first parameter represents `nextProps` while the second parameter represents `nextState`.

In our case, we could do something like this:

```
shouldComponentUpdate(nextProps, nextState) {
  return this.state.items !== nextState.items;
}
```

We return `true` only if the items are changed, while we stop the rendering in any other case. Suppose, for example, that `List` is a child of a component that gets updated frequently but its state does not affect the `List` in any way: We can use `shoudlComponentUpdate` to tell React to stop running the `render` methods from that component to its children.

Checking if all the props and all the state attributes are changed is a boring job, and it is sometimes hard to maintain the complex `shouldComponentUpdate` implementations, especially when the requirements change frequently.

For that reason, React gives us a special component from which we can inherit and which implements a shallow comparison of all the props and the state attributes for us.

Using it is pretty straightforward; we just have to extend `React.PureComponent` instead of `React.Component` when we create our component classes.

It is important to notice that the shallow comparison, as the name suggests, does not check for deep and nested properties in objects, and it can sometimes give unexpected results.

It works very well with immutable data structures, which we will see in more detail later in this chapter. It is worth saying that performing a deep comparison of complex objects can sometimes be more expensive than the `render` method itself.

That is why `PureComponent` should be used only when it is needed and only once the performance has been measured and you have figured out which components are taking too much time to be executed.

Stateless functional components

Another concept that is sometimes counterintuitive for beginners is the fact that stateless components do not give us any benefits regarding performance.

They are great for the many reasons that we saw in Chapter 3, *Create Truly Reusable Components*, and for the way they make our applications simpler and easier to reason about, but they do not have (as yet) any internal implementation that makes them faster.

It is easy to think that they are rendered quicker because they do not have an instance, a state, or event handlers, but at the moment that's not the case.

In the future, they might be optimized (according to the React team), but today they perform even worse because it is not possible to use the shouldComponentUpdate method that, as we have seen before, can help React render the tree faster.

Common solutions

We have seen how using PureComponent can help us to tell React whether a subtree has to be rendered or not. If utilized in the right way, it could improve the performance of our applications a lot. It is also important to stress that it should be used only after the application has been monitored and the bottleneck has been found.

There are some tricky situations where extending PureComponent does not give the expected results; usually, the cause is that our props or state attributes are changing even if we think they are not. Sometimes it is not easy to figure out which props are causing the component to re-render or we do not know which components can be optimized with PureComponent.

Most of the time, refactoring the components and putting the state in the right place can greatly assist the optimization of the application.

In this section, we will look at some common tools and solutions to solve re-rendering issues, figuring out which components can be optimized. We will also look at how to refactor complex components into small ones to achieve better performance.

Why did you update?

There are different things we can do to find out which components do not need to be updated. One of the easiest is to install a third-party library that can provide the information automatically.

First of all, we have to type the following command in the terminal:

```
npm install --save-dev why-did-you-update
```

And add the following snippet after the `import` statement of React in your App.js:

```
import React from 'react';
if (process.env.NODE_ENV !== 'production') {
  const { whyDidYouUpdate } = require('why-did-you-update');
  whyDidYouUpdate(React);
}
```

We are basically saying that, in development mode, we want to load the library and patch React using the `whyDidYouUpdate` method. It is important to say that this library should not be enabled in production.

If we now go back to the `List` example of the previous section and we change it a little bit, we can see the library in action.

The first thing we have to do is to modify the `render` method as follows:

```
render() {
  return (
    <div>
      <ul>
        {this.state.items.map(item => (
          <Item key={item} item={item} />
        ))}
      </ul>
      <button onClick={this.handleClick}>+</button>
    </div>
  );
}
```

Instead of rendering the single list items inside the `map` function, we return a custom `Item` component to which we pass the current item and we use the key to tell React which components existed before the update.

We can now implement the item component, extending `React.Component`:

```
class Item extends Component
```

At the moment, it only implements the `render` method, which does what we were doing inside the `render` method of `List`:

```
render() {
  return (
    <li>{this.props.item}</li>
  );
}
```

In the browser console, you can see the output from the `whyDidYouUpdate` function, which tells us that we can avoid re-rendering some components:

```
Item.props
  Value did not change. Avoidable re-render!
  before Object {item: "foo"}
  after Object {item: "foo"}

Item.props
  Value did not change. Avoidable re-render!
  before Object {item: "bar"}
  after Object {item: "bar"}
```

In fact, even if React does not touch the DOM for the `foo` and `bar` items, their `render` methods are still being called with the same props, which makes React perform an additional job. This is very useful information that is sometimes not easy to find.

Now, we can easily fix the issue by modifying the `extends` statement of the `Item` component from `extends` and `React.Component` to:

```
class Item extends PureComponent
```

If we now open the browser and run the application again, clicking the + button, we see that nothing is logged into the console, which means that we are not rendering any `Item` for which the props are not changed.

Regarding perceived performance, there is not much difference in this small example, but if you imagine a big application that shows hundreds of `list` items, this small change can represent a huge win.

Creating functions inside the render method

Now, let's keep on adding features to `List` as we would do in a real-world application and see whether, at some point, we manage to break the benefits given by `PureComponent`.

For example, we want to add a click event handler on each item so that, if the item gets clicked, we log its value into the console.

This is far from being a useful feature in a real application, but you can easily figure out how, with a small amount of effort, you can create a more complex operation (for example, showing a new window with the item's data).

To add the logging feature, we have to apply two changes: one to the `render` method of `List` and the other one to the `render` method of `Item`.

Let's start with the first one:

```
render() {
  return (
    <div>
      <ul>
        {this.state.items.map(item => (
          <Item
            key={item}
            item={item}
            onClick={() => console.log(item)}
          />
        ))}
      </ul>
      <button onClick={this.handleClick}>+</button>
    </div>
  );
}
```

We added an `onClick` prop to the `Item` component, and we set it to a function that, when called, logs the current item into the console.

To make it work, we have to add the logic on the `Item` components as well, and we can just use the `onClick` prop as the `onClick` handler of the `<li>` element:

```
render() {
  return (
    <li onClick={this.props.onClick}>
      {this.props.item}
```

```
      </li>
    );
  }
```

The component is still pure, and we expect it to not re-render if the values have not changed when baz is added to the list.

Unfortunately, if we run the component in the browser, we notice some new logs in DevTools. First of all, the whyDidYouUpdate library is telling us that there is a possibly avoidable re-render because the onClick function is always the same:

```
Item.props.onClick
   Value is a function. Possibly avoidable re-render?
   before onClick() {
     return console.log(item);
   }
   after onClick() {
     return console.log(item);
   }

Item.props.onClick
   Value is a function. Possibly avoidable re-render?
   before onClick() {
     return console.log(item);
   }
   after onClick() {
     return console.log(item);
   }
```

The reason React thinks that we are passing a new function on every render is because the arrow function returns a newly created function every time it is invoked, even if the implementation remains the same. This is a pretty common mistake when using React, and it can be easily fixed by refactoring the components a bit.

Unfortunately, we cannot define the logging function once in the parent because we need to know which child has fired it; that is why creating it inside the loop seems the best solution.

What we actually have to do is move part of the logic inside the item that knows the item that has been clicked.

Let's see the full implementation of Item, which extends PureComponent:

```
class Item extends PureComponent
```

It has `constructor`, where we bind the click handler, which is now part of its implementation:

```
constructor(props) {
  super(props);
  this.handleClick = this.handleClick.bind(this);
}
```

Inside the `handleClick` function, we call the `onClick` handler that we received from `props`, passing the current item that has been clicked within the `<li>` element:

```
handleClick() {
  this.props.onClick(this.props.item);
}
```

Finally, in the `render` method, we use the new local event handler:

```
render() {
  return (
    <li onClick={this.handleClick}>
      {this.props.item}
    </li>
  );
}
```

The last thing to do is change the `List` component render to make it not return a new function at every single render, as follows:

```
render() {
  return (
    <div>
      <ul>
        {this.state.items.map(item => (
          <Item key={item} item={item} onClick={console.log} />
        ))}
      </ul>
      <button onClick={this.handleClick}>+</button>
    </div>
  );
}
```

As you can see, we are passing the function we wanted to use, in this case `console.log`, which will be called inside the children with the right parameter. Doing so, the instance of the function in `List` is always the same and it does not fire any re-rendering.

If we now run the component in the browser and we click the + button to add the new item, which causes the `List` component to render, we can see that we are not wasting time anymore.

Also, if we click on any item in the list, we will see its value in the console as well.

As Dan Abramov says, it is not a problem by itself to use arrow functions inside the `render` method (or even to use `bind` to avoid binding in the constructor); we just have to be careful and make sure that it does not force any unnecessary re-rendering when `PureComponent` is in action.

Constants props

Let's keep on improving our list example, and see what happens when we add new features.

In this case, we will learn how to avoid a common error when using `PureComponent`, which makes it less effective.

Suppose we want to add a prop to our `Item` component, which represents a list of statuses that the item can have. There are many ways of implementing it, but our focus is more on the way we pass down the default values.

Change the `render` method of the `List` component as follows:

```
render() {
  return (
    <div>
      <ul>
        {this.state.items.map(item => (
          <Item
            key={item}
            item={item}
            onClick={console.log}
            statuses={['open', 'close']}
          />
        ))}
      </ul>
      <button onClick={this.handleClick}>+</button>
    </div>
  );
}
```

In the preceding code, for each Item, we set the key and the item prop to the current value of item. We fire console.log when the onClick event is fired inside Item, and we now have a new prop, which represents the possible statuses of item.

Now, if we render the List component inside the browser we see **foo** and **bar** as usual, and if we click the **+** button to add **baz**, we notice a new message in the console:

```
Item.props.statuses
   Value did not change. Avoidable re-render!
   before ["open", "close"]
   after ["open", "close"]
 Item.props.statuses
   Value did not change. Avoidable re-render!
   before ["open", "close"]
   after ["open", "close"]
```

The message is telling us that even if the values inside the array stay the same, on every render we are passing a new instance of the array to Item.

The reason behind this behavior is that all the objects return a new instance when created and a new array is never equal to another, even if they contain the same values:

```
[] === []
false
```

There is also a table printed on the console, which shows the time that React is wasting rendering the items with unchanged props when there is no need to touch the DOM.

What we can do to solve the issue here is to create the array once, and always pass the same instance to every render:

```
import React, { Component } from 'react';
import Item from './Item';

const statuses = ['open', 'close'];

class List extends Component {
  constructor(props) {
    super(props);

    this.state = {
      items: ['foo', 'bar']
    };

    this.handleClick = this.handleClick.bind(this);
  }
```

```
handleClick() {
  const items = this.state.items.slice();
  items.unshift('baz');

  this.setState({
    items
  });
}

render() {
  return (
    <div>
      <ul>
        {this.state.items.map(item => (
          <Item
            key={item}
            item={item}
            onClick={console.log}
            statuses={statuses}
          />
        ))}
      </ul>
      <button onClick={this.handleClick}>+</button>
    </div>
  );
}
}

export default List;
```

If we try the component again in the browser, we see that the console now contains no message, which means that the items do not re-render themselves unnecessarily when the new element is added.

Refactoring and good design

In the last part of this section, we will see how we can refactor an existing component (or design a new one in a better way) to improve the performance of our application.

Poor design choices often lead to issues, and, in the case of React, if we do not put the state in the right place, the risk is that our components are going to render more than needed.

As we said before, this is not a huge problem if a component renders itself more often than necessary. The problem becomes a real one only when we measure performance and realize that rendering a long list of items many times makes the application less responsive.

The component that we are going to create is similar to the previous one, a to-do list-like component with a form to let the users enter a new item.

As usual, we will start with a basic version, and we will optimize it step by step.

The component is called `Todos`, which is a class that is `extends` and `React.Component`:

```
class Todos extends Component
```

Inside `constructor`, we initialize the state and bind the event handlers:

```
constructor(props) {
  super(props);
  this.state = {
    items: ['foo', 'bar'],
    value: ''
  };
  this.handleChange = this.handleChange.bind(this);
  this.handleClick = this.handleClick.bind(this);
}
```

The `state` has two attributes:

- `items`: This is the list of items with a couple of default values, and it's also the array where the new items will be added
- `value`: This is the current value of the input that the users can fill to add new items

You should be now able to infer the functionalities of the event handlers from their names. We have `handleChange` that is fired every time a user types a character in the form:

```
handleChange({ target: { value } }) {
  this.setState({
    value
  });
}
```

As we saw in Chapter 6, *Write Code for the Browser*, the `onChange` handler receives the event with a target property that represents the input element, and we store its value inside the state to control the component.

Then, there is `handleClick` that is fired when the users submit the form to add a new item:

```
handleClick() {
  const items = this.state.items.slice();
  items.unshift(this.state.value);
  this.setState({
```

```
      items
    });
  }
```

The click handler is pretty similar to the previous one except that it uses the value from the state instead of a constant string, and it adds it as the first element on a copy of the current array.

Finally, we describe our view in the `render` method:

```
render() {
  return (
    <div>
      <ul>
        {this.state.items.map(item => <li key={item}>{item}</li>)}
      </ul>
      <div>
        <input
          type="text"
          value={this.state.value}
          onChange={this.handleChange}
        />
        <button onClick={this.handleClick}>+</button>
      </div>
    </div>
  );
}
```

We have the unordered list, where we loop through the items collection and we print every single item inside a `<li>` element. Then there is the controlled input field, and we set its current values as well as listen to the change event. Last, but not least, there is a + button, which we use to submit the value and add it to the array of items.

Now, this component works, and if we run it inside the browser, we'll see the list of items with the two default values and the form that we can use to add new items to the list. As soon as we click on the button, the new item is added to the top of the list.

There are no particular problems with this component unless we start adding hundreds of items. At that point, we realize that typing into the field becomes laggy. The reason for the reduction in performance as soon as the number of items grows is that the list re-renders every time a user types in the field. When we update the state with the new value of the controlled component, in fact, React calls the render again to see if the elements are different.

The only change is the value of the input element, and that is going to be the only mutation applied to the DOM; but, to figure out which operations are needed, React has to render the entire component and all its children, and rendering a big list of items many times over is expensive.

Now, if we look at the state object of the component, it's pretty clear that it is not well structured. In fact, we are storing the items as well as the value of the form field, which are two entirely different things.

Our goal is always to have components that do one thing very well, rather than components with multiple purposes.

The solution here is to split the component into smaller ones, each one with a clear responsibility and state.

We need a common parent because the components are related. In fact, if we don't want to re-render the list every time a user types in the field, we also do not want to render the list again as soon as the form is submitted and the new item is added.

To do so, we change the Todos component to store only the list of items, which is the part of the store that is shared between the list and the form.

Then we create a separate list that only receives the items and a form that has its state for controlling the input field. The field fires a callback on the common parent to update the list when the form is submitted.

Let's start changing the Todos component:

```
class Todos extends Component
```

In the constructor, we now define only the default items inside the state, and we bind a single submit handler, which is the callback of the Form component:

```
constructor(props) {
  super(props);
  this.state = {
    items: ['foo', 'bar']
  };
  this.handleSubmit = this.handleSubmit.bind(this);
}
```

The implementation of the submit handler is the same as we've seen before on the click handler:

```
handleSubmit(value) {
  const items = this.state.items.slice();
```

```
  items.unshift(value);
  this.setState({
    items
  });
}
```

The exception is that it receives the value of the new item as a parameter of the callback. It then clones the array and adds the value as its first element. When the array is updated, it gets added back to the state.

The `render` method is much cleaner now, because we just render two custom components, each one with their props:

```
render() {
  return (
    <div>
      <List items={this.state.items} />
      <Form onSubmit={this.handleSubmit} />
    </div>
  );
}
```

The `List` component receives the items from the state, and the `Form` receives the `handleSubmit` function as a callback, and it fires `onSubmit` when the user clicks the + button.

It is now time to create the subcomponents, and we will start from `List` just by extracting the part of the code from the previous `render` method.

`List` can be implemented as a class, and it inherits from `PureComponent` so that it gets re-rendered only when the items are changed:

```
class List extends PureComponent
```

The `render` method is pretty simple and it just loops through the items in the array to generate the list:

```
render() {
  return (
    <ul>
      {this.props.items.map(item => <li key={item}>{item}</li>)}
    </ul>
  );
}
```

Then, we have the `Form` component, which is a bit more complex because it handles the state of the controlled input element. It extends `PureComponent` as well so that it never gets re-rendered from the parent since the callback never changes:

```
class Form extends PureComponent
```

We define `constructor`, where we set the initial state and bind the change handler for the controlled input:

```
constructor(props) {
  super(props);
  this.state = {
    value: ''
  };
  this.handleChange = this.handleChange.bind(this);
}
```

The implementation of the change handler is very similar to any other controlled input we have seen so far:

```
handleChange({ target: { value } }) {
  this.setState({
    value
  });
}
```

It receives the target element, which is our input, and saves its value into the state.

Finally, in the `render` method, we declare the elements that compose our form:

```
render() {
  return (
    <div>
      <input
        type="text"
        value={this.state.value}
        onChange={this.handleChange}
      />
      <button onClick={() => this.props.onSubmit(this.state.value)}>+
      </button>
    </div>
  );
}
```

This includes the controlled input field, where we set the value, the change handler, and the + button, which fires the callback passing the current value. In this case, we can generate a function inside `render` because there are no pure children.

Done! If we now run the newly created `Todos` component in the page, we see that the behavior is the same as before, but the list and the form have two separate states and they render only when their props change.

For example, if we try to add hundreds of items inside the list, we see that the performance is not affected and the input field is not laggy. We've solved a performance issue just by refactoring the component and changing the design a bit by separating the responsibilities correctly.

Tools and libraries

In the next section, we will go through some techniques, tools, and libraries that we can apply to our code base to monitor and improve the performance.

Immutability

As we have seen, the most powerful tool we can use to improve the performance of our React application is `shouldComponentUpdate` using `PureComponent`.

The only problem is that `PureComponent` uses a shallow comparison method against the props and state, which means that if we pass an object as a prop and we mutate one of its values, we do not get the expected behavior.

In fact, a shallow comparison cannot find mutation on the properties and the components never get re-rendered, except when the object itself changes.

One way to solve this issue is using **immutable data**: Data that, once it gets created, cannot be mutated.

For example, we can set the state in the following mode:

```
const obj = this.state.obj;

obj.foo = 'bar';

this.setState({ obj });
```

Even if the value of the `foo` attribute of the object is changed, the reference to the object is still the same and the shallow comparison does not recognize it.

What we can do instead is create a new instance every time we mutate the object, as follows:

```
const obj = Object.assign({}, this.state.obj, { foo: 'bar' });

this.setState({ obj });
```

In this case, we get a new object with the `foo` property set to `bar` , and the shallow comparison would be able to find the difference.

With ES6 and Babel, there is another way to express the same concept in a more elegant way, and it is by using the object spread operator:

```
const obj = {
  ...this.state.obj,
  foo: 'bar'
};
this.setState({ obj });
```

This structure is more concise than the previous one, and it produces the same result; but, at the time of writing, it requires the code to be transpiled to be executed inside the browser.

React provides some immutability helpers to make it easy to work with immutable objects, and there is also a popular library called `immutable.js` , which has more powerful features but it requires you to learn new APIs.

Babel plugins

There are also a couple of interesting **Babel** plugins that we can install and use to improve the performance of our React applications. They make the applications faster, optimizing parts of the code at build-time.

The first one is the React constant elements transformer that finds all the static elements that do not change depending on the props and extracts them from the `render` method (or the functional stateless components) to avoid calling `createElement` unnecessarily.

Using a Babel plugin is pretty straightforward. We first install it with `npm`:

```
npm install --save-dev babel-plugin-transform-react-constant-elements
```

You need to create the .babelrc file and add a plugins key with an array that has the value with the list of the plugin that we want to activate:

```
{
    "plugins": ["transform-react-constant-elements"]
}
```

The second Babel plugin we can choose to use to improve performance is the React inline elements transform, which replaces all the JSX declarations (or the createElement calls) with a more optimized version of them to make execution faster.

Install the plugin with:

```
npm install --save-dev babel-plugin-transform-react-inline-elements
```

Next, you can easily add the plugin to the array of plugins in the .babelrc file, as follows:

```
{
    "plugins": ["transform-react-inline-elements"]
}
```

Both plugins should be used only in production because they make debugging harder in development mode.

Summary

Our journey through performance is finished, and we can now optimize our applications to give users a better UX.

In this chapter, we learned how the reconciliation algorithm works and how React always tries to take the shortest path to apply changes to the DOM. We can also help the library to optimize its job by using the keys.

Once you've found your bottlenecks, you can apply one of the techniques we have seen in this chapter to fix the issue. One of the first tools you can use is to extend PureComponent and use immutable data to make your component re-render only when strictly needed.

Don't forget to avoid the common mistakes that make PureComponent less effective, such as generating new functions inside the render method or using constant as props.

We have learned how refactoring and designing your components structure in the proper way could provide a performance boost. Our goal is to have small components that do one single thing in the best possible way.

At the end of the chapter, we talked about immutability, and we've seen why it's important not to mutate data to make `shouldComponentUpdate` and shallow compare do their job. Finally, we ran through different tools and libraries that can make your applications faster.

In the next chapter, we'll look at testing and debugging using Jest, Enzyme, and React Dev Tools.

About Testing and Debugging

React, thanks to its components, makes it easy to test our applications. There are many different tools that we can use to create tests with React, and here we'll cover the most popular ones to understand the benefits they provide.

Jest is an all-in-one testing framework solution, maintained by Christopher Pojer from Facebook and contributors within the community, and aims to give you the best developer experience. We will look at both ways of building the best test environment.

By the end of the chapter, you'll be able to create a test environment from scratch and write tests for your application's components.

In this chapter, we will look at the following topics:

- Why it is important to test our applications, and how this helps developers move faster
- How to set up a Jest environment to test components using Enzyme
- What Enzyme is and why it is a must-have for testing React applications
- How to test a real-world component
- How to test events
- The React developer tools and some error-handling techniques

The benefits of testing

Testing web UIs has always been a difficult job. From unit to end-to-end tests. The fact that the interfaces depend on browsers, user interactions, and many other variables makes it difficult to implement an effective testing strategy.

If you've ever tried to write end-to-end tests for the web, you'll know how complex it is to get consistent results and how the results are often affected by false negatives due to different factors, such as the network. Other than that, user interfaces are frequently updated to improve the experience, maximize conversions, or simply add new features.

If tests are hard to write and maintain, developers are less prone to cover their applications. On the other hand, tests are pretty important because they make developers more confident with their code, which is reflected in speed and quality. If a piece of code is well tested (and tests are well written), developers can be sure that it works and is ready to ship. Similarly, thanks to tests, it becomes easier to refactor the code because tests guarantee that the functionalities do not change during the rewrite.

Developers tend to focus on the feature they are currently implementing, and sometimes it is hard to know if other parts of the application are affected by those changes. Tests help to avoid regressions because they can tell if the new code breaks the old tests. Greater confidence in writing new features leads to faster releases.

Testing the main functionalities of an application makes the code base more solid, and whenever a new bug is found, it can be reproduced, fixed, and covered by tests so that it does not happen again in the future.

Luckily, React (and the component era) makes testing user interfaces easy and efficient. Testing components, or trees of components, is a less arduous job because every single part of the application has its responsibilities and boundaries.

If components are built in the right way, if they are pure and aim for composability and reusability, they can be tested as simple functions.

Another great power that modern tools bring us is the ability to run tests using Node and the console. Spinning up a browser for every single test makes tests slower and less predictable, degrading the developer experience; instead, running the tests using the console is faster.

Testing components only in the console can sometimes give unexpected behaviors when they are rendered in a real browser, but in my experience this is rare.

When we test React components, we want to make sure that they work properly and that, given different sets of props, their output is always correct.

We may also want to cover all the various states that a component can have. The state might change by clicking a button, so we write tests to check if all the event handlers are doing what they are supposed to do.

When all the functionalities of the component are covered, but we want to do more, we can write tests to verify its behavior on **edge cases**. Edge cases are states that the component can assume when, for example, all the props are `null`, or there is an error. Once the tests are written, we can be pretty confident that the component behaves as expected.

Testing a single component is great, but it does not guarantee that multiple individually tested components will still work once they are put together. As we will see later, with React we can mount a tree of components and test the integration between them.

There are different techniques that we can use to write tests, and one of the most popular ones is **test-driven development** (**TDD**). Applying TDD means writing the tests first and then writing the code to pass the tests.

Following this pattern helps us to write better code because we are forced to think more about the design before implementing the functionalities, which usually leads to higher quality.

Painless JavaScript testing with Jest

The most important way to learn how to test React components in the right way is by writing some code, and that is what we are going to do in this section.

The React documentation says that at Facebook they use Jest to test their components. However, React does not force you to use a particular test framework, and you can use your favorite one without any problems.

To see Jest in action, we are going to create a project from scratch, installing all the dependencies and writing a component with some tests. It'll be fun!

The first thing to do is to move into a new folder and run the following:

```
npm init
```

Once `package.json` is created, we can start installing the dependencies, with the first one being the `jest` package itself:

```
npm install --save-dev jest
```

To tell npm that we want to use the jest command to run the tests, we have to add the following scripts to package.json:

```
"scripts": {
  "build": "webpack",
  "start": "node ./dist/server",
  "test": "jest",
  "test:coverage": "jest --coverage"
}
```

To write components and tests using ES2015 and JSX, we have to install all Babel-related packages so that Jest can use them to transpile and understand the code.

The second set of dependencies is:

```
npm install --save-dev @babel/core @babel/preset-env @babel/preset-react
babel-jest
```

As you may know, we now have to create a .babelrc file, which is used by Babel to know the presets and the plugins that we would like to use inside the project.

The .babelrc file looks like the following:

```
{
  "presets": ["@babel/preset-env", "@babel/preset-react"]
}
```

Now, it is time to install React and ReactDOM, which we need to create and render components:

```
npm install --save react react-dom
```

The setup is ready, and we can run Jest against ES6 code and render our components into the DOM, but there is one more thing to do.

We need to install enzyme and enzyme-adapter-react-16.3:

```
npm install enzyme enzyme-adapter-react-16.3
```

After you have installed these packages, you have to add a jest configuration to package.json:

```
"jest": {
  "setupFilesAfterEnv": [
    "<rootDir>/jest/setupTestFramework.js"
  ],
  "collectCoverageFrom": [
```

```
    "src/**/*.{js,jsx}"
  ]
}
```

Then, let's create the `jest/setupTestFramework.js` file:

```
import { configure } from 'enzyme';
import Adapter from 'enzyme-adapter-react-16.3';

configure({ adapter: new Adapter() });
```

Now, let's imagine we have a `Hello` component:

```
import React from 'react';

const Hello = props => (
  <h1 className="Hello">Hello {props.name || 'World'}</h1>
);

export default Hello;
```

In order to test this component, we need to create a file with the same name but adding the `.test` (or `.spec`) suffix in the file. This will be our test file:

```
// Dependencies
import React from 'react';
import { shallow } from 'enzyme';

// Component to test...
import Hello from './index';

describe('Hello', () => {
  const wrapper = shallow(<Hello />);
  const wrapperWithProps = shallow(<Hello name="Carlos" />);

  it('should render Home component', () => {
    expect(wrapper.length).toBe(1);
  });

  it('should render by default Hello World', () => {
    expect(wrapper.text()).toBe('Hello World');
  });

  it('should render the name prop', () => {
    expect(wrapperWithProps.text()).toBe('Hello Carlos');
  });

  it('should has .Home class', () => {
```

```
    expect(wrapper.find('h1').hasClass('Hello')).toBe(true);
  });
});
```

Then, in order to run the `test`, you need to execute the following command:

```
npm test
```

You should see this result:

```
[→  testing git:(master) × npm test

> geolocation@0.1.0 test /Users/czantany/projects/React-Design-Patterns-and-Best-Practices-2nd-Edition/Chapter10/testing
> jest

 PASS   src/components/Hello/index.test.js
  HelloWorld
    ✓ should render Home component (3ms)
    ✓ should render by default Hello World (1ms)
    ✓ should render the name prop
    ✓ should has .Home class (4ms)

Test Suites: 1 passed, 1 total
Tests:       4 passed, 4 total
Snapshots:   0 total
Time:        1.472s, estimated 2s
Ran all test suites.
```

The PASS label means that all tests have been passed successfully; if you failed at least on one test, you would see the FAIL label. Let's change one of our tests to make it fail:

```
it('should render Home component', () => {
  expect(wrapper.length).toBe(0);
});
```

This is the result:

```
[→ testing git:(master) × npm test

> geolocation@0.1.0 test /Users/czantany/projects/React-Design-Patterns-and-Best-Practices-2nd-Edition/Chapter10/testing
> jest

 FAIL  src/components/Hello/index.test.js
  Hello
    × should render Home component (4ms)
    ✓ should render by default Hello World (1ms)
    ✓ should render the name prop
    ✓ should has .Home class (2ms)

  ● Hello › should render Home component

    expect(received).toBe(expected) // Object.is equality

    Expected: 0
    Received: 1

      11 |
      12 |     it('should render Home component', () => {
    > 13 |       expect(wrapper.length).toBe(0);
         |                              ^
      14 |     });
      15 |
      16 |     it('should render by default Hello World', () => {

      at Object.toBe (src/components/Hello/index.test.js:13:30)

Test Suites: 1 failed, 1 total
Tests:       1 failed, 3 passed, 4 total
Snapshots:   0 total
Time:        1.466s, estimated 2s
Ran all test suites.
npm ERR! Test failed.  See above for more details.
```

As you can see, the FAIL label is specified with an X. Also, the expected and received values provide useful information, and you can see which value is expected and which value is being received.

If you want to see the coverage percentage of all your unit tests, you can execute the following command:

```
npm run test:coverage
```

The result is the following:

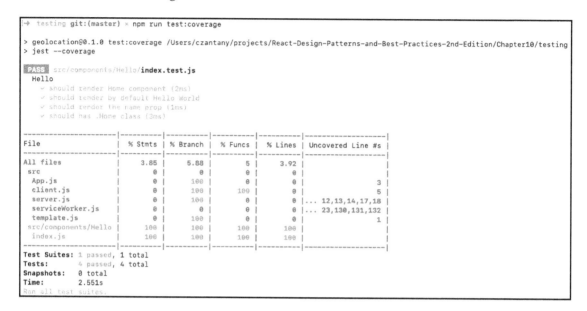

The coverage also generates an HTML version of the result; it creates a directory called `coverage` and inside another called `Icov-report`. If you open the `index.html` file in your browser, you will see the HTML version like this:

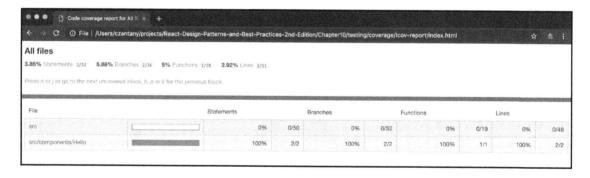

Testing events

The events are very common in any web application and we need to test them as well, so let's learn how to test events. For this, let's create a new `ShowInformation` component:

```
import React, { Component } from 'react';

class ShowInformation extends Component {
  state = {
    name: '',
    age: 0,
    show: false
  };

  handleOnChange = ({ target: { value, name } }) => {
    this.setState({
      [name]: value
    });
  }

  handleShowInformation = () => {
    this.setState({
      show: true
    });
  }

  render() {
    if (this.state.show) {
      return (
        <div className="ShowInformation">
          <h1>Personal Information</h1>

          <div className="personalInformation">
            <p><strong>Name:</strong> {this.state.name}</p>
            <p><strong>Age:</strong> {this.state.age}</p>
          </div>
        </div>
      );
    }
    return (
      <div className="ShowInformation">
        <h1>Personal Information</h1>

        <p><strong>Name:</strong></p>

        <p>
          <input
```

```
                    name="name"
                    type="text"
                    value={this.state.name}
                    onChange={this.handleOnChange}
                />
            </p>

            <p>
              <input
                    name="age"
                    type="number"
                    value={this.state.age}
                    onChange={this.handleOnChange}
                />
            </p>

            <p>
              <button onClick={this.handleShowInformation}>
                Show Information
              </button>
            </p>
          </div>
        );
      }
    }

    export default ShowInformation;
```

You will probably get the following error when you try to run this code:

```
ERROR in ./src/components/ShowInformation/index.js
Module build failed (from ./node_modules/babel-loader/lib/index.js):
SyntaxError: /Users/czantany/projects/React-Design-Patterns-and-Best-Practices-2nd-Edition/Chapter10/events/src/components/ShowInformation/index.js: Support for the experimental syntax 'classProperties' isn't currently enabled (4:9)

  2 |
  3 | class ShowInformation extends Component {
> 4 |   state = {
    |         ^
  5 |     name: '',
  6 |     age: 0,
  7 |     show: false

Add @babel/plugin-proposal-class-properties (https://git.io/vb4SL) to the 'plugins' section of your Babel config to enable transformation.
```

To fix this issue, you need to install the following package:

```
npm install @babel/plugin-proposal-class-properties
```

And then you need to add it to your `.babelrc` file as a plugin:

```
{
  "presets": [
    "@babel/preset-env",
    "@babel/preset-react"
  ],
```

```
    "plugins": ["@babel/plugin-proposal-class-properties"]
  }
```

Now, let's create the test file at `src/components/ShowInformation/index.test.js`:

```javascript
// Dependencies
import React from 'react';
import { shallow } from 'enzyme';

// Component to test...
import ShowInformation from './index';

describe('ShowInformation', () => {
  const wrapper = shallow(<ShowInformation />);

  it('should render ShowInformation component', () => {
    expect(wrapper.length).toBe(1);
  });

  it('should modify the state onChange', () => {
    wrapper.find('input[name="name"]').simulate('change', {
      target: {
        name: 'name',
        value: 'Carlos'
      }
    });

    wrapper.find('input[name="age"]').simulate('change', {
      target: {
        name: 'agé',
        value: 31
      }
    });

    // Getting the values of the name and age states
    expect(wrapper.state('name')).toBe('Carlos');
    expect(wrapper.state('age')).toBe(31);
  });

  it('should show the personal information when user clicks on the
button', () => {
    // Simulating the click event
    wrapper.find('button').simulate('click');

    // The show state should be true...
    expect(wrapper.state('show')).toBe(true);
  });
});
```

If you run the test and it works fine, you should see this:

```
→ events git:(master) × npm test

> geolocation@0.1.0 test /Users/czantany/projects/React-Design-Patterns-and-Best-Practices-2nd-Edition/Chapter10/events
> jest

 PASS  src/components/ShowInformation/index.test.js
  ShowInformation
    ✓ should render ShowInformation component (3ms)
    ✓ should modify the state onChange (8ms)
    ✓ should show the personal information when user clicks on the button (1ms)

Test Suites: 1 passed, 1 total
Tests:       3 passed, 3 total
Snapshots:   0 total
Time:        1.549s, estimated 2s
Ran all test suites.
```

React DevTools

When testing in the console is not enough, and we want to inspect our application while it is running inside the browser, we can use the React Developer Tools.

You can install them as a Chrome extension at the following URL: `https://chrome.google.com/webstore/detail/react-developer-tools/fmkadmapgofadopljbjfkapdkoienihi?hl=en`.

The installation adds a tab to the Chrome DevTools called React, where you can inspect the rendered tree of components and check which properties they have received and what their state is at a particular point in time.

Props and states can be read, and they can be changed in real time to trigger updates in the UI and see the results straightaway.

This is a must-have tool, and in the most recent versions it has a new feature that can be enabled by ticking the **Trace React Updates** checkbox.

When this functionality is enabled, we can use our application and visually see which components get updated when we perform a particular action. The updated components are highlighted with colored rectangles, and it becomes easy to spot possible optimizations.

Redux DevTools

If you are using Redux in your application probably, you want to use Redux DevTools to be able to debug your Redux flow. You can install it at the following URL: `https://chrome.google.com/webstore/detail/redux-devtools/lmhkpmbekcpmknklioeibfkpmmfibljd?hl=es`.

Also, you need to install the `redux-devtools-extension` package:

```
npm install --save-dev redux-devtools-extension
```

Once you have installed the React Developer Tools and Redux DevTools, you will need to configure them.

If you try to use Redux DevTools directly, it won't work; this is because we need to pass the `composeWithDevTools` method into the Redux store; this should be the `configureStore.js` file:

```js
// Dependencies
import { createStore, applyMiddleware } from 'redux';
import thunk from 'redux-thunk';
import { composeWithDevTools } from 'redux-devtools-extension';

// Root Reducer
import rootReducer from '@reducers';

export default function configureStore({
  initialState,
  reducer
}) {
  const middleware = [
    thunk
  ];
  return createStore(
    rootReducer,
    initialState,
    composeWithDevTools(applyMiddleware(...middleware))
  );
}
```

Summary

In this chapter, you learned about the benefits of testing, and the frameworks you can use to cover your React components with tests.

You learned how to implement and test components and events with Enzyme, how to use the Jest coverage, and how to use React and Redux Dev Tools.

It is important to bear in mind common solutions when it comes to testing complex components, such as higher-order components or forms with multiples nested fields.

In the next chapter, you will learn about how to implement routes in your application using React Router.

11
React Router

React, unlike Angular, is a library instead of a framework, meaning specific functionalities (for example, routing `propTypes`) are not part of the React core. Instead, routing is handled by a third-party library called **React Router**.

In this chapter, you will see how to implement React Router in your application, and by the end of the relevant sections, you will be able to add dynamic routes and understand how React Router works.

In this chapter, we will cover the following topics:

- Understanding the differences between the `react-router`, `react-router-dom`, and `react-router-native` packages
- How to install and configure React Router
- Adding the `<Switch>` component
- Adding the `exact` property
- Adding parameters to the routes

Installation and configuration

After you create a new React application using `create-react-app`, the first thing you need to do is to install React Router v4.x, using this command:

```
npm install react-router-dom
```

You probably are confused about why we are installing `react-router-dom` instead of `react-router`. React Router contains all the common components of `react-router-dom` and `react-router-native`. That means that if you are using React for the web, you should use `react-router-dom`, and if you are using React Native, you need to use `react-router-native`. The `react-router-dom` package was created originally to contain version 4, and `react-router` was using version 3. The `react-router-dom` has some improvements over `react-router`. They are listed here:

- The improved `<Link>` component (which renders `<a>`).
- Includes `<BrowserRouter>`, which interacts with the browser `window.history`.
- Includes `<NavLink>`, which is a `<Link>` wrapper that knows whether it's active or not.
- Includes `<HashRouter>`, which uses the hash in the URL to render the components. If you have one static page, you should use this component instead of `<BrowserRouter>`.

Creating our sections

Let's create some sections to test some basic routes. We need to create four stateless components (`About`, `Contact`, `Home`, and `Error404`) and name them as `index.jsx` in their directories.

You can add the following to the `src/components/Home.jsx` component:

```jsx
import React from 'react';

const Home = () => (
  <div className="Home">
    <h1>Home</h1>
  </div>
);

export default Home;
```

The `src/components/About.jsx` component can be created with the following:

```
import React from 'react';

const About = () => (
  <div className="About">
    <h1>About</h1>
  </div>
);

export default About;
```

The following creates the `src/components/Contact.jsx` component:

```
import React from 'react';

const Contact = () => (
  <div className="Contact">
    <h1>Contact</h1>
  </div>
);

export default Contact;
```

Finally, the `src/components/Error404/index.jsx` component is created as follows:

```
import React from 'react';

const Error404 = () => (
  <div className="Error404">
    <h1>Error404</h1>
  </div>
);

export default Error404;
```

After we have created all the stateless components, we need to modify our `index.js` file to import our route file, which we will create in the next step:

```
// Dependencies
import React from 'react';
import { render } from 'react-dom';
import { BrowserRouter as Router } from 'react-router-dom';

// Styles
import './index.css';

// Routes
```

```
import AppRoutes from './routes';

render(
  <Router>
    <AppRoutes />
  </Router>,
  document.getElementById('root')
);
```

Now, we need to create the route file, where we will render our `Home` component when the user accesses to the root path (/):

```
// Dependencies
import React from 'react';
import { Route } from 'react-router-dom';

// Components
import App from './components/App';
import Home from './components/Home';

const AppRoutes = () => (
  <App>
    <Route path="/" component={Home} />
  </App>
);

export default AppRoutes;
```

After that, we need to modify our `App.jsx` file to render the route components as children:

```
import React from 'react';
import { element } from 'prop-types';
import './App.css';

const App = ({ children }) => (
  <div className="App">
    {children}
  </div>
);

App.propTypes = {
  children: element
};

export default App;
```

If you run the application, you will see the `Home` component in the root (/):

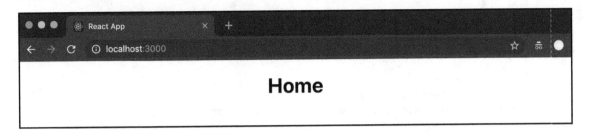

Now, let's add `Error404` when the user tries to access any other route:

```
// Dependencies
import React from 'react';
import { Route } from 'react-router-dom';

// Components
import App from './components/App';
import Home from './components/Home';
import Error404 from './components/Error404';

const AppRoutes = () => (
  <App>
    <Route path="/" component={Home} />
    <Route component={Error404} />
  </App>
);

export default AppRoutes;
```

Let's run the application again. You will see that both the `Home` and `Error404` components are being rendered:

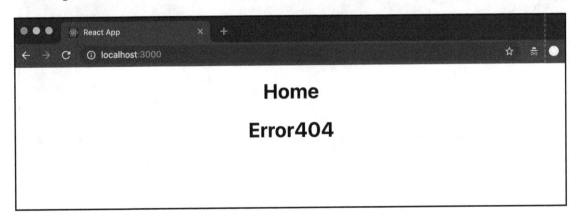

You are probably wondering why this is happening. It's because we need to use the `<Switch>` component to execute just one component if it matches the path. For this, we need to import the `Switch` component and add it as a wrapper for our routes:

```
// Dependencies
import React from 'react';
import { Route, Switch } from 'react-router-dom';

// Components
import App from './components/App';
import Home from './components/Home';
import Error404 from './components/Error404';

const AppRoutes = () => (
  <App>
    <Switch>
      <Route path="/" component={Home} />
      <Route component={Error404} />
    </Switch>
  </App>
);

export default AppRoutes;
```

Now, if you got to the root (/), you will see the `Home` component and `Error404` won't be executed at the same time (it will just be executed in the `Home` component), but if we go to `/somefakeurl`, we will see that the `Home` component is executed as well, and this is a problem:

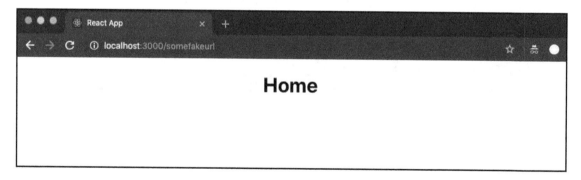

To fix the problem, we need to add the `exact` prop in the route that we want to match. The problem is that `/somefakeurl` will match our root path (`/`), but if we want to be very specific about the paths, we need to add the `exact` prop to our `Home` route:

```
const AppRoutes = () => (
  <App>
    <Switch>
      <Route path="/" component={Home} exact />
      <Route component={Error404} />
    </Switch>
  </App>
);
```

Now, if you go to `/somefakeurl` one more time, you will be able to see the **Error404** component:

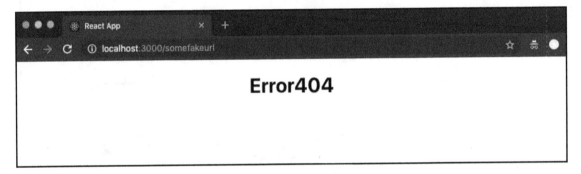

Now, we can add our other components (`About` and `Contact`):

```
// Dependencies
import React from 'react';
import { Route, Switch } from 'react-router-dom';

// Components
import App from './components/App';
import About from './components/About';
import Contact from './components/Contact';
import Home from './components/Home';
import Error404 from './components/Error404';

const AppRoutes = () => (
  <App>
    <Switch>
      <Route path="/" component={Home} exact />
      <Route path="/about" component={About} exact />
      <Route path="/contact" component={Contact} exact />
```

```
            <Route component={Error404} />
        </Switch>
    </App>
);

export default AppRoutes;
```

Now, you can visit /about:

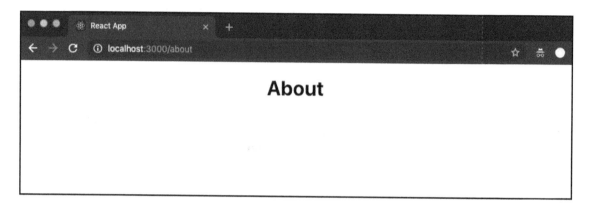

Alternatively, you can now visit /contact:

Adding parameters to the routes

So far, you have learned how to use React Router for basic routes (one-level routes). Now, I will show you how to add some parameters to the routes and get them into our components.

For this example, we will create a Contacts component to display a list of contacts when we visit /contacts route, but we will show the contact information (name, phone, and email) when the user visits /contacts/:contactId.

The first thing we need to do is to create our `Contacts` component. Let's use this skeleton:

```javascript
import React, { Component } from 'react';
import './Contacts.css';

class Contacts extends Component {
  // For now we are going to add our contacts to our
  // local state, but normally this should come
  // from some service.
  state = {
    contacts: [
      {
        id: 1,
        name: 'Carlos Santana',
        email: 'carlos.santana@dev.education',
        phone: '415-307-3112'
      },
      {
        id: 2,
        name: 'John Smith',
        email: 'john.smith@dev.education',
        phone: '223-344-5122'
      },
      {
        id: 3,
        name: 'Alexis Nelson',
        email: 'alexis.nelson@dev.education',
        phone: '664-291-4477'
      }
    ]
  };

  render() {
    return (
      <div className="Contacts">
        <h1>Contacts</h1>
      </div>
    );
  }
}

export default Contacts;
```

Let's use these CSS styles:

```css
.Contacts ul {
  list-style: none;
  margin: 0;
```

```
  margin-bottom: 20px;
  padding: 0;
}

.Contacts ul li {
  padding: 10px;
}

.Contacts a {
  color: #555;
  text-decoration: none;
}

.Contacts a:hover {
  color: #ccc;
  text-decoration: none;
}
```

Once you have created the `Contacts` component, you need to import it into our route file:

```
// Dependencies
import React from 'react';
import { Route, Switch } from 'react-router-dom';

// Components
import App from './components/App';
import About from './components/About';
import Contact from './components/Contact';
import Home from './components/Home';
import Error404 from './components/Error404';
import Contacts from './components/Contacts';

const AppRoutes = () => (
  <App>
    <Switch>
      <Route path="/" component={Home} exact />
      <Route path="/about" component={About} exact />
      <Route path="/contact" component={Contact} exact />
      <Route path="/contacts" component={Contacts} exact />
      <Route component={Error404} />
    </Switch>
  </App>
);

export default AppRoutes;
```

Now, you will be able to see the **Contacts** component if you go to the /contacts URL:

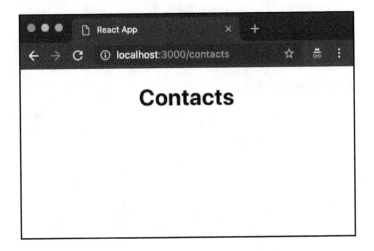

Now that the Contacts component is connected to React Router, let's render our contacts as a list:

```
import React, { Component } from 'react';
import { Link } from 'react-router-dom';
import './Contacts.css';

class Contacts extends Component {
  // For now we are going to add our contacts to our
  // local state, but normally this should come
  // from some service.
  state = {
    contacts: [
      {
        id: 1,
        name: 'Carlos Santana',
        email: 'carlos.santana@dev.education',
        phone: '415-307-3112'
      },
      {
        id: 2,
        name: 'John Smith',
        email: 'john.smith@dev.education',
        phone: '223-344-5122'
      },
      {
        id: 3,
        name: 'Alexis Nelson',
        email: 'alexis.nelson@dev.education',
```

```
        phone: '664-291-4477'
      }
    ]
  };

  renderContacts = contacts => (
    <ul>
      {contacts.map((contact, key) => (
        <li key={key}>
          <Link to={`/contacts/${contact.id}`}>{contact.name}</Link>
        </li>
      ))}
    </ul>
  );

  render() {
    const { contacts } = this.state;

    return (
      <div className="Contacts">
        <h1>Contacts</h1>

        {this.renderContacts(contacts)}
      </div>
    );
  }
}

export default Contacts;
```

As you can see, we are using the `<Link>` component, which will generate an `<a>` tag that points to `/contacts/contact.id`, and this is because we will add a new nested route into our route file to match the ID of the contact:

```
const AppRoutes = () => (
  <App>
    <Switch>
      <Route path="/" component={Home} exact />
      <Route path="/about" component={About} exact />
      <Route path="/contact" component={Contact} exact />
      <Route path="/contacts" component={Contacts} exact />
      <Route path="/contacts/:contactId" component={Contacts} exact />
      <Route component={Error404} />
    </Switch>
  </App>
);
```

React Router has a special prop called `match`, which is an object that contains all the data related to the route, and if we have parameters, we will be able to see them in the `match` object:

```
import React, { Component } from 'react';
import { Link } from 'react-router-dom';
import './Contacts.css';

class Contacts extends Component {
  // For now we are going to add our contacts to our
  // local state, but normally this should come
  // from some service.
  state = {
    contacts: [
      {
        id: 1,
        name: 'Carlos Santana',
        email: 'carlos.santana@dev.education',
        phone: '415-307-3112'
      },
      {
        id: 2,
        name: 'John Smith',
        email: 'john.smith@dev.education',
        phone: '223-344-5122'
      },
      {
        id: 3,
        name: 'Alexis Nelson',
        email: 'alexis.nelson@dev.education',
        phone: '664-291-4477'
      }
    ]
  };

  renderSingleContact = ({ name, email, phone }) => (
    <>
      <h2>{name}</h2>
      <p>{email}</p>
      <p>{phone}</p>
    </>
  )

  renderContacts = () => (
    <ul>
      {this.state.contacts.map((contact, key) => (
        <li key={key}>
          <Link to={`/contacts/${contact.id}`}>{contact.name}</Link>
```

```
        </li>
      ))}
    </ul>
  );

  render() {
    // Let's see what contains the props object.
    console.log(this.props);

    // We got the noteId param from match object.
    const { match: { params: { contactId } } } = this.props;
    const { contacts } = this.state;

    // By default our selectedNote is false
    let selectedContact = false;

    if (contactId > 0) {
      // If the contact id is higher than 0 then we filter it from our
      // contacts array.
      selectedContact = contacts.filter(
        contact => contact.id === Number(contactId)
      )[0];
    }

    return (
      <div className="Contacts">
        <h1>Contacts</h1>

        {/* We render our selectedContact or all the contacts */}
        {selectedContact
          ? this.renderSingleContact(selectedContact)
          : this.renderContacts()}
      </div>
    );
  }
}

export default Contacts;
```

The `match` prop looks like this:

```
▼ {match: {…}, location: {…}, history: {…}, staticContext: undefined} ⓘ
  ▶ history: {length: 3, action: "POP", location: {…}, createHref: ƒ, push: ƒ, …}
  ▶ location: {pathname: "/contacts/2", search: "", hash: "", state: undefined, key: "3c5xbh"}
  ▼ match:
      isExact: true
    ▶ params: {contactId: "2"}
      path: "/contacts/:contactId"
      url: "/contacts/2"
    ▶ __proto__: Object
    staticContext: undefined
  ▶ __proto__: Object
```

As you can see, the `match` props contains a lot of useful information. React Router also includes the object's history and location. Also, we can get all the parameters we pass within the routes; in this case, we are receiving the `contactId` parameter.

If you run the application again, you should see your contacts like this:

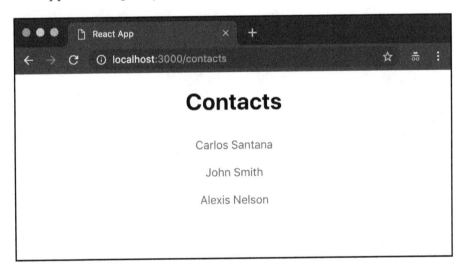

If you click on **John Smith** (whose `contactId` is 2), you will see the contact information:

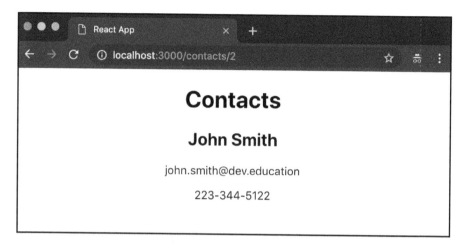

After this, you can add a navbar in the `App` component to access to all the routes:

```
import React from 'react';
import { element } from 'prop-types';
import { Link } from 'react-router-dom';
import './App.css';

const App = ({ children }) => (
  <div className="App">
    <ul className="menu">
      <li><Link to="/">Home</Link></li>
      <li><Link to="/about">About</Link></li>
      <li><Link to="/contacts">Contacts</Link></li>
      <li><Link to="/contact">Contact</Link></li>
    </ul>

    {children}
  </div>
);

App.propTypes = {
  children: element
};

export default App;
```

Now, let's modify our `App` styles:

```css
.App {
  text-align: center;
}

.App ul.menu {
  margin: 50px;
  padding: 0;
  list-style: none;
}

.App ul.menu li {
  display: inline-block;
  padding: 0 10px;
}

.App ul.menu li a {
  color: #333;
  text-decoration: none;
}

.App ul.menu li a:hover {
  color: #ccc;
}
```

Finally, you will see something like this:

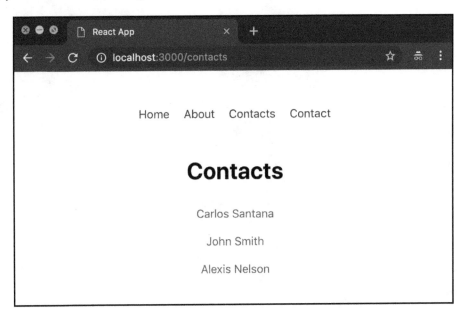

Summary

The journey through React Router has come to an end, and now you know how to install and configure React Router, how to create basic routes and how to add parameters to the nested routes.

In the next chapter, we will see how to avoid some of the most common anti-patterns in React.

Anti-Patterns to be Avoided

12

In this book, you've learned how to apply best practices when writing a React application. In the first few chapters, we revisited the basic concepts to build a solid understanding, and then we took a leap into more advanced techniques in the following chapters.

You should now be able to build reusable components, make components communicate with each other, and optimize an application tree to get the best performance. However, developers make mistakes, and this chapter is all about the common anti-patterns we should avoid when using React.

Looking at common errors will help you to avoid them and will aid your understanding of how React works and how to build applications in the React way. For each problem, we will see an example that shows how to reproduce and solve it.

In this chapter, we will cover the following topics:

- Initializing the state using properties
- Mutating the state
- Using indexes as a key
- Spreading properties on DOM elements

Initializing the state using properties

In this section, we will see how initializing the state using properties received from the parent is usually an anti-pattern. I have used the word usually because, as we will see, once we have it clear in our mind what the problems with this approach are, we might still decide to use it.

One of the best ways to learn something is by looking at the code, so we will start by creating a simple component with a + button to increment a counter.

The component is implemented using a `class`, as shown in the following snippet of code:

```
class Counter extends Component
```

It has a `constructor`, where we initialize the `state` using the `count` property, and we bind the event handler:

```
constructor(props) {
  super(props);
  this.state = {
    count: props.count
  };
  this.handleClick = this.handleClick.bind(this);
}
```

The implementation of the click handler is pretty straightforward—we just add 1 to the current count value and store the resulting value back into the `state`:

```
handleClick() {
  this.setState({
    count: this.state.count + 1
  });
}
```

Finally, in the `render` method, we describe the output, which is composed of the current value of the `count`, and the button to increment it:

```
render() {
  return (
    <div>
      {this.state.count}
      <button onClick={this.handleClick}>+</button>
    </div>
  );
}
```

Now, let's render this component, passing 1 as the `count` property:

```
<Counter count={1} />
```

It works as expected—each click on the + button increments the current value. So, what's the problem?

There are two main errors, which are outlined as follows:

- We have a duplicated source of truth
- If the `count` property passes to the component changes, the state does not get updated

If we inspect the `Counter` element using the React DevTools, we notice that `Props` and `State` hold a similar value:

```
<Counter>
Props
   count: 1
State
   count: 1
```

This makes it unclear which is the current and trustworthy value to use inside the component, and to display to the user.

Even worse, clicking **+** once makes the values diverge. An example of this divergence is shown in the following code:

```
<Counter>
Props
   count: 1
State
   count: 2
```

At this point, we can assume that the second value represents the current count, but this is not explicit and can lead to unexpected behaviors, or wrong values down in the tree.

The second problem centers on how the class is created and instantiated by React. The `constructor` function of the class gets called only once when the component is created.

In our `Counter` component, we read the value of the `count` property and we store it into the state. If the value of that property changes during the life cycle of the application (let's say, it becomes `10`), the `Counter` component will never use the new value, because it has already been initialized. This puts the component into an inconsistent state, which is not optimal and hard to debug.

What if we really want to use the prop's value to initialize the component, and we know for sure that the value does not change in the future?

In that case, it's a best practice to make it explicit and give the property a name that makes your intentions clear, such as `initialCount`. For example, let's say we change the `constructor` of the `Counter` component in the following way:

```
constructor(props) {
  super(props);
  this.state = {
    count: props.initialCount
  };
  this.handleClick = this.handleClick.bind(this);
}
```

If we use it like so, it is clear that the parent only has a way to initialize the counter, but any future values of the `initialCount` property will be ignored:

```
<Counter initialCount={1} />
```

Mutating the state

React comes with a very clear and straightforward API to mutate the internal state of components. Using the `setState` function, we can tell the library how we want the state to be changed. As soon as the state is updated, React re-renders the component, and we can access the new state through the `this.state` property—that's it.

Sometimes, however, we could make the mistake of mutating the state object directly, leading to dangerous consequences for the component's consistency and performance.

First of all, if we mutate the state without using `setState`, two bad things can happen:

- The state changes without making the component re-render
- Whenever `setState` gets called in the future, the mutated state gets applied

If we go back to the counter example and change the click handler to the following, we can see that clicking + does not affect the rendered value in the browser. However, if we look into the component using the React DevTools, the value of the state is correctly updated. This is an inconsistent state and we surely do not want it in our applications:

```
handleClick() {
  this.state.count++;
}
```

If you are doing it by mistake, you can easily fix it by using the `setState` API; but if you find yourself doing it on purpose, for example, to avoid the component re-rendering, you had better re-think the structure of your components.

As we saw in `Chapter 3`, *Create Truly Reusable Components*, one of the reasons why we use the state object is to store values that are needed inside the `render` method.

The second problem that occurs when the state is mutated directly is that, whenever `setState` is called in any other part of the component, the mutated state gets applied unexpectedly.

For example, if we keep on working on the `Counter` component and we add the following button, which updates the state creating a new `foo` property, we can see that clicking the + does not have any visible effect. However, as soon as we click **Update**, the count value in the browser makes a jump, displaying the current hidden state count value:

```
<button onClick={() => this.setState({ foo: 'bar' })}>
  Update
</button>
```

This uncontrolled behavior is something we want to avoid as well.

Last but not least, mutating the state has a severe impact on performance. To show this behavior, we are going to create a new component, similar to the list we used in `Chapter 9`, *Improve the Performance of Your Applications*, when we learned how to use `keys` and `PureComponent`.

Changing the value of the state has a negative impact when using `PureComponent`. To understand the problem, we are going to create the following `List`:

```
class List extends PureComponent
```

Inside its `constructor`, we initialize the list with two items and bind the event handler:

```
constructor(props) {
  super(props);
  this.state = {
    items: ['foo', 'bar']
  };
  this.handleClick = this.handleClick.bind(this);
}
```

The click handler is pretty simple—it just pushes a new element into the array (we will see later why that is wrong) and then it sets the array back into the `state`:

```
handleClick() {
  this.state.items.push('baz');
  this.setState({
    items: this.state.items
  });
}
```

Finally, we use the `render` method to display the current length of the list and the button that triggers the handler:

```
render() {
  return (
    <div>
      {this.state.items.length}
      <button onClick={this.handleClick}>+</button>
    </div>
  );
}
```

Looking at the code, we might think that there are no issues; however, if we run the component inside the browser, we'll notice that the value doesn't get updated when we click **+**.

Even in this case, by checking the state of the component using the React DevTool, we can see how the state has been updated internally, without causing a re-render:

```
<List>
State
  items: Array[3]
    0: "foo"
    1: "bar"
    2: "baz"
```

The reason why we experience this inconsistency is that we mutated the array instead of providing a new value.

Pushing a new item into the array, in fact, does not create a new array.
The `PureComponent` decides if the component should be updated by checking whether the values of its properties and state are changed but, in this case, we passed the same array again. This can be counter-intuitive in the beginning, especially if you are not used to working with immutable data structures.

The point here is to always set a new value of the `state` property, which means we can easily fix the issue by changing the click handler of the `List` component in the following way:

```
handleClick() {
  this.setState({
    items: this.state.items.concat('baz')
  });
}
```

The `concat` function of the array returns a new array, thus appending the new item to the previous ones. In this way, `PureComponent` finds a new array in the state and re-renders itself correctly.

Using indexes as a key

In Chapter 9, *Improve the Performance of Your Applications*, which talks about performance and the reconciler, we saw how we can help React figure out the shortest path to update the DOM by using the `key` prop.

The key property uniquely identifies an element in the DOM, and React uses it to check if the element is new, or if it has to be updated when the component properties or state change.

Using keys is always a good idea and, if you don't do it, React gives a warning in the console (in development mode). However, it is not simply a matter of using a key; sometimes, the value that we decide to use as a key can make the difference. In fact, using the wrong key can give us unexpected behaviors in some instances. In this section, we will see one of those instances.

Let's, again, create a `List` component, as shown here:

```
class List extends PureComponent
```

In the `constructor`, the items are initialized and the handlers are bound to the component:

```
constructor(props) {
  super(props);
  this.state = {
    items: ['foo', 'bar']
  };
  this.handleClick = this.handleClick.bind(this);
}
```

The implementation of the click handler is slightly different from the previous one, because in this case, we need to insert a new item at the top of the list:

```
handleClick() {
  const items = this.state.items.slice();
  items.unshift('baz');
  this.setState({
    items
  });
}
```

Finally, in the render method, we show the list and the + button to add the **baz** item at the top of the list:

```
render() {
  return (
    <div>
      <ul>
        {this.state.items.map((item, index) => (
          <li key={index}>{item}</li>
        ))}
      </ul>

      <button onClick={this.handleClick}>+</button>
    </div>
  );
}
```

If you run the component inside the browser, you will not see any problems; clicking the + button inserts a new item at the top of the list. But let's do an experiment.

Let's change the render method in the following way, adding an input field near each item. We then use an input field because we can edit its content, making it easier to figure out the problem:

```
render() {
  return (
    <div>
      <ul>
        {this.state.items.map((item, index) => (
          <li key={index}>
            {item}
            <input type="text" />
          </li>
        ))}
      </ul>
      <button onClick={this.handleClick}>+</button>
```

```
        </div>
    );
}
```

If we run this component again in the browser, copy the values of the items in the input fields, and then click **+**, we will get unexpected behavior.

As shown in the following screenshot, the items shift down while the input elements remain in the same position, in such a way that their value does not match the value of the items anymore:

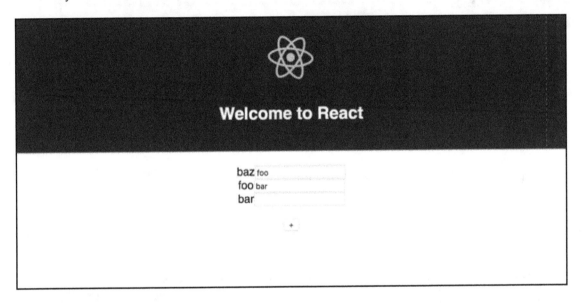

Running the component, clicking **+**, and checking the console should give us all the answers we need.

What we can see is that React, instead of inserting the new element on top, swaps the text of the two existing elements, and inserts the last item at the bottom as if it was new. The reason it does that is because we are using the index of the map function as the key.

In fact, the index always starts from 0, even if we push a new item to the top of the list, so React thinks that we changed the values of the existing two, and added a new element at index 2. The behavior is the same as it would have been without using the key property at all.

This is a very common pattern because, we may think that providing any key is always the best solution, but it is not like that at all. The key has to be unique and stable, identifying one, and only one, item.

To solve this problem we can, for example, use the value of the item if we expect it not to be repeated within the list, or create a unique identifier.

Spreading properties on DOM elements

There is a common practice that has recently been described as an anti-pattern by Dan Abramov; it also triggers a warning in the console when you do it in your React application.

It is a technique that is widely used in the community and I have personally seen it multiple times in real-world projects. We usually spread the properties to the elements to avoid writing every single one manually, which is shown as follows:

```
<Component {...props} />
```

This works very well and it gets transpiled into the following code by Babel:

```
React.createElement(Component, props);
```

However, when we spread properties into a DOM element, we run the risk of adding unknown HTML attributes, which is bad practice.

The problem is not related only to the spread operator; passing non-standard properties one by one leads to the same issues and warnings. Since the spread operator hides the single properties we are spreading, it is even harder to figure out what we are passing to the element.

To see the warning in the console, a basic operation we can do is render the following component:

```
const Spread = () => <div foo="bar" />;
```

The message we get looks like the following because the foo property is not valid for a div element:

Unknown prop `foo` on <div> tag. Remove this prop from the element

In this case, as we said, it is easy to figure out which attribute we are passing and remove it but, if we use the spread operator, as in the following example, we cannot control which properties are passed from the parent:

```
const Spread = props => <div {...props} />;
```

If we use the component in the following way, there are no issues:

```
<Spread className="foo" />
```

This, however, is not the case if we do something like the following. React complains because we are applying a non-standard attribute to the DOM element:

```
<Spread foo="bar" className="baz" />
```

One solution we can use to solve this problem is create a property called domProps that we can spread safely to the component because we are explicitly saying that it contains valid DOM properties.

For example, we can change the Spread component in the following way:

```
const Spread = props => <div {...props.domProps} />;
```

We can then use it as follows:

```
<Spread foo="bar" domProps={{ className: 'baz' }} />
```

As we have seen many times with React, it's always good practice to be explicit.

Summary

Knowing all the best practices is always a good thing, but sometimes being aware of anti-patterns helps us avoid taking the wrong path. Most importantly, learning the reasons why some techniques are considered bad practice helps us understand how React works, and how we can use it effectively.

In this chapter, we covered four different ways of using components that can harm the performance and behavior of our web applications.

For each one of those, we used an example to reproduce the problem and supplied the changes to apply, in order to fix the issue.

We learned why using properties to initialize the state can result in inconsistencies between the state and the properties, and we discovered why mutating the state is bad for performance. We also saw how using the wrong key attribute can produce bad effects on the reconciliation algorithm. Finally, we learned why spreading non-standard properties to DOM elements is considered an anti-pattern.

Deploying to Production

13

Now that you have completed your first React application, it is time to learn how to deploy it to the world. For this purpose, we will use the cloud service called Digital Ocean.

In this chapter, you will learn how to deploy your React application using Node.js and Nginx on an Ubuntu server from Digital Ocean.

In this chapter, we will cover the following topics:

- Creating a Digital Ocean Droplet and configuring it
- Deploying our React application to production
- Configuring nginx, PM2, and a domain
- Implementing CircleCI for Continuous Integration

Creating our first Digital Ocean Droplet

I have used Digital Ocean for the last four years and I can say that it is one of the best cloud services I have tried, not just because of the cheap costs, but also because it is super easy and fast to configure, and the community has a lot of updated documentation to fix most of the common issues related to the server configuration.

At this point, you will need to invest some money to get this service. I will show you the cheapest way to do this, and if in the future you want to increase the power of your Droplets, you will be able to increase the capacity without redoing the configuration. The lowest price for the very basic Droplet is $5.00 per month ($0.007 per hour).

The latest LTS version of Ubuntu is 18.04; you will need to know some basic Linux commands to be able to configure your Droplet. If you're a beginner using Linux, don't worry—I'll try to show you each step in a very easy way.

Signing up to Digital Ocean

If you don't have a Digital Ocean account, you can sign up at `https://cloud.digitalocean.com/registrations/new`.

You can sign up with your Google account, or by registering manually. Once you register with Google, you will see the billing info view, as follows:

You can pay with your credit card or by using PayPal. Once you configured your payment information, Digital Ocean will ask you for some information about your project so that it can configure your Droplet faster:

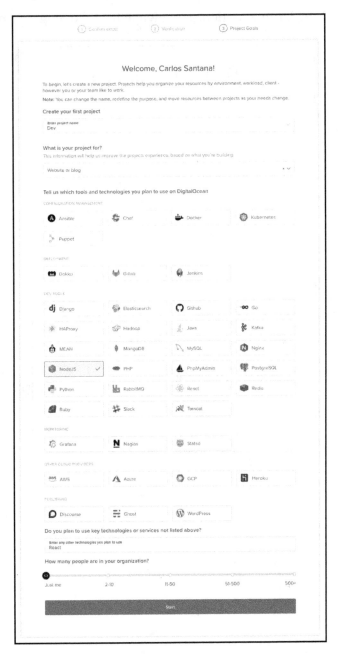

Creating our first Droplet

Nevertheless, we will create a new Droplet from scratch; follow these steps to do so:

1. Select the **New Droplet** option, as shown in the following screenshot:

2. Choose **Ubuntu 18.04.2 x64**, as follows:

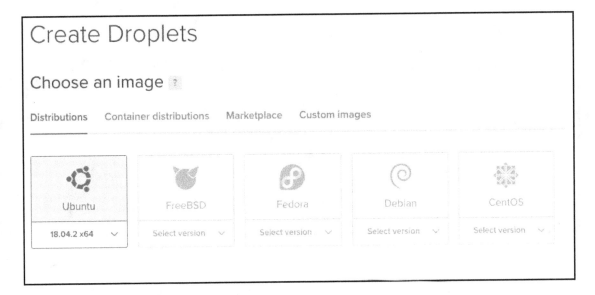

3. Then, choose the **Standard** plan, as shown here:

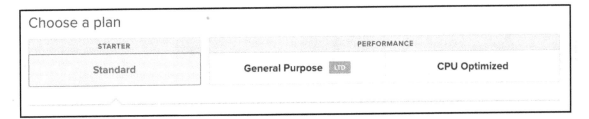

4. You can then choose **$5/mo** in the payment option:

5. Select a region. In this case, we will select the **San Francisco** region:

6. Add the name of your Droplet and then click on the **Create** button, as follows:

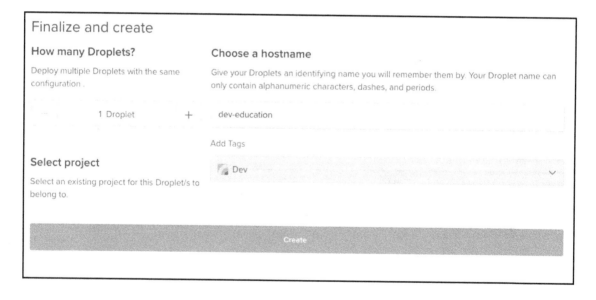

7. It will take around 30 seconds to create your Droplet. Once it has been created, you will be able to see it:

8. Following its creation, you should get an email with your Droplet credentials:

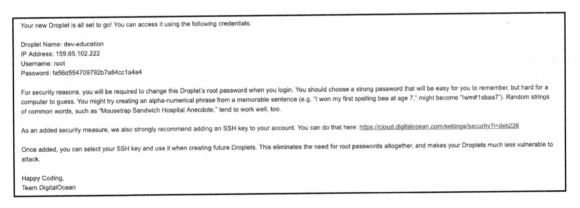

9. Now, in your Terminal, you can access to the droplet by using the following command:

```
ssh root@THE_DROPLET_IP
```

10. The first time you log in, you will get a message to add this IP to your known hosts. Then, you will be asked for your Droplet password (the one you got in your email), and then you need to define a new password:

```
Last login: Fri Mar  8 10:41:33 on console
⇒ ~ ssh root@159.65.102.222
The authenticity of host '159.65.102.222 (159.65.102.222)' can't be established.
ECDSA key fingerprint is SHA256:/DBwYKX88DDJlyYvtOPy1LKz+ODR0Q0gLsMjNbMvllA.
Are you sure you want to continue connecting (yes/no)? yes
Warning: Permanently added '159.65.102.222' (ECDSA) to the list of known hosts.
root@159.65.102.222's password:
You are required to change your password immediately (root enforced)
Welcome to Ubuntu 18.04.2 LTS (GNU/Linux 4.15.0-45-generic x86_64)

 * Documentation:  https://help.ubuntu.com
 * Management:     https://landscape.canonical.com
 * Support:        https://ubuntu.com/advantage

  System information as of Sun Mar 10 08:25:27 UTC 2019

  System load:  0.0                Processes:            83
  Usage of /:   5.0% of 24.06GB    Users logged in:      0
  Memory usage: 12%                IP address for eth0:  159.65.102.222
  Swap usage:   0%

  Get cloud support with Ubuntu Advantage Cloud Guest:
    http://www.ubuntu.com/business/services/cloud

48 packages can be updated.
30 updates are security updates.



The programs included with the Ubuntu system are free software;
the exact distribution terms for each program are described in the
individual files in /usr/share/doc/*/copyright.

Ubuntu comes with ABSOLUTELY NO WARRANTY, to the extent permitted by
applicable law.

Changing password for root.
(current) UNIX password:
```

Installing Node.js

Now that you're connected to your droplet, let's configure it. First, we need to install the latest version of Node.js using a PPA. The current version of Node as at the time of writing this book is 11.11.x. Follow these given steps to install Node.js:

1. If, when you are reading this paragraph, Node has a new version, change the version in the `setup_11.x` command:

```
cd ~
curl -sL https://deb.nodesource.com/setup_11.x -o nodesource_setup.sh
```

2. Once you get the `nodesource_setup.sh` file, run the following command:

```
sudo bash nodesource_setup.sh
```

3. Then, install Node by running the following command:

```
sudo apt install nodejs -y
```

4. If everything works fine, verify the installed version of Node and npm with the following commands:

```
node -v
v11.11.0
npm -v
6.7.0
```

Configuring Git and GitHub

I created a special repository for helping you to deploy your first React application to production (`https://github.com/D3vEducation/production`).

In your Droplet, you need to clone this Git repository or your own repository if you have your React application ready to be deployed. The production repository is public, but normally you will use a private repository; in this case, you need to add the SSH key of your Droplet to your GitHub account. To create this key, follow these steps:

1. Run the `ssh-keygen` command and then press *Enter* three times without writing any passphrase:

```
root@dev-education:~# ssh-keygen
Generating public/private rsa key pair.
Enter file in which to save the key (/root/.ssh/id_rsa):
Enter passphrase (empty for no passphrase):
Enter same passphrase again:
Your identification has been saved in /root/.ssh/id_rsa.
Your public key has been saved in /root/.ssh/id_rsa.pub.
The key fingerprint is:
SHA256:S89wOBZXesI0o0P1S/0gDXoMFWkQahqXpENo1DLMa8g root@dev-education
The key's randomart image is:
+---[RSA 2048]----+
|    +.o. o.0+=o   |
|     B..+ * Xo+   |
|   . o ++ O *.B + |
|    E o  * = = o o |
|      .  . S . .   .|
|         o B       |
|          . o      |
|                   |
|                   |
+----[SHA256]-----+
```

If you left your Terminal inactive for more than five minutes, your Droplet connection will probably be closed, and you will need to connect again.

2. Once you have created your droplet SSH key, you can see it by running the following command:

```
vi /root/.ssh/id_rsa.pub
```

You will see something like this:

```
ssh-rsa AAAAB3NzaC1yc2EAAAADAQABAAABAQC7IZfQe4TKFDcvvJfDkyLQqFj09mK7sawMDX
BeB3h8t5j9b5LijsIXrZ2nvwSQteDrfYzokjQhUjO3eopHoQc8l0y36ry+omyvurX3qg5IhfPw
BHbbP/yMoAASV+vyjmgT+dRee8NCGcQqFnw9pswVoVJlZVx2L+OHk9o3z4Gm/ZG6pb+dXkAUgd
5Q+kgSRmtwnzGul+gwKyuUTjryfAVkRLVv2ebQ7rO6f8ESP8xgFJQxSUb+7mxc1y5NDC8L0fJx
lsfdSN8+WKpr1xH4MSgkaYM1pVSznsaYW10NfgVZp4XrrleB8+gi/bmsW6b4tkYJ+Z1puylYx1
fUnYZMm/b9 root@dev-education
```

3. Copy your SSH key and then visit your GitHub account. Go to **Settings** I **SSH and GPC Keys** (`https://github.com/settings/ssh/new`). Then, paste your key in the text area and add your title to the key:

SSH keys / **Add new**

Title

Dev Education Droplet

Key

ssh-rsa
AAAAB3NzaC1yc2EAAAADAQABAAABAQC7IZfQe4TKFDcvvJfDkyLQqFj09mK7sawMDXBeB3h8t5j9b5LijsIXrZ2
nvwSQteDrfYzokjQhUjO3eopHoQc8l0y36ry+omyvurX3qg5IhfPwBHbbP/yMoAASV+vyjmgT+dRee8NCGcQqFn
w9pswVoVJlZVx2L+OHk9o3z4Gm/ZG6pb+dXkAUgd5Q+kgSRmtwnzGul+gwKyuUTjryfAVkRLVv2ebQ7rO6f8ES
P8xgFJQxSUb+7mxc1y5NDC8L0fJxlsfdSN8+WKpr1xH4MSgkaYM1pVSznsaYW10NfgVZp4XrrleB8+gi/bmsW6b
4tkYJ+Z1puylYx1fUnYZMm/b9 root@dev-education

Add SSH key

4. Once you click on the **Add SSH key** button, you will see your SSH key, like so:

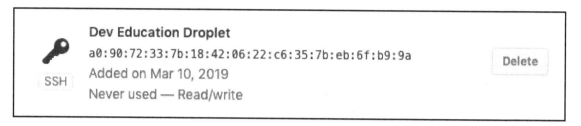

5. Now you can clone our repository (or yours) using the following command:

```
git clone git@github.com:D3vEducation/production.git
```

6. Once you clone it for the first time, you will get a message, asking you to allow the RSA key fingerprint:

```
root@dev-education:~# git clone git@github.com:D3vEducation/production.git
Cloning into 'production'...
The authenticity of host 'github.com (192.30.255.112)' can't be establishe
d.
RSA key fingerprint is SHA256:nThbg6kXUpJWGl7E1IGOCspRomTxdCARLviKw6E5SY8.
Are you sure you want to continue connecting (yes/no)?
```

7. You have to write yes and then hit *Enter* to be able to clone it:

```
Warning: Permanently added 'github.com,192.30.255.112' (RSA) to the list of known hosts.
remote: Enumerating objects: 18, done.
remote: Counting objects: 100% (18/18), done.
remote: Compressing objects: 100% (18/18), done.
remote: Total 18 (delta 0), reused 18 (delta 0), pack-reused 0
Receiving objects: 100% (18/18), 146.84 KiB | 3.50 MiB/s, done.
```

8. Then, you have to go to the production directory and install the npm packages:

```
cd production
npm install
```

9. If you want to test the application, just run the `start` script:

```
npm start
```

10. Then open your browser and go to your droplet IP and add the port number. In my case, it is `http://159.65.102.222:3000`:

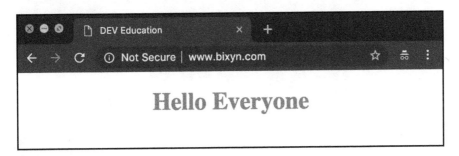

11. This will run the project in development mode. If you want to run the production mode, then you can run the following command:

```
npm run start:production
```

You should see PM2 running, as shown in the following screenshot:

```
^Croot@dev-education:~/production# npm run start:production

> production@1.0.0 start:production /root/production
> npm run stop && npm run build && NODE_ENV=production pm2 start --interpreter babel-node src/backend

> production@1.0.0 stop /root/production
> pm2 kill


            -------------

__/\\\\\\\\\\\\___/\\_____/\\\___/\\\\\\\\\_____
_\/\\\///////\\\_\/\\\_____/\\\\_/\\\///////\\\__
 _\/\\_____\/\\\_\/\\\/\\\___/\\\/\\\_\///_____\//\\\__
  _\/\\\\\\\\\\\/__\/\\\//\\\/\\\/\\_____/\\\/___
   _\/\\\//////////____\/\\\\////\\\/\\_____/\\\//_____
    _\/\\_____\/\\\___\///___\/\\\____/\\\//_____
     _\/\\_____\/\\_____\/\\\__/\\\/_____
      _\/\\_____\/\\_____\/\\\_/\\\\\\\\\\\\\\\_
       _\///_____\///_____\///_\///////////////__


            Runtime Edition

    PM2 is a Production Process Manager for Node.js applications
                 with a built-in Load Balancer.

            Start and Daemonize any application:
            $ pm2 start app.js

            Load Balance 4 instances of api.js:
            $ pm2 start api.js -i 4

            Monitor in production:
            $ pm2 monitor

            Make pm2 auto-boot at server restart:
            $ pm2 startup

            To go further checkout:
            http://pm2.io/


            -------------

[PM2] Spawning PM2 daemon with pm2_home=/root/.pm2
[PM2] PM2 Successfully daemonized
[PM2] [v] Modules Stopped
[PM2][WARN] No process found
[PM2] [v] All Applications Stopped
[PM2] [v] PM2 Daemon Stopped

> production@1.0.0 build /root/production
> NODE_ENV=production node -r @babel/register node_modules/.bin/webpack --progress --display-modules --config webpack.config.js

Hash: 6561e493277e6c3b30ee
Version: webpack 4.29.6
Time: 3646ms
Built at: 03/13/2019 3:17:29 AM
            Asset       Size  Chunks             Chunk Names
../css/main.css   77 bytes       0  [emitted]  main
  main.bundle.js   4.6 KiB       0  [emitted]  main
vendor.bundle.js   117 KiB       1  [emitted]  vendor
Entrypoint main = vendor.bundle.js ../css/main.css main.bundle.js
   [0] /root/production/node_modules/react/index.js 190 bytes {1} [built]
   [1] /root/production/node_modules/object-assign/index.js 2.06 KiB {1} [built]
   [2] /root/production/node_modules/react-dom/index.js 1.33 KiB {1} [built]
   [3] /root/production/node_modules/prop-types/index.js 710 bytes {1} [built]
   [4] ./components/Hello/Hello.scss 104 bytes {0} [built]
   [5] multi ./index.jsx 28 bytes {0} [built]
   [6] /root/production/node_modules/react/cjs/react.production.min.js 6.67 KiB {1} [built]
   [7] /root/production/node_modules/react-dom/cjs/react-dom.production.min.js 106 KiB {1} [built]
   [8] /root/production/node_modules/scheduler/index.js 198 bytes {1} [built]
   [9] /root/production/node_modules/scheduler/cjs/scheduler.production.min.js 4.88 KiB {1} [built]
  [10] (webpack)/buildin/global.js 472 bytes {1} [built]
  [11] /root/production/node_modules/prop-types/factoryWithThrowingShims.js 1.58 KiB {1} [built]
  [12] /root/production/node_modules/prop-types/lib/ReactPropTypesSecret.js 314 bytes {1} [built]
  [13] ./index.jsx + 2 modules 6.06 KiB {0} [built]
      | ./index.jsx 349 bytes [built]
      | ./App.jsx 2.71 KiB [built]
      | ./components/Hello/index.jsx 2.99 KiB [built]
      + 1 hidden module
Child mini-css-extract-plugin ../../node_modules/css-loader/dist/cjs.js??ref--5-1!../../node_modules/sass-loader/lib/loader.js!components/Hello/Hello.
scss:
    Entrypoint mini-css-extract-plugin = *
       [0] /root/production/node_modules/css-loader/dist/cjs.js??ref--5-1!/root/production/node_modules/sass-loader/lib/loader.js!./components/Hello/Hell
o.scss 306 bytes {0} [built]
       [1] /root/production/node_modules/css-loader/dist/runtime/api.js 2.35 KiB {0} [built]
[PM2] Spawning PM2 daemon with pm2_home=/root/.pm2
[PM2] PM2 Successfully daemonized
[PM2] Starting /root/production/src/backend in fork_mode (1 instance)
[PM2] Done.

| App name | id | version | mode | pid   | status | restart | uptime | cpu | mem     | user | watching |
| backend  | 0  | 1.0.0   | fork | 28161 | online | 0       | 0s     | 0%  | 33.0 MB | root | disabled |
```

12. If you run it and you view the **Network** tab in your Chrome Dev Tools, you will see the bundles being loaded:

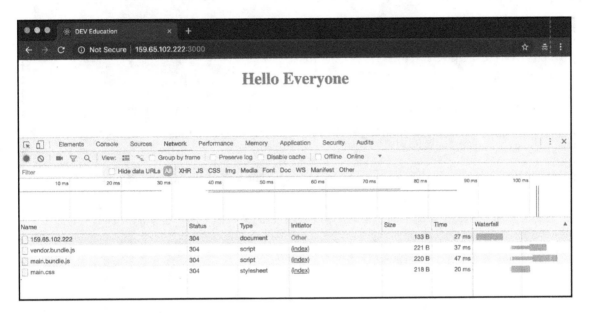

Turning off our droplet

To turn off the droplet, follow these steps:

1. If you want to turn off your droplet, you can go to the **Power** section, or you can use the **ON/OFF** switch:

2. Digital Ocean will charge you only when your droplet is **ON**. If you click on the **ON** switch to turn it off, then you will get the following message:

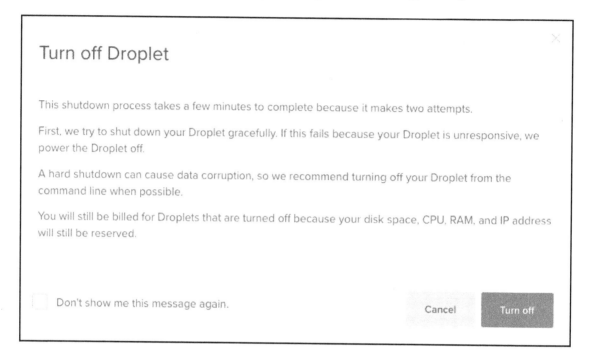

Configuring nginx, PM2, and a domain

Our Droplet is ready to be used for production, but as you can see, we are still using port 3000. We need to configure nginx and implement a proxy to redirect the traffic from port 80 to 3000; this means we won't need to specify the port directly anymore. **Node Production Process Manager** (**PM2**) will help us run the Node server in production securely. Generally, if we run Node directly with the `node` or `babel-node` command, and there is an error in the app, then it will crash and will stop working; PM2 restarts the node server if an error occurs.

First, in your droplet, you need to install PM2 globally:

```
npm install -g pm2
```

Installing and configuring nginx

To install nginx, you need to execute the following command:

```
sudo apt-get update
sudo apt-get install nginx
```

After you have installed nginx, then you can start the configuration:

1. We need to adjust the firewall to allow the traffic for port 80. To list the available application configurations, you need to run the following command:

    ```
    sudo ufw app list
    Available applications:
      Nginx Full
      Nginx HTTP
      Nginx HTTPS
      OpenSSH
    ```

2. `Nginx Full` means that it will allow the traffic from port 80 (HTTP) and port 443 (HTTPS). We haven't configured any domain with SSL, so, for now, we should restrict the traffic to send the traffic just through port 80 (HTTP):

    ```
    sudo ufw allow 'Nginx HTTP'
    Rules updated
    Rules updated (v6)
    ```

If you try to access the droplet IP, you should see nginx working:

3. You can manage the nginx process with these commands:

```
Start server: sudo systemctl start nginx
Stop server: sudo systemctl stop nginx
Restart server: sudo systemctl restart nginx
```

Setting up a reverse proxy server

As I mentioned previously, we need to set up a reverse proxy server to send the traffic from port 80 (HTTP) to port 3000 (React app). To do this, you need to open the following file:

```
sudo vi /etc/nginx/sites-available/default
```

The steps are as follows:

1. In the `location` / block, you need to replace the code in the file with the following:

```
location / {
  proxy_pass http://localhost:3000;
  proxy_http_version 1.1;
  proxy_set_header Upgrade $http_upgrade;
  proxy_set_header Connection 'upgrade';
  proxy_set_header Host $host;
  proxy_cache_bypass $http_upgrade;
}
```

2. Once you have saved the file, you can verify whether there is a syntax error in the nginx configuration with the following command:

```
sudo nginx -t
```

3. If everything is fine, then you should see this:

```
root@dev-education:~# sudo nginx -t
nginx: the configuration file /etc/nginx/nginx.conf syntax is ok
nginx: configuration file /etc/nginx/nginx.conf test is successful
```

4. Finally, you need to restart the nginx server:

```
sudo systemctl restart nginx
```

Now, you should be able to access the React application without the port, as shown in the following screenshot:

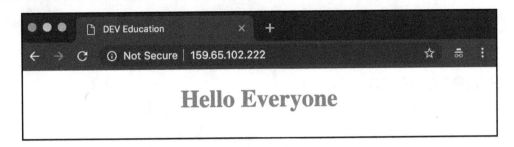

Adding a domain to our droplet

Using an IP for a website is not nice; we always need to use a domain to help users find our website easier. If you want to use a domain on your droplet, you need to change the nameservers of your domain to point to Digital Ocean DNS. I normally use GoDaddy to register my domains. To do so using GoDaddy, follow these steps:

1. Go to `https://dcc.godaddy.com/manage/YOURDOMAIN.COM/dns`, and then go to the **Nameservers** section:

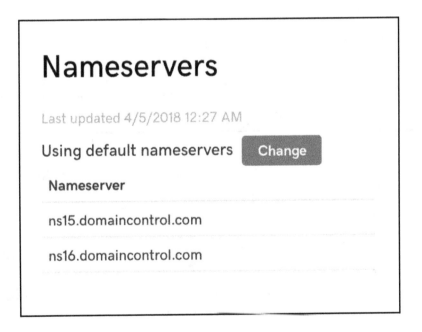

2. Click on the **Change** button, select **Custom**, and then specify the Digital Ocean DNS:

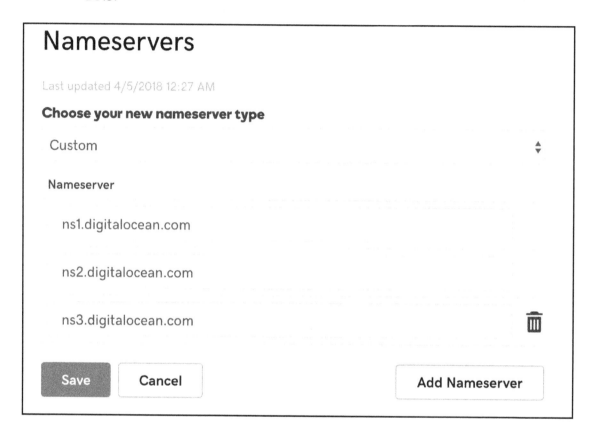

3. Normally, this takes between 15 and 30 minutes for the DNS changes to be reflected; for now, after you have updated your **Nameservers**, go to your droplet dashboard, and then choose the **Add a domain** option:

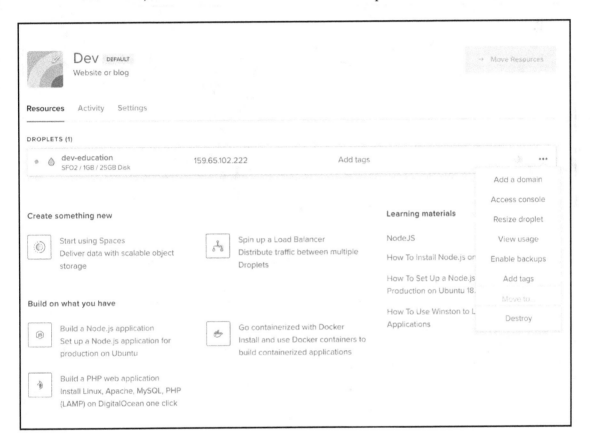

4. Then, write your domain name, select your droplet, and click on the **Add Domain** button:

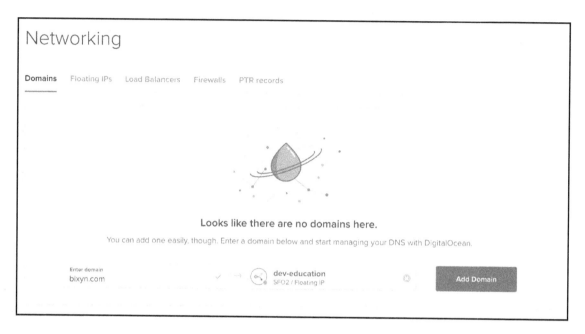

Now, you have to create a new record for **CNAME**. Select the **CNAME** tab, in the **HOSTNAME** write www, in the alias field write @, and by default, the **TTL** is 43200; this is to enable access to your domain using the www prefix:

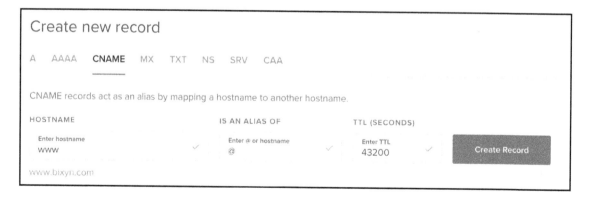

If you did everything correctly, you should be able to access your domain and see the React application working. As I said before, this process can take up to 30 minutes, but in some cases, it can take up to 24 hours, depending on the DNS propagation speed:

Implementing CircleCI for continuous integration

I've been using CircleCI for a while and I can tell you that it is one of the best CI solutions: it is free for personal use, giving you unlimited repositories and users, you have 1,000 builds minutes per month, one container, and one concurrent job; if you need more, you can upgrade the plan with an initial price of $50 per month.

The first thing you need to do is **Sign Up** on the site using your GitHub account (or Bitbucket, if you prefer). If you choose to use GitHub, you need to authorize CircleCI in your account, as shown in the following screenshot:

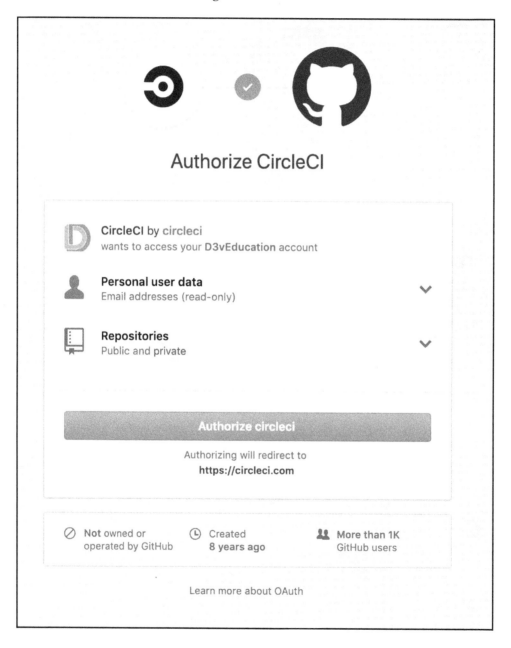

Adding an SSH key to CircleCI

Now that you have created your account, CircleCI needs a way to log in to your Digital Ocean droplet to run the deploy script. Follow these steps to complete this task:

1. Create a new SSH key inside our droplet using the following command:

```
ssh-keygen -t rsa
# Then save the key as /.ssh/id_rsa_droplet with no password.
```

2. After that, let's add the key to our `autorhized_keys`:

```
cat id_rsa_droplet.pub >> authorized_keys
```

3. Now, you need to download the private key. To verify that you can log in with the new key, you need to copy it to your local machine, as follows:

```
# In your local machine do:
scp root@YOUR_DROPLET_IP:/root/.ssh/id_rsa_droplet ~/.ssh/
ssh-add id_rsa_droplet
ssh -v root@YOUR_DROPLET_IP
```

If you did everything correctly, you should be able to log in to your droplet without a password, and that means CircleCI can have access to our droplet:

1. Copy the content of your `id_rsa_droplet.pub` key and then go to your repository settings (the gear icon next to the name of your repository):

2. Then, go to **SSH Permissions**, as follows:

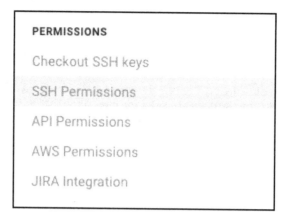

3. You can also access on the
   URL https://circleci.com/gh/**YOUR_GIT_USER**/**YOUR_REPOSITORY**/edit#ssh,
   and then click on the **Add SSH Key** button:

4. Paste your private key, and then put a name to the hostname; we will name it
   Digital Ocean Droplet.

Configuring CircleCI

Now that you have configured the CircleCI access to your droplet, you need to add a `config` file to your project to specify the jobs you want to execute for the deployment process. This process is shown in the following steps:

1. For this, you need to create the `.circleci` directory and add the following inside the file `config.yml`:

```
version: 2
jobs:
  build:
    branches:
      only:
        - master
    working_directory: ~/tmp
    docker:
      - image: circleci/node:10
    steps:
      - checkout
      - run: npm install
      - run: npm run lint
      - run: npm test
      - run: ssh -o StrictHostKeyChecking=no
$DROPLET_USER@$DROPLET_IP 'cd production; git checkout master; git
pull; npm install; npm run start:production;'
```

2. When you have a `.yml` file, you need to be careful with the indentation; since it is similar to Python, if you don't indent correctly you will get an error. Let's see how this file is structured:

```
version: 2
```

3. Specify the CircleCI version we will use. In this case, you are using version 2 (the latest one, at the time of writing this book):

```
jobs:
```

4. Inside `jobs`, we will specify that it needs to configure the container; we will create it using Docker, and also outline the steps to follow for the deployment process:

```
build:
  branches:
    only:
      - master
```

5. In this block, we are specifying that we will use only the `master` branch of the repository. Of course, you can change it for any branch you want to deploy:

```
working_directory: ~/tmp
```

6. The `working_directory` will be the temporal directory we will use to install the NPM packages and run our deploy scripts. In this case, I decided to use the `tmp` directory, as follows:

```
docker:
  - image: circleci/node:10
```

7. As I said before, we will create a Docker container, and in this case, I selected an existing image that includes `node: 10`. If you want to know about all the available images, you can visit `https://circleci.com/docs/2.0/circleci-images`:

```
steps:
  - checkout
  - run: npm install
  - run: npm run lint
  - run: npm test
  - run: ssh -o StrictHostKeyChecking=no $DROPLET_USER@$DROPLET_IP
'cd production; git checkout master; git pull; npm install; npm run
start:production;'
```

For code case, the checkout is a simple git checkout to master, then on each run sentence, you need to specify the scripts you want to run. Follow these steps:

1. `npm install`: First, you need to install the NPM packages to be able to perform the next tasks.
   1. `npm run lint`: Executes the ESLint validation; if it fails, it will break the deployment process, otherwise, it continues with the next run.
2. `npm run test`: Executes the jest validations; if it fails, it will break the deployment process, otherwise, it continues with the next run.
3. In the last step, we connect to our Digital Ocean Droplet, passing the `StrictHostKeyChecking=no` flag to disable the strict host key checking, then we use the `$DROPLET_USER` and `$DROPLET_IP` ENV variables to connect it (we will create those in the next step), and finally, we will specify all the commands we will perform inside our droplet using single quotes. These commands are listed as follows:
   - `cd production`: Grants access to the production (or your Git repository name)

- `git checkout master`: This will checkout the master branch
- `git pull`: Pulls the latest changes from our repository
- `npm run start:production`: This is the final step, which runs our project in production mode

Creating ENV variables in CircleCI

As you saw previously, we are using the `$DROPLET_USER` and `$DROPLET_IP` variables, but do we define those? Follow these steps:

1. You need to go to your project settings again and select the `Environment Variables` option. Then, you need to create the `DROPLET_USER` variable:

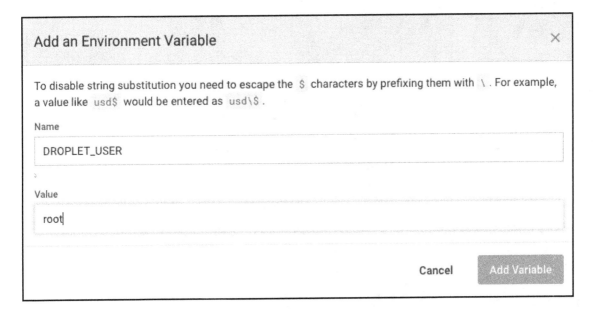

2. Then, you need to create the `DROPLET_IP` with your droplet IP:

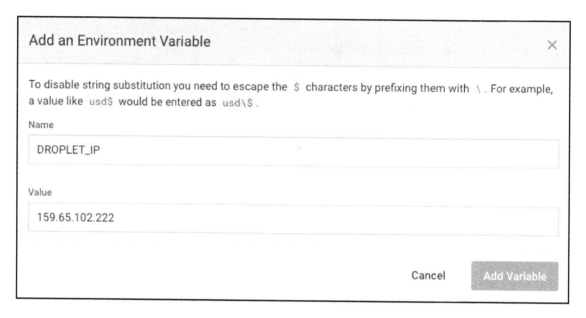

3. Now, you need to push the `config` file to your repository, and you will be ready for the magic. Now that CircleCI is connected to your repository, every time you push changes to master, it will fire a build. Normally, the first two or three builds can fail due to syntax errors, or indent errors in our config, or maybe because we have linter errors, or unit test errors; if you have a failure, you will see something like this:

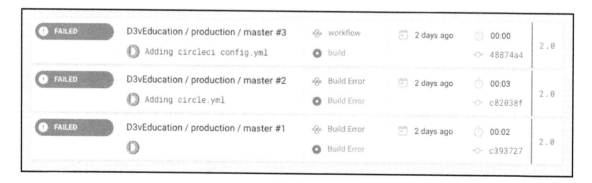

4. As you can see from the preceding screenshot, the first two build failures say **Build Error**, and the third one says **workflow**, basically meaning that in the first build, the `config.yml` file didn't exist, in the second, I had a **syntax error** in the `config.yml`, and then in the third one, everything was fine with the `config.yml`, but I got a **workflow** error, meaning that some of the scripts failed (linter or tests).

5. After you fix all the syntax errors in the `config.yml` file, and all the issues with the linter or the unit tests, you should see a **SUCCESS** build, like this:

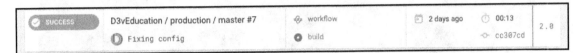

6. If you click on the build number, you can see all the steps that CircleCI executed before publishing the new changes in your droplet:

7. As you can see, the order of the steps is the same as we specified in our `config.yml` file; you can even see the output of each step by clicking on it:

```
♡  npm run lint                                                    00:01

    $ #!/bin/bash -eo pipefail                              Exit code: 0
      npm run lint


    > production@1.0.0 lint /home/circleci/tmp
    > eslint --ext .jsx,.js src


♡  npm test                                                        00:03

    $ #!/bin/bash -eo pipefail                              Exit code: 0
      npm test


    > production@1.0.0 test /home/circleci/tmp
    > jest --no-cache

     PASS  src/frontend/components/Hello/index.test.jsx
      Hello
        ✓ should render Hello component (3ms)
        ✓ should render by default Hello World (1ms)
        ✓ should render the name prop (1ms)
        ✓ should has .Hello class (2ms)

    Test Suites: 1 passed, 1 total
    Tests:       4 passed, 4 total
    Snapshots:   0 total
    Time:        1.755s
    Ran all test suites.
```

8. Now, let's suppose you have an error on your linter validation or in some unit tests. Let's see what happen in that case, as follows:

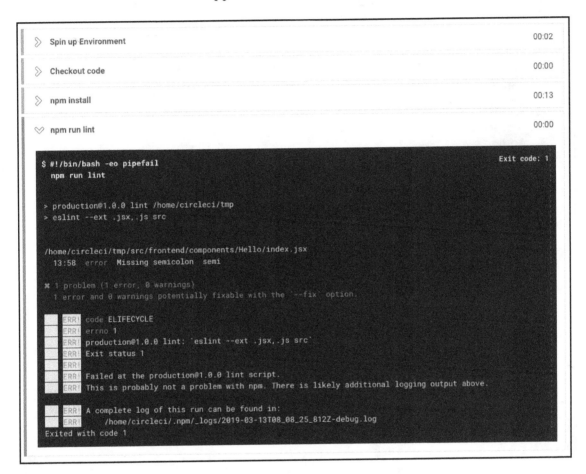

As you can see, once an error is detected, it will exit with code 1. This means it will abort the deployment and will mark it as a failure, and as you can see, all the steps after `npm run lint` are not executed.

Another cool thing is that now, if you go to your GitHub repository and check your commits, you will see all the commits that have a success build and all the commits that have a failed build:

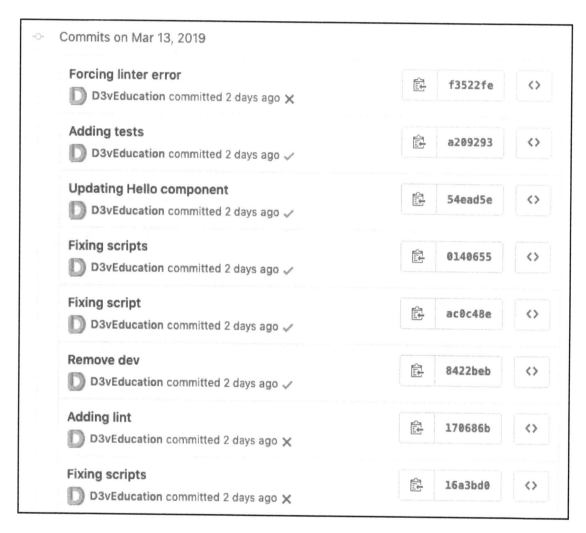

Summary

The journey through the deployment process has come to an end, and now you know how to deploy your React application to the world (production), and also how to implement CircleCI for continuous integration.

In the next chapter, we will learn how to publish npm packages.

14
Next Steps

React is one of the most amazing libraries that has been released in the last few years, not only because of the library itself and its great features but, most importantly, due to the ecosystem that has been built around it.

Following the React community is very exciting and inspiring; there are new projects and tools to learn and play with every single day. Not just that, there are conferences and meetups where you can talk to people in real life and build new relationships, blog posts that you can read to improve your skills and learn more, and many other ways to become a better developer.

React and its ecosystem are encouraging best practices and love for open source in developers, which is fantastic for the future of our careers.

In this chapter, we will cover the following topics:

- How to contribute to the React library by opening issues and **pull requests**
- Why it is important to give back to the community and share your code
- The most important aspects to keep in mind when pushing open source code
- How to publish an npm package and how to use semantic versioning

Contributing to React

One thing that people often want to do when they've used React for a while is contribute to the library. React is open source, which means that its source code is public and anyone who's signed the **Contributor License Agreement** (**CLA**) can help to fix bugs, write documentation, or even add new features.

You can read the full terms of the CLA at the following URL: `https://code.facebook.com/cla.`

You need to make sure that any bug you post in React's GitHub repository is 100% replicable. Once you verify this, and if you want to file an issue on GitHub, you can go to `https://github.com/facebook/react/issues/new`.

As you'll see, the issue comes with some pre-filled instructions, with one of those being to set up the minimal demo. The other questions help you to explain the problem, and to describe current and expected behaviors.

It is important for you to read the **Facebook Code of Conduct** before participating or contributing to the repository at `https://code.facebook.com/codeofconduct`. The document lists good behaviors that are expected from all community members and that everyone should follow.

Once the issue is filed, you have to wait for one of the core contributors to examine it and tell you what they've decided to do with the bug. Depending on the severity of it, they might fix it, or ask you to fix it.

In the second case, you can fork the repository and write code to solve the problem. It is important to follow the coding style guides and write all the tests for the fix. It is also crucial that all the old tests pass to make sure the new code does not introduce regressions in the codebase.

When the fix is ready and all the tests are green, you can submit a pull request, and wait for the core team members to review it. They may decide to merge it, or ask you to make some changes.

If you did not find a bug but you still want to contribute to the project, you can look into the issues tagged with the **good first issue** label on GitHub: `https://github.com/facebook/react/labels/good%20first%20issue`.

This is a great way to start contributing and it is fantastic that the React team gives everyone, especially new contributors, the possibility of being part of the project.

If you find a good first bug issue that has not already been taken by someone, you can add a comment on the issue saying that you are interested in working on it. One of the core members will get in touch with you. Make sure to discuss your approach, and the path you want to take with them before starting coding, so that you do not have to rewrite the code multiple times.

Another way of improving React is by adding new features. It is important to say that the React team has a plan to follow, and the main features are designed and decided by the core members.

If you are interested in knowing the next steps that the library will take, you can find some of them under the label **Type: Big Picture** on GitHub: `https://github.com/facebook/react/labels/Type%3A%20Big%20Picture`.

That said, if you have some good ideas about features that should be added to the library, the first thing to do is open an issue, and start talking with the React team. You should avoid spending time writing code and submitting a pull request before asking them, because the feature you have in mind might not fit into their plans, or might conflict with other functionalities they are working on.

Distributing your code

Contributing to the React ecosystem does not only mean pushing code into the React repository. To give back to the community and help developers, you can create packages, blog posts, answer questions on Stack Overflow, and perform many other activities.

Suppose, for example, you created a React component that solves a complex problem, and you think that other developers would benefit from using it instead of investing time in building their solutions. The best thing to do is to publish it GitHub and make it available for everyone to read and use. However, pushing the code to GitHub is only a small action within a big process, and it comes with some responsibilities. So, you should have a clear idea in mind about the reasons behind your choice.

The motivation behind why you want to share your code contributes to improving your skills as a developer. Sharing your code, on the one hand, forces you to follow best practices and write better code. On the other hand, it exposes your code to feedback and comments from other developers. This is a big opportunity for you to receive tips and improve your code to make it better.

Other than the suggestions related to the code itself, by pushing your code to GitHub, you benefit from other people's ideas. In fact, you might have thought about a single problem that your component can solve, but another developer may use it in a slightly different way, finding new solutions for it. Moreover, they might need new features and they could help you implement them, so that everyone, yourself included, can benefit from it. Building software together is a great way to improve both your skills and your packages, and that is why I strongly believe in open source.

Another significant opportunity that open source can give you is letting you get in touch with smart and passionate developers from all around the world. Working closely with new people who have different backgrounds and skill sets is one of the best ways to keep our minds open and improve ourselves.

Sharing code also gives you some responsibilities and it could be time-consuming. In fact, once the code is public and people can use it, you have to maintain it.

Maintaining a repository requires commitment because the more popular it gets and the more people use it, the higher the number of questions and issues. For example, developers may encounter bugs and open issues, so you have to go through all of them and try to reproduce the problems. If the problems exist, then you have to write the fix and publish a new version of the library. You could receive pull requests from developers, which could be long and complex, and they need to be reviewed.

If you decide to ask people to co-maintain the project and help you with issues and pull requests, you have to coordinate with them to share your vision and make decisions together. With this in mind, we can go through some good practices that can help you make a better repository, and avoid some of the common pitfalls.

First of all, if you want to publish your React component, you have to write a comprehensive set of tests. With public code and many people contributing to it, tests are very helpful for many reasons:

- They make the code more robust
- They help other developers understand what the code does
- They make it easier to find regression when new code is added
- They make other contributors more confident in writing the code

The second important thing to do is add a README with a description of the component, an example of its use, and documentation of the APIs and props that can be used.

This helps users of the package, but it also avoids people opening issues and asking questions about how the library works and how it should be used.

It is also essential to add a LICENSE file to your repository to make people aware of what they can and cannot do with your code. GitHub has a lot of ready-made templates to choose from.

Whenever you can, you should keep the package small and add as few dependencies as you can. Developers tend to think carefully about size when they have to decide whether to use a library or not. Remember that heavy packages have a bad impact on performance.

Not only that, depending on too many third-party libraries can create problems if any of them are not maintained or have bugs.

One tricky part in sharing React components comes when you have to decide about the styling. Sharing JavaScript code is pretty straightforward, while attaching the CSS is not as easy as you may think. In fact, there are many different paths you can take to provide it: from adding a CSS file to the package, to using inline styles. The important thing to keep in mind is that CSS is global and generic class names may conflict with the ones that already exist in the project where the component is imported.

The best choice is to include the fewest possible styles and make the component highly configurable for end users. In this way, developers will be more likely to use it because it can be adapted to their custom solutions.

To show that your component is highly customizable, you can add one or more examples to the repository to make it easy for everyone to understand how it works and which props it accepts. Examples are also useful so that you can test new versions of the component and see if there are unexpected breaking changes.

As we saw in Chapter 3, *Create Truly Reusable Components*, tools such as **React Storybook** can help you create living style guides, which are easier for you to maintain, and for the consumer of your package to navigate and use.

An excellent example of a highly customizable library that uses Storybook to show all these variations is react-dates from Airbnb. You should take that repository as the perfect example of how to publish React components to GitHub.

As you can see, they use Storybook to show the different options of the component:

Last but not least, you might not only want to share your code—you may also want to distribute your package. The most popular package manager for JavaScript is npm, which we've used throughout this book to install packages and dependencies.

In the next section, we will see how easy it is to publish a new package with npm.

Other than npm, some developers may need to add your component as a global dependency and use it without a package manager.

As we saw in Chapter 1, *Taking Your First Steps with React*, you can easily use React by just adding a script tag pointing to unpkg.com. It is important to give the users of your library the same option.

So, to offer a global version of your package, you should build the **Universal Module Definition** (**UMD**) version as well. With webpack, this is pretty straightforward; you just have to set the libraryTarget in the output section of the configuration file.

Publishing an npm package

The most popular way of making a package available to developers is by publishing it to npm, the package manager for Node.js.

We used it in all the examples in this book and you have seen how easy it is to install a package; it is just a matter of running the npm install package, and that is it. What you may not know is how easy it is to publish a package as well.

First of all, let's say you move into an empty directory and write the following in your Terminal:

```
npm init
```

A new package.json will be created and some questions will be displayed. The first one is the package name, which defaults to the folder name, and then the version number. These are the most important ones, because the first is the name that the users of your package will refer to when they install and use it; the second helps you release new versions of your package safely and without breaking other people's code.

The version number is composed of three numbers separated by a dot, and they all have a meaning. The last number of the package on the right represents the patch, and it should be increased when a new version of the library that contains bug fixes is pushed to npm.

The number in the middle indicates the minor version of the release, and it should be changed when new features are added to the library. Those new features should not break existing APIs.

Finally, the first number on the left represents the major version, and it has to be increased when a version containing breaking changes is released to the public.

Following this approach, called **Semantic Versioning (SemVer)**, is good practice and it makes your users more confident when they have to update your package.

The first version of a package is usually 0.1.0.

To publish an npm package, you must have an npm account, which you can easily create by running the following command in the console, where $username is the name of your choice:

```
npm adduser $username
```

Once the user is created, you can run the following command:

```
npm publish
```

A new entry will be added to the registry with the package name and the version you specified in `package.json`.

Whenever you change something in your library and you want to push a new version, you just have to run `$type`, where one patch is minor or major:

```
npm version $type
```

This command will bump the version automatically in your `package.json` and it will also create a commit and a tag if your folder is under version control.

Once the version number is increased, you just have to run `npm publish` again, and the new version will be available to users.

Summary

In the last stop on this trip around the React world, we have seen some of the aspects that make React great—its community and its ecosystem, and how to contribute to them.

You learned how to open an issue if you find a bug in React, and the steps to take to make it easier for its core developers to fix it. You now know the best practices when making code open source, and the benefits and the responsibilities that come with it.

Finally, you saw how easy it is to publish packages on the `npm` registry, and how to choose the right version number to avoid breaking other people's code.

Other Books You May Enjoy

If you enjoyed this book, you may be interested in these other books by Packt:

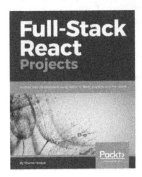

Full-Stack React Projects
Shama Hoque

ISBN: 9781788835534

- Set up your development environment and develop a MERN application
- Implement user authentication and authorization using JSON Web Tokens
- Build a social media application by extending the basic MERN application
- Create an online marketplace application with shopping cart and Stripe payments
- Develop a media streaming application using MongoDB GridFS
- Implement server-side rendering with data to improve SEO
- Set up and use React 360 to develop user interfaces with VR capabilities
- Learn industry best practices to make MERN stack applications reliable and scalable

Hands-on Full-Stack Web Development with GraphQL and React
Sebastian Grebe

ISBN: 9781789134520

- Resolve data from multi-table database and system architectures
- Build a GraphQL API by implementing models and schemas with Apollo and Sequelize
- Set up an Apollo Client and build front end components using React
- Use Mocha to test your full-stack application
- Write complex React components and share data across them
- Deploy your application using Docker

Leave a review - let other readers know what you think

Please share your thoughts on this book with others by leaving a review on the site that you bought it from. If you purchased the book from Amazon, please leave us an honest review on this book's Amazon page. This is vital so that other potential readers can see and use your unbiased opinion to make purchasing decisions, we can understand what our customers think about our products, and our authors can see your feedback on the title that they have worked with Packt to create. It will only take a few minutes of your time, but is valuable to other potential customers, our authors, and Packt. Thank you!

Index

testing
  benefits 242
theming 192

U

uncontrolled components 139, 140, 141, 142
universal applications 196
Universal Module Definition (UMD) 326

V

Visual Studio Code (VSC) 47

W

Webpack 4
  using 177

CPSIA information can be obtained
at www.ICGtesting.com
Printed in the USA
FSHW011724090820
72821FS